A HANDBOOK FOR TRAINING STRATEGY
Second edition

DEDICATION

For the staff of the IPD Library and Information Services – with special thanks to Marilyn Arnott, who headed the service for over twenty-five years, and to Steve Corbett.

A HANDBOOK FOR TRAINING STRATEGY
Second edition

Martyn Sloman

First edition published 1994
This edition published by
Gower Publishing Limited
Gower House
Croft Road
Aldershot
Hampshire GU11 3HR
England

Gower
Old Post Road
Brookfield
Vermont 05036
USA

Martyn Sloman has asserted his right under the Copyright, Designs and Patent Act 1988 to be identified as the author of this work.

British Library Cataloguing in Publication Data
Sloman, Martyn
   A handbook for training strategy. – 2nd ed.
   1. Employees – Training of – Handbooks, manuals, etc.
   I. Title
   658.3'124

   ISBN 0 566 08128 8

Library of Congress Cataloging-in-Publication Data
Sloman, Martyn
      A handbook for training strategy/Martyn Sloman. – 2nd ed.
         p.   cm.
      Includes bibliographical references and index.
      ISBN 0-566-08128-9 (hc.)
      1. Employees–Training of Handbooks, manuals, etc.   I. Title.
   HF5549.5.T7S62   1999
   658.3' 124–dc21   99–34482
                                                                                        CIP

Typeset in Century Old Style by IML Typographers, Chester and printed in Great Britain at the University Press, Cambridge.

Contents

Part III   Managing the Training Function

Figures

Preface to the second edition

I wrote this book from the viewpoint of the practising training manager. The driving force for the production of the first edition was a belief that the literature, while of value, did not always reflect the practical difficulties faced by those of us who carry responsibility for the training and development function in an organization. This motivation is even stronger now, and I was pleased to respond to the publisher's request for a revised text. Much has changed. New opportunities are emerging. Translating the seemingly endless stream of perspectives and ideas into hard practical steps is increasingly demanding. I hope this volume helps.

The first edition was written while I was Head of Training for a large investment bank. This second edition was written in my current role of Director of Management Education and Training at a leading business advisory firm. There have been similarities in the roles, but some radical differences in the acceptance of the importance of training between the two organizations. This has led me, not only to develop new material, but to reconsider some of my thoughts on ways of promoting training and defining its role. The five-year interval has also led to the introduction of whole topics (for example, knowledge management) which did not feature in the trainers' world in 1994.

The demands of my job and other pressures mean that I owe a debt of gratitude to a large number of people. My colleagues at Ernst & Young provided the stimulation and challenge which led me to focus my thoughts and develop the underlying models. Particular thanks go to Geoff Pye, Des Woods, Mike Laws, Julie Holden, Hilary Farrar and Caroline Davis.

The following people offered expert advice or assisted by reading drafts: Caroline Davis, Melanie Donaldson, Graeme Finnie, Richard Gartside, Roy Harrison, Moira Palmer and Iain Thomson. Jennifer Taylor made a significant contribution to Part II of the book. Anna Stawinska-Bassim undertook much of the research, particularly for the section on Training for the global workforce. Anna also carried out the work on the survey of best practice companies reported in Appendix IV: I am grateful to her and to all the representatives from the companies who found the time to provide such valuable input. The influential work of Anthony Carnevale of the American Society for Training and Development has migrated from the first to the second edition. Cedar Consultants supplied a number of training modules which are reproduced as figures. Helen Pitcher, Cedar's Managing Director, contributed greatly with the section on Training and equal opportunities. My thanks to them. All these people have helped shape my ideas but this does not necessarily mean that they agree with my arguments or conclusions. Kim Andrews, who typed the manuscript, showed immense patience in interpreting my handwriting and coping with multiple rewrites and repositioning of text.

Thanks are also due to the staff of the Institute of Personnel and Development (IPD) Library and Information Services – especially to Steve Corbett. The IPD has a valuable asset for uprating the quality of human resource professionalism in the comprehensiveness of this service and the capabilities of its staff. I owe a debt of gratitude to my employers for encouraging me to publish and allowing me to include information from the workplace, and to my wife for tolerating sustained holiday and weekend work on the book. Our visits to our cottage in Norfolk have produced a beautiful home and garden (her efforts) and a second edition for the bookshelves (my efforts).

I have acknowledged sources where possible and am grateful for permission to reproduce work drawn from so many places. I apologize for any errors and omissions and, as any good training manager should, accept responsibility for any inadequacies.

Martyn Sloman

Introduction

Although we may not realize it, this is potentially a golden age for the training professional. The late 1990s have been a period of economic growth in the US and Europe; people are seen as paramount to securing competitive advantage; resources are available for future investment. The current UK government has made the uprating of workforce skills through training a central tenet of economic policy. New approaches to training design and delivery are emerging; new management ideas from international gurus are filling airport bookstores. All emphasize the fundamental importance of developing people. Additionally, social pressures have prompted a reaction to competition based on sweating human assets. Staff are demanding training to enhance their future employment prospects – now called employability. The lean, tough training environment of the early 1990s has been overtaken by the exciting and demanding, but confused environment that is evident today.

Shortly after the first edition of this book was published in 1994, the following advertisement appeared in the *Sunday Times*:

Unpleasant training manager

City c. £40,000 + package

If you only really care about people and the fulfilment of human potential, perhaps you should be a missionary. This is an opportunity for somebody who wants to be judged on results. We are a multinational company driven by a profit motive so pure that it hurts. We have some of the Square Mile's highest of high flyers, but they can be devils to work with. They don't like passengers and they don't suffer fools at all, let alone gladly.

When it comes to training, all they're interested in is training that helps them rub their competitors' faces further into the dirt. Your immediate job would be to build a brand new training function from the ground up. We don't give a damn about national training awards: we want training that will drive our business.

Don't underestimate the challenge. You'll be attempting to add value to slick operators who already know it all, and probably resent wasting any of their previous lolly-making time with you. If you're going to cut any ice at all, you'll need to be as least as difficult and demanding as they are.[1]

An equivalent advertisement in the year 2005 could well read:

Thames Valley/c.90,000 Euros + options

If you believe that the fulfilment of human potential and business success are complementary activities, you will be attracted to our culture. We are a transnational company that competes through its people. We employ some of the brightest and most committed knowledge workers. They work very hard. They demand appropriate development and we are determined to give it to them.

When it comes to training, they need the key tools to keep them ahead of the competition. Your job is to define the function so that training is delivered at the right time and in a cost-effective manner. State of the art processes are only of interest to us if it can be proved that they add value. Most of our course delivery is outsourced.

Don't underestimate the challenge. Our people drive themselves hard and resent anything that wastes their time. If you're going to cut any ice at all you'll need to demonstrate not only professionalism in your function but a real understanding of modern business.

A superficial comparison of the two (one real, one speculative) suggests a great contrast. In fact, although much is changing for the better, some underlying questions remain unresolved. Training must still achieve an appropriate organizational fit, and the role of the function must be defined. The training manager must be prepared to justify the investment of resources devoted to training. The pressures may be different, but they are no less acute.

There have, however, been some significant changes in the approach and style needed to deliver effective training within an organization. Arguably – and this is an important change from the first edition – one size no longer fits all. Trainers must choose their own most effective model – one which works for their organization. This book assists in that choice and helps the training manager define the desired approach and style. In particular, it:

- discusses what is meant by best training practice in a modern organization
- reviews and develops models for the place of the training function in the organization.

The aim of this book is to help those involved in the delivery of training in organizations – whether training managers, trainers, other human resource professionals, or committed line managers. As well as discussing the new approach to training, guidance on how to proceed is offered. Above all else the new model of training must be capable of translation into practical action.

A basic premise of this book is that new approaches should be firmly embedded in operating experience: to be of value, models should be determined by the realities of decision-making. How many times, for example, have trainers been told that for an important programme to be effective 'top management support is essential'? In today's progressive training climate, top management may be sympathetic and acquiescent but they often have more important problems demanding their immediate attention. They have a right to expect a professional trainer to drive the training function from below without recourse to decrees from above.

The need to move from models to implementation has led to the inclusion, particularly in Part II, of a series of questionnaires, survey instruments and other related schedules. All are drawn from similar documents used by myself and my colleagues and are intended to be examples and illustrations; any training manager worthy of the name would wish to develop his or her own instruments. Moreover, the effective training manager will already have a clear idea of what is likely to work in the culture of the organization.

Banks and business advisers are not typical organizations – but no training environment is typical. One justification for the inclusion of the instruments is that if they can work in these fast-moving environments they can be adapted to work elsewhere.

Some preliminary comments on the structure of the book and also on the terminology used may help the reader. The book is divided into three parts and some appendices:

Part I outlines the new role which training must fulfil. The changing organizational requirements for training will be discussed, together with the way in which the position of the training function is changing within the wider context of human resources. This part includes a review of some models of the training function and concludes with a consideration of how improved models can be developed.

In **Part II**, attention will shift to more practical issues – what the training manager should be doing to promote training in the organization. Needs identification will be considered at both the organizational and individual levels. At the higher level, the requirement to develop training within the context of the business plan will be discussed. So too will the need to capture human resource benefits beyond narrow skills enhancement – the limited traditional preserve of the trainer. Instruments that could prove successful in increasing the effectiveness of needs identification, performance appraisal and evaluation will be introduced. Underpinning much of the argument is a recognition that training must be a joint responsibility of broader line management and other human resource professionals as well as the training specialist.

Part III looks at the role of the training function and the place of the trainer. No single all-embracing model is proposed; the way forward must depend on the situation that the organization is facing. However, it is recommended that the modern training manager should fulfil the role of strategic facilitator: planning training and managing what will be described as the organization's training culture. The skills required to achieve this objective are considered in the concluding section of the book.

In the first three concluding Appendices, key features of the British training environment are presented – on national trends, UK government policies and employers' response to the policies. To many readers the content of these Appendices will be familiar; for those less aware of the current environment they contain essential background material. The fourth and final Appendix reports on a brief survey of how some leading organizations in the UK are responding to the current challenges.

Throughout the book the analyses, arguments and recommendations advanced are directed at the training and development of managerial, supervisory and clerical staff. Characteristically such staff are able to exercise some choice and discretion at work. In recent literature the term 'knowledge workers' has become popular, but it is used in three senses. First, it is used to describe those people whose work is in some part intellectual in content. Their basic task is to share ideas and to meet customer needs. Second, it is used to describe a broad movement among the workforce away from routine operations towards more demanding tasks. Third, it is used to describe the small group of people in sophisticated organizations who work in knowledge management – capturing and communicating the firm's intellectual capital.

This book is more concerned with the training of knowledge workers in the first sense. It is not concerned with training programmes for operatives, or for other workers whose tasks are mainly repetitive and allow little scope for discretion. The issues that arise in this form of training have been well addressed in the existing literature.

While these exclusions limit the scope of the book, it is universally accepted that the workforce of the future will contain a far greater proportion of employees who will exercise choice and discretion. This is where the main challenges for the trainer will lie.

Another semantic topic best dealt with at this stage is the use of the term 'training' as shorthand for both training and development. The most comprehensive survey undertaken in the UK[2] defined training as:

> the process of acquiring the knowledge and skills related to work requirements by formal, structured or guided means, but excluding general supervision, job specific innovations and learning by experience.

Development is much broader in ambition. It is concerned with the growth of the individual through a series of jobs, not just the current role, and also with the provision for the company of a flexible and trained workforce which will meet future requirements. Both training and development are involved with conscious activities that take place within an organization to enhance the effectiveness of the employees. They are interventions. As we move towards a more sophisticated workforce, the distinction between training and development will become increasingly blurred. In this book, 'training' will be used to describe interventions which are more likely to yield results in the short-term than longer-term developmental activity, but the difference will be one of degree. Both are part of the organization's human resource development programme.

By contrast, education is the structured, formal learning process which commonly takes place in an institutional framework. Most of the issues of management education can only be resolved beyond the boundary of the organization – within the further and higher education system and by government intervention. Hence they fall outside the scope of this book, which deals principally with the domain where the training manager carries responsibility.

Learning can be defined as 'the physical and mental processes involved in changing one's normal behavioural patterns and habits from the norm' (p. 580).[3] There is, of course, a whole literature about the learning processes. For our purposes a simple distinction can be adopted. Learning lies within the domain of the individual, can result from a whole range of experiences, and can be positive, negative or neutral from the organization's point of view. Training lies within the domain of the organization: it is an intervention designed to produce behaviours from individuals that have positive organizational results.

The primary audience for this book are those responsible for managing training in an organization. As will be discussed at various stages in the text, such individuals can position their roles in a number of different ways. Training can be delivered by a team led by a training manager, by a sole (and perhaps isolated) trainer, or by someone who carries responsibility for broader human resource activity. Since most of the topics considered relate to the management of training interventions, the term 'training manager' will be used; 'trainer' and 'training professional' will also appear and there is no difference intended in the use of these three terms. The analysis discusses the appropriate form of intervention, and the label of the person responsible is of secondary importance.

Given the deliberate focus of the book, it does not purport to be comprehensive. It is not a textbook or manual on training in its widest form. Instead, it looks at the issues involved in developing a new framework in which training can be successfully managed and delivered in the modern organization. It presents approaches and instruments that are likely to be effective. Although the intention is to offer practical guidelines and advice, a polemic tone is bound to emerge on occasions. Readers may not concur with the author's comments on existing models, policies and approaches, but it is hoped that they will agree that such discussion is of value.

In developing the approach, evidence is drawn from a number of academic and quasi-academic works and from published reports. These have been introduced not in an attempt to provide a comprehensive view of thinking on training, but because they have been instrumental in shaping the current debate. References have therefore been identified by source so that the reader can visit or revisit them and draw his or her own conclusions on the best way forward. This process is thoroughly worthwhile. Drawing on the thoughts of others to chart your own journey is one of the real pleasures of a creative job.

REFERENCES

1. My thanks to the HR recruitment consultancy, Courtenay, for permission to reproduce this advertisement which originally appeared in the *Sunday Times* in March 1994.
2. The Training Agency (1989), *Training in Britain, a Study of Funding, Activity and Attitudes*, London: HMSO. See also: The Training Agency (1989), *Training in Britain, a set of Research Reports*, London: HMSO.
3. Kelly, Robert, J. in J. Prior (ed.) (1994), *Gower Handbook of Training and Development*, Second Edition, Aldershot: Gower.

Part I
The Role of Training

Introduction to Part I

The premise underlying this book is that there is a need for a reappraisal of the role of training in the modern organization. This need has arisen from a number of factors that, taken together, demand a thorough review of the identification of training needs, the design and delivery of training activity, and the post-training evaluation and reinforcement. Most importantly, this combination of factors has raised questions on the validity of traditional models of training management: a review of the organizational position of the training function is needed, and the skills required of the training professional must be reassessed.

A great deal of rethinking is taking place, but it often lacks structure. Managers responsible for the delivery of training in an organization (whether training specialists or not) are thoughtful and conscientious and are aware that important changes are taking place in the training environment. In recent years, more so than ever before, they have been subjected to a barrage of ideas. Most are conceptually complex and it is often hard to see how, if at all, they fit together. Most have been concerned with strategy and competition. The human resource implications have been implicit rather than explicit. To illustrate this point, consider the following questions which are all exercising the training manager's thinking:

- it is accepted that training should be closely linked with business strategy, but what does this mean in practice? How should it be done?
- how should training relate to corporate culture?
- should the training manager be operating as an internal consultant and, if so, what does this mean?
- how important a breakthrough are competencies? What is the link with National Vocational Qualifications?
- how important are the opportunities offered by knowledge management and open and distance learning?
- should the company be attempting to become a learning organization and, if so, how?

All these are important questions. Regrettably, it is hard – however many articles are examined or conferences attended – to find simple operational guidelines indicating what should be done in the organization on Monday morning. Many training managers are therefore left feeling inadequate and confused.

There are sound reasons for such confusion. Delivering effective training in a modern organization requires new thinking, new relationships, new models, a new approach and new instruments and mechanisms. Grafting current 'isms' onto old frameworks is unlikely to be effective. It is necessary, therefore, at the outset to consider fully the new context in which the training manager must operate. This is carried out in Chapter 1, where I consider the new approach to competition through people, and Chapter 2, where I discuss the implications for human resources.

Once this analysis has been undertaken, the training manager's confusion is explained. He or she is operating in an uncertain environment and only partial guidance is offered by the existing conceptual models. These models are reviewed in Chapter 3 and the characteristics of a new approach are presented.

1   Competition through people

A new confidence is evident throughout the training profession. Changes in the corporate and business environment in which the training manager operates have created opportunities for a significant new organizational contribution. Although many problems and challenges lie ahead, there are clear indications that the competitive demands of today's economy will bring training and development centre stage. The training department will no longer be required to justify its existence: it will no longer need to fight for support and attention from the Chief Executive. From now on it will be seen as a key player in the creation and maintenance of competitive strategy.

For many training managers the sentiments outlined in the paragraph above are attractive, even seductive. Regrettably these sentiments represent a battle cry rather than a description of current reality. An opportunity exists for advancing the role and credibility of training in organizations. However, a great deal of serious analysis must take place if the opportunity is to be grasped. The forces that give rise to the new opportunity must be understood, the challenge articulated, models, techniques and processes must be developed. Moreover, these models, techniques and processes are situational: they must reflect the circumstances that apply in any particular organization. If a new exciting future can be glimpsed, there is considerable effort required to make that exciting future a reality. If necessary efforts are not made, both by the training profession as a whole and by the individual training manager in his or her organization, the exciting future could turn out to be a mirage.

In this chapter I begin the fundamental analysis: what is the justification for the claim that the changing corporate environment has created new opportunities for the training profession? This analysis first shows how the development of people could become the new source of competitive advantage. Next it looks closely at the underlying business and organizational trends that have given rise to this possibility. I then review the perspectives offered by some influential commentators.

Finally, I summarize the major issues and questions facing the profession and individual training managers.

TRAINING AND COMPETITIVE STRATEGY

Summary: *A new meaning has been given to the phrase 'people are our most important asset'. Economic pressures have prompted developed economies to see the skills and capabilities of their employees as the key to business survival. As a result a new competitive model has emerged – one that enhances the role of training.*

The phrase 'people are our most important asset' has, in the era of involuntary redundancy and corporate downsizing (and similar euphemisms), been greeted with much cynicism. However, current thinking on competitive strategy has given the phrase a new credibility. A new competitive model is emerging, in which training has a significant role to play.

There is a simple articulation of the new model in Figure 1.1: it consists of the six elements, none of which should be accepted without challenge. All require scrutiny and demand that hard evidence be produced to support the underlying assumptions. Where appropriate, such evidence as is available is presented in the course of this book. At this stage all that is needed is: first, a recognition that each of the elements has a strong immediate credibility; second, that taken together the elements provide a powerful argument for promoting training both nationally and within organizations.

This new competitive model is central to the promotion of training nationally as an examination of Government policy statements demonstrates. Two promotional publications written during the last few years illustrate the point. In 1994 the

---

TRAINING IS KEY TO COMPETITIVE STRATEGY BECAUSE

1. The new global economy, reinforced by the information/telecommunications revolution and by deregulation, has changed the nature of competition
2. As barriers to international trade disappear, developed countries cannot compete through costs
3. Survival for these countries must be sought through developing a sophisticated workforce which can apply individual skills and knowledge
4. The true source of competitive advantage for companies, therefore, is embedded in the skills and capabilities of their employees
5. Retaining, rewarding and motivating these knowledge workers *requires* a new approach to human resource management
6. Developing the skills of these knowledge workers *demands* that the training function is given a new enhanced organisational role.

Figure 1.1   Elements of the new competitive model

Department of Trade and Industry (DTI) together with the Confederation of British Industry (CBI) published *Competitiveness – How the Best UK Companies are Winning;*[1] in 1997 the Department of Trade and Industry and the Department of Education and Employment (DfEE) published *Competitiveness through Partnerships with People.*[2]

Winning argued that the UK contained many excellent companies: these produced the right goods and services of the right quality, at the right price and at the right time, meeting customers' needs more efficiently and effectively than other firms. This is a reasonable, if somewhat bland, description of the ingredients of short-term commercial success. Not enough of these excellent companies existed, however. Accordingly, the DTI and CBI commissioned the Warwick Manufacturing Group at Warwick University to study one hundred of these best companies and identify shared characteristics. These elements of 'ingredients for success' are presented in Figure 1.2.

Partnerships with People took as an assumption that competitiveness could only be improved if 'we work together to improve every aspect of our performance. This partnership is at the heart of what constitutes a responsible and successful organisation.' The DTI and DfEE carried out an investigation into how this was achieved in practice. The Centre for Research into Innovation Management at the University of Brighton set the framework for research, which was carried out through focus groups and interviews by a large number of partner organizations (including, once again, the CBI). Five main broad bands of management practices were identified as 'producing a balanced environment in which employees thrived and sought success for themselves and their organisations'. These 'paths to sustained success' are also reproduced in Figure1.2.

The two reports had a great deal in common in terms of intention, approach and (as can be seen from Figure 1.2) in findings. Neither set out to be a description of the reality of UK practice in general: both simply claimed that best practice existed. The extent to which these excellent companies are representative was not dealt with. Both offered a checklist to allow organisations to benchmark themselves against best practice.

Both recognized that different organizational situations (size, markets, etc.) could require different processes but argued that the key elements of success are the same and any organization could benefit from their findings. Both were firmly unitarist in perspective, reflecting a philosophy that all employees are committed to the same ends and that different groups should willingly work together to deliver organizational performance. Both were firmly grounded in what will be later described as the 'new human resources'. This concept will be developed in Chapter 2. The framework for the 'new human resources' involves a clear set of goals, leading to motivation, supported by training, reinforced by communication and delivered through teamwork.

WINNING: INGREDIENTS FOR SUCCESS

Winning UK companies

Are led by visionary, enthusiastic champions of change

Unlock the potential of their people by
- creating a culture in which employees are genuinely empowered and focused on the customer
- investing in people through good communications, teaming and training
- flattening and inverting the organisational pyramid.

Know their customers by
- constantly learning from others
- welcoming the challenge of demanding customers to drive innovation and competitiveness.

Constantly introduce new, differentiated products and services by
- deep knowledge of their competitors
- encouraging innovation to successfully exploit new ideas
- focusing on core businesses complemented by strategic alliances.

Exceed their customers' expectations with new products and services

Partnerships with people: five paths to sustained success

1. *Shared goals*
   Understanding the business we are in
2. *Shared culture*
   Agreed values binding us together
3. *Shared learning*
   Continuously improving ourselves
4. *Shared effort*
   One business driven by flexible teams
5. *Shared information*
   Effective communication throughout the company

Figure 1.2   Extracts from Government publications on competitiveness

Most importantly, from the point of view of the arguments to be developed in this book, both saw learning, development and training as a key driver of *business success*. To quote:

> Training is seen as a key component in achieving empowerment of the individual and in maintaining focus on the customer in order to remain competitive. Not only is 'training the epicentre of empowerment' with as much as 10% of employees' time spent on it, but 'successful companies use education as a competitive weapon' (*Winning*).

and

> As the workforce becomes more skilled, the visions of the company can become more ambitious because the full potential of the people is released into an environment of achievement ... Companies report that training and learning steadily develop an atmosphere of problem solving and creativity (*Partnerships with People*).

The 'new human resources' goes hand in hand with recognition of and commitment to customer needs which permeates the organization. Knowledge of customer requirements links back to improved services and products from increasingly skilled employees.

Significantly the two reports were issued by UK Governments of opposite political persuasions (Conservative and New Labour). In the intervening period between the publications a vigorously fought general election had taken place. Yet there is scarcely any perceptible difference between the two – save the Trades Union Congress as a signatory to *Partnerships with People*. Cynically one could dismiss both publications as example of 'exhortative voluntarism': an attempt to describe best practice in the hope it is accepted and becomes adopted as universal reality – a politically attractive alternative to compulsion.

However, there is something important to be gained from looking beyond the propaganda hype. A new opportunity for training is beckoning. The challenge is to move from a recognition of the opportunity to specify and implement the new approaches to training which will be particular to each organization. How this can be achieved will be developed in this and later chapters, starting with an overview of the changes in the market economy.

KEY BUSINESS TRENDS

Summary: *It is universally accepted that competition has become more intense. Two forces that have given rise to this growing intensity are an increasingly global economy underpinned by an information/telecommunications revolution. There is incontrovertible evidence that these forces have exerted a powerful influence on the competitive environment in which all large organizations operate. An important issue facing the training manager is to consider how the influence will be felt in the case of his or her organization.*

A helpful start to analysing the significant changes in market conditions that have influenced competitive strategy has been presented by Michael de Kare-Silver in *Strategy in Crisis*.[3] He offered the following list: which is reproduced with illustrative quotations from his text.

- *Power in nearly every industry, has firmly shifted to the customer* 'effective customer management and 'customer service' specifically appear to be prime routes for competitive success.'
- *Scale is not necessarily an advantage* 'until even quite recently the trend in business has been for size – the big just got bigger, aiming through scale to dominate their markets. But the new global arena is more demanding. Right now being the biggest doesn't necessarily mean a company can dominate.'

- *Borders and boundaries have collapsed* 'the general effects [of globalization are] well known ... but less attention is typically given to the nevertheless equally dramatic collapse of more traditional business boundaries – those within an organization and those between its previously separate and discrete suppliers and customers. This erosion of former boundaries is giving rise to new sources of advantage and competitive opportunity.'

- *Technology is ever more quickly copied* 'recent research goes on to show that imitations succeed as often as innovations and being 'first-in' a market is no guarantee whatsoever of future success.'

- *There is a constant stream of new low-cost competitors* 'the rush of low-priced competition from Asia, Eastern Europe and Latin America and elsewhere has been well-documented. What this has done is put price firmly on the agenda and reconfirmed views that simply having scale is now irrelevant in the modern day.'

- *Information technology has revolutionized what can be done and what can be accessed* 'what is clear for strategy makers is that IT has created an environment where customers perceive almost anything is possible. Indeed it has encouraged the view that there can be continuous improvement in doing things faster, or making tasks easier or services more convenient and generally that it will all get cheaper.'

- *The global spread has now made it even more difficult for a corporate centre to manage the company* 'Management was never easy. Now there are often diverse operating companies headquartered in different countries, speaking different languages, with different cultures and spread across often 50 or more countries around the world.'

Michael de Kare-Silver used this list as a background in his review of existing tools and his formulation of a new approach to strategy. Most business leaders and all strategic planners will be aware of the pressures that these changes in market conditions have had on their organization. These pressures have led to a reaction to the aggressive cost-cutting and downsizing. The Chief Executive must formulate a different style of response.

Against this background of growing pressures, the human resource function (and training in particular) has been given a window of opportunity. It can assist the Chief Executive in formulating his or her response. What form that response will take will obviously depend on the nature of the business.

As de Kare-Silver has argued, globalization and technology are irreversible trends and affect all businesses. The emphasis is therefore on speed to market, and to markets where boundaries are blurred. The traditional market place is obsolete as a concept; it has been replaced by market spaces – opportunities to satisfy customers with products and services which did not exist a decade earlier.

These customers are becoming far more sophisticated and new thinking is taking place on the concept of customer service. Customer loyalty is paramount: particularly in the service sector it is much more profitable to retain existing customers and sell different products to them than to attract new customers.

The Board and Chief Executive must therefore decide how to position their firms. They will be trying to increase revenues, while coping with far-reaching transformations brought about by technological changes. There has, for example, been a significant convergence in broadcast media, computer and telecommunications. The relationship between the pharmaceutical industry as provider and health care as user has become blurred. In addition the Board and Chief Executive must manage pressure from key parties – government regulation will have a decisive effect on the pattern of competition in sectors such as the two just mentioned.

Overall, therefore, the focus has shifted from cost reduction to growth. The former was the focus for much of the 1990s where the emphasis was on doing the same things better and more cost-effectively. Re-engineering processes were introduced to increase efficiency, but have broadly disappointed. Similarly, attempts to alter corporate cultures have not always succeeded. Cost efficiency will always be important but now the emphasis has shifted to a planned use of outsourcing – where non-critical activities are undertaken on a contractual basis by an outside body. Outsourcing started as a way of cutting costs. It is now seen as an opportunity to focus management time on developing the core activities which are critical to the business.

If the attractions and potential for cost reduction have reduced, profitability must be achieved through growing revenues. Boards and Chief Executives are therefore considering options which include: growing organically or by acquisition; entering new product markets (which build on existing capabilities); expanding into new territories which are more and more global. Each of these options may be achieved in part by building strategic alliances with other firms. All business leaders will be looking for the next big step forward – that breakthrough that redefines the nature of competition in the market. The potential rewards are huge and can allow the successful (for example, Microsoft in software) a period of market domination.

Why does all this offer human resources and training a window of opportunity? First, because firms are increasingly trying to identify and consolidate their core activities or capabilities. Second, because firms are trying to innovate, using these capabilities as a starting point. Both of these place more emphasis on managing and developing the critical knowledge workers. In addition, the softer issues of management are recognized as serious challenges. Firms need to develop the right sort of culture and clear communication is required both upwards and downwards. This demands effective people management and more responsibility at lower levels for development of subordinates.

All the above has given rise to what will be described throughout this book as the new human resources. This concept is developed in the next chapter. First, however, the views of a number of leading management thinkers are considered. They, too, offer a perspective on the changing business environment, which will assist the training manager in forming his or her response in the particular circumstances of their organization. If the current opportunity is to be taken, the Chief Executive must be convinced that training is a key part of survival and prosperity; training must be seen to contribute to the active management of the appropriate organizational response to continual changes.[4]

THE CHANGING ORGANIZATIONAL RESPONSE

Summary: *Changes in the global market have not only redefined the rules of competition. They have affected the structures of the organization and the appropriate style of management. Other societal factors, through their influence on attitudes to job and careers, have also made an impact here. To complete the initial analysis of the concept of competition through people the views of some leading management commentators will be reviewed.*

Studying the work of the best writers on management offers fertile territory for the trainer. There is an underlying emphasis on competition through people – though this is often implicit rather than explicit. This leads to the identification of some common themes which will shape the approach to the management of training in the organization.

Such a review was undertaken in the previous edition of this book. The common themes identified there continue to be relevant and are reproduced as Figure 1.3.

RELEVANT FEATURES OF THE CURRENT ORGANIZATIONAL ENVIRONMENT ARE:

- people issues are growing in prominence and there is greater emphasis on enhancing the skills of the workforce
- 'management' is decreasingly seen as a status position: growing numbers of people have authority and require management and interpersonal skills to do their job
- organizations are becoming more dependent on self-aware, capable individuals and must recognize their aspirations; new processes will take the place of traditional career management
- communication and feedback skills are critical, as shared objectives become both more important and more difficult to formulate and maintain
- it is less easy to achieve results through hierarchical control; operation through alliances and coalition is required and appropriate influencing skills are needed.

These should be taken into account when determining the approach to training.

Figure 1.3   Relevant features of the current organizational environment

In this second edition the management thinkers will be selected on a different basis.

Two of the three sources reviewed will be taken from the business strategy literature. This reflects the importance of changing the focus of the contribution for training to a more proactive one of building competitive advantage through people.

The first set of authors, Gary Hamel (a professor at the London Business School) and C.K. Prahalad (whose chair is at the University of Michigan), have co-authored a decisive set of contributions to the strategy debate. Three Harvard Business Review articles[5,6,7] were followed by *Competing for the Future*.[8]

Hamel and Prahalad argue that in the long term success is about creating unimagined, but soon to be essential, products and services. They have observed that similar companies have shown marked differences in resource effectiveness, which could not be explained by differences in operational efficiency. Therefore, simply embarking on cost cutting to create leaner organizations is not the answer. In fact, successful companies simply get more out of their resources by setting ambitious goals. Most importantly they make a commitment to develop particular components of competitive advantage – these they call *core competencies*.

Hamel and Prahalad regard core competencies as a bundle of skills and tech-nologies that enable a company to provide a particular benefit to customers. These core competencies are the gateways to future opportunities. Competing for the future involves pre-emptive building of the competencies that provide tomorrow's opportunities, as well as finding novel applications of current ones.

Successful companies are not only aware of their competencies; they can stretch and leverage them. They stretch them by getting more competitive advan-tage through their competencies, which involves considerable commitment from their resources. They leverage them by creating strategic alliances with other organizations that can offer complementary competencies. There may be between five and fifteen core competencies in an organization.

To be regarded as a core competency an organizational skill or attribute must pass three tests. First, it must make a disproportionate contribution to perceived customer value. Second, it must be competitively unique. Third, it must be extendible – it should be possible to derive a new array of products and services from the competency.

Hamel and Prahalad therefore take the idea of competing through people a stage further. While their key core competencies are more than simply people-based skills, retaining and nurturing human resources are most important for competitive advantage.

The second set of authors, Christopher A. Bartlett and Sumantra Ghoshal, are also a transatlantic combination: the former is a professor at Harvard; the latter a professor at the London Business School. Both are academic teachers and consultants: neither is a human resource specialist. Yet their work is of considerable significance for the way in which human resource policies can contribute to business success. Through a number of publications, always reinforced by practical illustrations, they have sought to identify how the successful firms manage the competitive process. In so doing, they have necessarily moved away from traditional organizational systems – a movement which has profound significance for human resources and training professionals.

In a series of articles in the Harvard Business Review,[9,10,11] Bartlett and Ghoshal have presented a powerful argument along the following lines. Companies which have renewed themselves think that the real challenge lies not in revamping strategies, structures or systems, but in changing individual employees' behaviour: they encourage employees to strive voluntarily to meet and extend their own commitments. Hence leaders of today's large enterprises must build a framework based on purposes, processes and people. They must: build on corporate purpose; develop and deploy key people; develop personal values and interpersonal relationships that encourage self-monitoring; and develop personal communication to replace information systems. They must create a corporate work ethic that encourages individual entrepreneurship, collaboration and learning.

I would advise reading the original of all the works considered in this section for an adequate appreciation of the argument. However, it is evident from the above brief summary that competitive advantage must be secured through people, through capturing their 'hearts and minds'. In a subsequent article,[12] Bartlett and Ghoshal argued that radical changes in their internal and external environments had caused organizations to innovate a new organizational form. This form is firmly rooted in a perception that knowledge and expertise rather than capital or scale is now the key strategic resource. The multi-divisional corporate model, in which a corporate parent allocates assets and holds divisions accountable is no longer appropriate. In the new model resources will be decentralized to front-line units that operate with limited dependence on the corporate parent but with considerable independence among themselves.

The culmination of Ghoshal and Bartlett's recent thinking was expressed in a 1998 book.[13] By this stage their ideas on the significance of the new competitive pressures had led them to postulate an emerging corporate model. This they styled 'The Individualized Corporation' which became the title of their book. The book was sub-titled *A Fundamentally New Approach to Management*.

Three core capabilities distinguish 'The Individualized Corporation'. 'The first is its ability to inspire individual creativity and initiative in all its people, built on a fundamental faith in individuals ... The second ... is its ability to link and leverage pockets of entrepreneurial activity and individual expertise by building an integrated process of organizational learning ... The third core feature of the new corporate model [is] its ability to continuously renew itself' (p. 14). Inevitably 'this different conceptualization of the organization has radical implications for the roles of frontline, senior and top-level managers of a company, and for the relationships that are needed among them to tie these new roles together into a high-performing management system' (p. 15).

Several of these implications, particularly on the importance of organizational learning and shared knowledge, are considered later in this book – especially in Chapter 3 (p. 58) and Chapter 7 (p. 169).

The UK-based writer, Charles Handy, has drawn his views from a wide social perspective. He investigated and discussed the concept of corporate culture well in advance of the current interest in the subject; he has considered the place of the individual in the overall employment context.

His reflections led him to argue that organizations of the future will need to adapt their managerial philosophy to the needs and aspirations of individuals – leading to a far-reaching reorganization of the structure of organizations and their work. In his early works Handy talked in terms of a move from the employment organization to a combination of professional partnership, contractual organization and a federal state. This shift has considerable implications for the task of management. Extending the federal structure of corporate organizations into an analogy of centres and villages, Handy argues that the centre will be dominated 'by the need to prepare plans, reach agreement on plans, disseminate the plans and co-ordinate the village efforts to implement the plans' and, so that the individual needs of the villages are not threatened 'the process therefore is one of bargaining, adaptation, persuasion and compromise. Vision and imagination are required, but so are sensitivity, the ability to understand other points of view, patience, tact, the skill to weld groups and fuse perceptions.' (p. 200).[14]

Management in this context is seen as a task for a time, not a career. The individual in such an organization will have a variety of interests and will belong to different groups; balances of power and priorities will be shifting according to the problems in hand. Decisions will emerge rather than be made.

In the *The Age of Unreason*[15] Handy extended his thoughts on changing structures by introducing the concept of the shamrock organization. Today's corporations are made up of three different groups of people – who have different expectations, and must be paid and managed differently. These three groups, analogous to the three leaves of the shamrock, are:

- the core workers, the qualified professionals, technicians and managers – the people who own the knowledge that gives the organization its character
- the contractual fringe, who make a speciality of providing appropriate services for the organization, and range from the cleaners through to consultants
- the flexible labour force, part-time and temporary workers who are hired in as appropriate.

Each part of this labour force requires a different management approach. Professionals and technicians in the core think in terms of advancement and the future. They wish to make a contribution and they need to be asked for their input. Life at the core of organizations is going to resemble a consultancy firm, with early promotion and few layers of management. At the contractual fringe, by contrast, payment is for results, not time – and this situation needs control to specify the outcome. The most important aspect to managing the third leaf, the flexible labour force, is to take them seriously, and to treat them with respect as a valuable part of the organization. Handy suggests that they should be included in any company training plans. In the same book he also foreshadows the 'Triple I' organization (information, intelligence, ideas) in which competitive advantage is based on knowledge and the ability to use that knowledge.

The knowledge worker will have different aspirations from the status-conscious executive of the past. Handy has placed considerable attention on career development for this group, identifying a shift from lifetime employment in a single company to 'portfolio' work which will be less secure but more satisfying.

Over time, Charles Handy has developed his thinking and positioned his management theory in a wider social philosophy. His two most recent books, *The Empty Raincoat*[16] and *The Hungry Spirit*[17] are works of considerable scope and ambition. Handy highlights the role of the individual in the organization of the future: his exploration leads him to identify the changes that will be needed in individual attitudes and organizational structure.

The Empty Raincoat is a spiritual work in which Handy examines the paradoxes of modern corporate life. He identifies the indications that material prosperity has fitted uneasily with personal development. Low-level jobs give neither economic reward nor personal dignity; at the other end jobs are exhilarating, well paid but totally demanding. Individuals, families and societies suffer. The challenge is 'to find our human selves again, amid all the pressures for progress and economic success' (p. 129). This gives Handy an agenda that is wide in scope, embracing many aspects of the relationship of work and society. Part of this agenda concerns the meaning of business in society. Here, Handy argues that 'focused intelligence, the ability to acquire and apply knowledge and know-how, is the new source of wealth' (p. 23) and this will alter the shape of the organization of the future, because 'When intelligence is the primary asset the organisation becomes more like a collection of project groups, some fairly permanent, some temporary, some in alliance with other parties. Instead of an organisation being a castle, a home for life for its defenders, it will be more like a condominium, an association of temporary residents gathered together for their mutual convenience' (p. 38–39).

In *The Hungry Spirit*, Handy again challenges the endless quest for growth and identifies failings of the market-driven economy – though he sees it the best of the alternatives. A deeper purpose to living is needed beyond materialism. For the individual this requires acceptance of 'a responsibility for making the most of oneself by, ultimately, finding a purpose beyond and bigger than oneself' (p. 9). This Handy calls 'proper selfishness': an altruistic and individual striving. He argues that this is the sort of individualism that, operating within a capitalist framework, is needed to make the world a better place.

Where Handy's work is of particular relevance to this book is when he applies his principles to institutions – especially companies. These he compares to nation states and draws a powerful analogy between the rights of citizens and employees. Organizations must now come to terms with a new face as 'individuals begin to expect from their work communities the same collection of freedoms, rights and responsibilities that they have in the wider society. People are property no more' (p. 179).

Handy's belief that organizations should adopt a new attitude towards their employees is a consequence of his ethical values. However, there are strong practical reasons for the new approach since much competition is now about intangible property, 'the brands, the research, the networks, the reputation, the know-how, and the "core competencies" of the place' (p. 160). Much of this intangible property can only belong to the individuals who have the skills and the expertise.

The practical steps, that can be taken to implement the new attitude are based on partnership and trust. Most controversially he argues for the guarantee of employment for a fixed period of years – he suggests a decade. Organizations need to distinguish between mercenaries (who have loyalty only to themselves and no commitment to the organization beyond the immediate project) and their citizens. The organization must be careful in its management of the psychological contract with the latter. The term 'psychological contract' will be considered more fully in Chapter 2. At this stage it can be defined as the undocumented understanding that exists between an organization and its employees.

THE IMPLICATIONS FOR TRAINING

Summary: *Competition through people offers the trainer a new opportunity. The new optimism is well founded. However, much of the new thinking and ideas have been generated outside the human resource profession. The training manager will need to determine how these significant trends and new ideas have affected his or her organization if the opportunity is to be grasped.*

This chapter has reviewed the changing context in which training will be delivered in most modern organizations. It is now appropriate to summarize some of the implications for the training manager. What are the significant issues and questions facing the profession?

An outline is presented as Figure 1.4. The work of Hamel and Prahalad and their formulation of core competencies suggest that the development and retention of key staff is critical. This places a greater value in effective training. However, competition through people extends beyond training. Bartlett and Ghoshal seek, through their Individualized Corporation, to indicate the importance of inspiration, the encouragement of creativity and of organizational learning and the inevitability of continuous change.

These underpin what they describe as the high-performing management system. These terms have a resonance in the training community. Handy reminds us that relationships between the organization and the individual cannot be taken for granted. Respect and trust must be earned and organizations must treat their people as partners not property. Surely training must play a part in building this trust.

IN MOST MODERN ORGANIZATIONS

- there is a new opportunity for positioning training as one of the key forces in driving business success
- such opportunity extends across the whole of the human resource discipline
- the seeds of this new opportunity lie in a recognition of the growing importance of competition through people – this has also given rise to a need for a new high-performing management system
- other social forces, through their effect on the employment relationship, have also led to revised opinions on the best approach to developing the workforce.

First of all, the training manager needs to consider how the above trends have affected his or her organization.

Figure 1.4 Implications of current trends for training

All the trends seem to be creating a new opportunity: the new confidence referred to in the opening sentence of this chapter is therefore justified. People are indeed the organization's most important assets; they must be properly trained. Would that life were that simple!

The trends are opening up opportunities but they are diverse and their impact is frequently unclear. They are often not fully appreciated by line managers, or even by chief executives. When they are understood, the link with training is not immediately apparent.

Moreover, very little analysis has come from the training profession. The influential literature and accompanying discussion has not been written by trainers; indeed, most of it has come from outside the human resource discipline. Hence, the implications for corporate training are implicit, but are rarely made explicit. There is a lot to be understood and analysed to form practical guidance for the trainer in his or her day-to-day work. The emergence of new models of competitive strategy, high-performing (and high-commitment) systems, the psychological contract, and knowledge (broadly, the management of Handy's information intelligence and ideas (see Chapter 7, p. 169) as subjects of interest are indeed good news. They must, however, be understood and discussed further if they are to influence practical plans for training. Their impact on human resources has therefore been considerable and the changes in the perception of the discipline and its contribution are considered next.

REFERENCES

1. Department of Trade and Industry/Confederation of British Industry (1994), *Competitiveness – How the Best UK Companies are Winning*, London: Crown Copyright.
2. Department of Trade and Industry/Department for Education and Employment (1997), *Competitiveness through Partnerships with People*, London: Crown Copyright.
3. de Kare-Silver, M. (1997), *Strategy in Crisis*, London: MacMillan Business, p. 22–35.
4. I am grateful to Richard Dicketts, a Partner in Ernst & Young's Management Consultancy Practice, for his analysis, which contributed to this section.
5. Hamel, G. and Prahalad, C.K. (1989), 'Strategic Intent', *Harvard Business Review,* **67** (3).
6. Hamel, G. and Prahalad, C.K. (1993), 'Strategy as Stretch and Leverage', *Harvard Business Review,* **71** (2).
7. Hamel, G. and Prahalad, C.K. (1994), 'Competing for the Future', *Harvard Business Review,* **72** (4).
8. Hamel, G. and Prahalad, C.K. (1994), *Competing for the Future*, Boston: Harvard Business School Press.
9. Bartlett, C.A. and Ghoshal, S. (1994), 'Changing the Role of Top Management: Beyond Strategy to Purpose', *Harvard Business Review,* **72** (6) p. 79–88.
10. Ghoshal, S. and Bartlett, C.A. (1995), 'Changing the Role of Top Management: Beyond Structure to Processes', *Harvard Business Review* **73** (1) pp. 86–96.
11. Bartlett, C.A. and Ghoshal, S. (1995), 'Changing the Role of Top Management: Beyond Systems to People', *Harvard Business Review,* **73** (3) pp. 32–142.
12. Bartlett, C.A. and Ghoshal, S. (1993), 'Beyond the M-Form: Toward a Managerial Theory of the Firm', *Strategic Management Journal*, Special Issue, **14**: 23–46.
13. Ghoshal, S. and Bartlett, C.A. (1998) *The Individualized Corporation*, London: Heinemann.
14. Handy, C. (1978), *Gods of Management*, London: Souvenir Press.
15. Handy, C. (1989), *The Age of Unreason*, London: Hutchinson.
16. Handy, C. (1994), *The Empty Raincoat*, London: Hutchinson.
17. Handy, C. (1997), *The Hungry Spirit*, London: Hutchinson.

2 The new human resources

In the previous chapter I considered the claim that training will play an exciting new role in the organization of the future. Training can become essential to competitive strategy because the source for advantage is embedded in the skills and the capabilities of knowledge workers. There is a deliberate attempt by Government to encourage best practice, which could work to reinforce the training managers' efforts. I identified the implications of these current trends and urged the training manager to consider the impact of these trends on his or her organization.

In later sections of this book, I consider the way in which these trends can be translated into training practice. First, however, it is necessary to examine and develop further three of the bullet points included in Figure 1.4 (p. 18). In particular, we must ask:

● what does 'competition through people' mean and how can it find an expression in human resource policies?
● given that the new competitive opportunity extends beyond training to include the whole of the human resource discipline, what is best practice human resources?
● what are the social forces affecting the employment relationship, and how could they affect day-to-day training activity?

These are wide-ranging questions. Their answers will lead to a reconsideration of the role of training in the organization. The analysis in this chapter embraces three important topics. First, I outline the strategy debate and the growing prominence of resource-based strategy. Second, I introduce new thinking on the role of human resources in the business. Third, I consider in detail one particular force which shapes the new human resources: this is the revised perception of careers and the emergent interest in the psychological contract. After consideration of these three topics, some implications for the training manager will be presented.

THE STRATEGY DEBATE: RESOURCE-BASED STRATEGY

Summary: *One of the forces that have shaped the new human resources is the emergence of what is now called resource-based strategy. This shifts the competitive emphasis from an external response to market conditions to an internal response based on the development of capabilities.*

It is impossible to understand the emergence of the new human resources – or to appreciate its significance – without some appreciation of the changing perspectives in business strategy. Part II of this book considers the practical side of linking training with strategy and outlines the new training processes. This section reviews the broad parameters of the debate that has taken place within the strategy profession. A starting point is the following simple definition of strategy, a matching process:

> Strategy matches what a company can do (organizational strengths and weaknesses) within the competitive context of what it might do (environmental opportunities and threats).

Broadly, the concept of strategy was transferred from the military arena to the business arena in the 1960s. The early emphasis was on prescriptive, linear strategy – a set of methodical, rational and sequential actions involved in planning from above, with formulation preceding implementation. Subsequently there has been a movement to a more descriptive, adaptive strategy, with far more flexibility between formulation and implementation.

Nowadays there are a number of different approaches adopted to strategy formulation. Some strategists focus strictly on operating issues, linking planning with other tools – for example benchmarking the comparison of internal performance with best practice elsewhere inside and outside the organization. Others look to the future and consider alternative scenarios and their consequences. A third group will focus on organizational culture and its implications (this concept is considered further in Chapter 4, p. 80). The compelling new concept of resource-based strategy is compatible with all these approaches and is particularly compelling to the human resource professional.

At its simplest, resource-based strategy is only another way of saying that 'people are our most important asset'. It is helpful to consider the definition of strategy as 'matching' which was offered at the start of this section. In resource-based approaches to strategy, the emphasis is on using what a company can do – the organizational strengths are developed, stretched, extended and leveraged for competitive advantage. Arguably, the weakness of resource-based strategy, and the source of much criticism of this approach, is that it fails to take sufficient account of the other half of the strategy definition: the competitive context in which the company operates. Resource-based approaches to strategy, the argument goes, may understate the environmental threats and opportunities; at their crudest they may disregard the market.

John Kay, Director of the Said Business School at Oxford University, has described the importance of resource-based strategy in the following terms.[1]

Resource-based strategy

> examines the dynamics of the successes and failures of firms by reference of their distinctive capabilities – the factors, often implicit and intangible which differentiate them from their competitors in the same markets and which cannot be reproduced by these competitors even after the advantages they offer are recognized (p. vi)

Effective strategy must start from

> what the company is distinctively good at, not from what it would like to be good at, and is adaptive and opportunistic in exploiting what is distinctive in these capabilities (p. 43).

And the main elements of resource-based strategy are:

- firms are essentially collections of capabilities
- the effectiveness of a firm depends on the match between these capabilities and the market it serves
- the growth, and appropriate boundaries, of a firm are limited by its capabilities
- some of these capabilities can be purchased or created and are available to all firms
- others are irreproducible or reproducible only with substantial difficulty, by other firms, and it is on these that competitive advantage depends
- such capabilities are generally irreproducible because they are a product of the history of the firm or by virtue of uncertainty (even within the firm itself) about their nature (pp. 33–4).

John Kay places great value on resource-based strategy and indeed argues that the resource-based theory 'unifies most of what is substantial and significant in our existing knowledge of business behaviour' (p. 33).

Hamel and Prahalad's advocacy of the core competency approach (see p. 13) is a practical expression of the concept underlying resource-based strategy. They adopt a tight approach when they suggest that there may be between five and fifteen core competencies in an organization; other commentators take looser approaches. Either way, resource-based strategy is a powerful and attractive concept.

STRATEGIC HUMAN RESOURCES

Summary: *The debate on the role of the function has moved beyond the transition from 'personnel management' to 'human resources management' (HRM). A new human resources (HR) is emerging; this positions the function as a key business* *driver playing a strategic role. It involves much more than enhanced training and development. Some descriptions and definitions are offered and the views of leading-edge commentators considered. Finally a practical instrument designed to assess the position of the human resource function in an organization is presented.*

Appropriate human resources policies are now recognized as essential for the success of the modern organization. Personnel/human resources programmes and activities contribute to the organization in three ways:

- by ensuring that employees possess the characteristics required for effective performance, achieved by appropriate recruitment at the outset, promotion, and development and training
- by providing cues and reinforcements to guide and motivate behaviour, most obviously a function of remuneration but also achieved through a performance review or appraisal process
- by creating an appropriate framework for the interaction between the individual and the organization.

This description of the role of personnel/human resources could have been presented at any time over the last thirty years. The three basic activities of resourcing the firm's needs for people, ensuring that they perform effectively, and regulating the interchange must be fulfilled in any organization beyond the size of a small partnership. While objectives have remained the same, there has been a changing perception of the best approaches. Tools and techniques have emerged and been discarded. Labels have changed.

The move from 'personnel management' to 'human resources management' is an example of such a change – but it is a significant one. The tendency towards the use of 'human resource management' (HRM) rather than personnel management marked a significant realignment in the way the function perceives, or would wish to perceive, itself. There are some important issues at the heart of the change – and these issues are essential for the determination of best training practice. In the following analysis 'human resources' (HR) will be used to describe the function or discipline and 'human resources management' (HRM) to describe the activities undertaken by that function or discipline.

The terms gained increased currency in the 1980s in organizations and business schools in the United States. In some quarters in the UK the new terminology was initially resisted as a transatlantic import and arguments have been advanced for regarding HRM as simply an evolutionary stage in the discipline of personnel management. This challenge has receded with time and emphasis has now shifted on determining the constituent elements of best practice HRM.

Torrington and Hall offer a useful starting definition:

Human resources management is resource centered, directed mainly at management needs for human resources (not necessarily employees) to be provided and deployed. Demand rather than supply is emphasized. There is greater emphasis on planning, monitoring and control rather than mediation ... It is totally identified with management interests being a general management activity, and is relatively distant from the workforce as a whole (pp. 15–16).[2]

Two broader management trends underline the need for such a change of perspective. First, line managers themselves undertake as part of day-to-day management many of the tasks traditionally labelled 'personnel'. The shift is particularly marked in training and development. Second, success depends on organizational policies and procedures becoming closely linked with the achievement of corporate objectives and strategic plans.

A most interesting analysis of these trends was offered in the 1990 Price Waterhouse/Cranfield project on international strategic human resource management. This report was based on a survey of 6000 employing organizations in five European countries. The report sought to examine the impact of major economic developments on the way that companies recruit, pay, train and develop their staff. One of their important findings was that 'personnel responsibility is increasingly being devolved to line managers – the trend is particularly marked in training and development' (p. 4).[3]

This trend was also emphasized a year later in the 1991 Price Waterhouse/Cranfield report, which found that the respective roles of line management and personnel specialist were changing, with more human resource responsibility take up by the line. While responsibility for industrial relations was retained by the human resources function, training and development 'is typically allocated to some combination of the HR Department in consultation with the line'. Generally 'decentralization in the level of decisions within the organisation and devolution to line management continues apace' (p. 8).[4]

The earlier (1990) Price Waterhouse/Cranfield survey uncovered one other feature that is central to the analysis of strategic human resources developed later in this section: the emergence of a new and pivotal human resource function:

characterised by its full involvement in the process of corporate decision-making. This evolving role will focus the organization's attention on vital human resource issues. Consequently, employers will be better placed to create coherent and consistent policies which contribute directly to the organisation's strategic goals (p. 4).[3]

Pivotal functions were distinguished by their influence at the strategic level of the organization; clear and consistent policies; adaptability to circumstances; the value they add to the organization; and their knowledge of, and commitment to, the evaluation of results. A characteristic of pivotal functions 'is not their acceptance of the importance of the people in the organisation – but their ability to make acceptance of that importance count' (p. 6).[3]

The arguments presented so far in this book have sought to demonstrate that human resource programmes are now an integral part of the process of building competitive advantage. Human resources management must be seen to play an essential role. This follows from a recognition of the importance of competition through people and an appreciation of resource-based strategy. Effective HRM is needed to develop the internal capabilities: to nurture and protect the core-led competencies. However, the role of HR extends beyond a focus on internal competencies. The function must play an expanded organizational role. In Chapter 1 (p. 7) the framework for this 'new human resources' was identified as a clear set of goals, leading to motivation, supported by training, reinforced by communication and delivered through teamwork. John Kay, whose work has been cited to introduce the concept of resource-based strategy, talked of the broader themes suggested by this view of strategy, 'that theory leads on to emphasis on the importance of corporate personality, the routines and cultures, relationships and reputations which are not simply associated with successful companies but which are the essence of what makes them successful' (p. vi).[1]

Clearly HR should play a role in building up the corporate personality and the associated culture, developing competitive advantage through people, and reinforcing it through appropriate policies to encourage involvement and commitment. Two views from leading-edge commentators will clarify the concept.

Jeffrey Pfeffer, Professor of Organizational Behavior at Stanford University in California, argues that competitive success involves altering fundamentally how we think about the workforce and employment relationships. In a series of articles and books he has examined what has led to sustained advantage for successful firms. This he sees as relying not on technology, patents or strategic position, but on how the workforce is managed. In a paper[5] adapted from an earlier book,[6] Pfeffer lists thirteen practices that 'seem to characterize companies that are effective in achieving competitive success through how they manage people' (p. 57).[5] These thirteen practices are reproduced in Figure 2.1. In his 1998 book he has reduced the list to seven 'dimensions that seem to characterize most if not all of the systems producing profit through people' (pp. 64–5).[7] The two lists cover similar ground and it is the fuller earlier list that will be considered here.

Pfeffer argues that achieving competitive advantage through the workforce takes time to accomplish, but once achieved it can be enduring and difficult to duplicate. The way in which each of the thirteen practices can be applied in any particular case will vary. However, the importance of this approach lies in its recognition that using HR as a competitive weapon involves putting in place a variety of parallel initiatives. Hopefully they will be mutually self-reinforcing.

Dave Ulrich, a professor at the University of Michigan, also adopts a broad perspective when he argues that what is required is organizational excellence and 'to state it plainly: achieving organizational excellence must be the work of HR'

Jeffrey Pfeffer has identified the following interrelated practices characterizing companies that achieve competitive success through the management of people (see Ref. 5):

- employment security
- selectivity in recruiting
- high wages
- incentive pay
- employee ownership
- information sharing
- participation and empowerment
- self-managed teams
- training and skill development
- cross utilization and cross training (having people do multiple jobs)
- symbolic egalitarianism (signalling to insiders and outsiders that there is comparative equality)
- wage compression
- promotion from within.

(Adapted from Jeffrey Pfeffer, *Competitive Advantage through People*, Harvard Business School Press, and reproduced by permission of the author and Harvard Business School Press.)

Figure 2.1   **Effective practices for managing people**

(p. 124).[8] He identifies four ways in which HR can achieve operational excellence. HR should become:

- a partner with senior and line managers in strategy execution
- an expert in the way work is organized and executed delivering administrative efficiency
- a champion for employees, both vigorously representing their concerns to senior management and also increasing their commitment to the organization and their ability to deliver
- an agent of continuous transformation, shaping processes and culture that improve an organization's capacity for change.

Ulrich argues that this new agenda would mark a radical departure for HR. It would move it away from 'policy police and regulatory watchdog' and 'every one of HR's activities would in some concrete way help the company better serve its customers or otherwise increase shareholder value' (p. 125).

Not all HR professionals would agree with Ulrich's four components of organizational excellence. Certainly the role of employee champion would not find ready acceptance in some quarters. It would mark a radical departure from recent trends where the profession has sought (some would argue too eagerly) to be purely an instrument of management. Ulrich's suggestion that HR should deliver administrative efficiency raises an important point. The new HR must not be achieved at the expense of neglecting the elements of the 'old' personnel administration (payroll, recruitment, induction and termination, for example), which are essential to the organization and must be delivered efficiently. Much of the credibility of the function depends on success in this area. Moreover, if these basic administrative activities are deficient, the HR Department will be spending inordinate amounts of time and effort in a reactive role rather than a proactive one of developing competitive advantage through people.

In the earlier discussion on the trends that have led to emergence of the new human resources, I outlined the Price Waterhouse/Cranfield project. This project has provided a useful new model of the place of the HR department in the organization, proceeding from a recognition of the issues raised by the centralizing and decentralizing tendencies.

Chris Brewster and Henrik Holt Larsen, drawing on the Price Waterhouse/Cranfield research, suggest that HR practices in the European countries surveyed can be categorized, *inter alia*, by the degree of integration of HRM with business strategy and the degree of devolvement to line managers.[9] Their two-by-two matrix is reproduced as Figure 2.2, and allows an analysis of both the role of the specialist HR department and the position of human resource management as a general management activity; it offers a valuable insight on how the ambitious HR Department may attain its strategic role – and what to avoid.

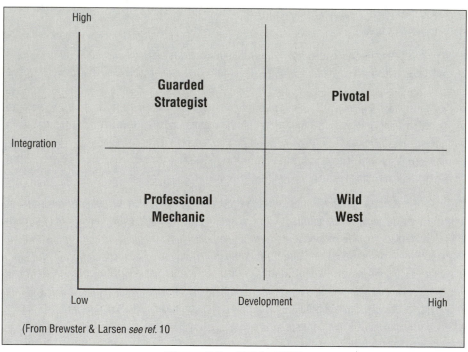

Figure 2.2   Models of HRM

Note: I have defined the position of Business Operative as a transitional stage between Professional Mechanic and Pivotal.

If the HR Department operates at a low level of integration we end up with either the Professional Mechanic or the Wild West. In neither case does the department play a strategic role. The Professional Mechanic emphasizes 'the specialist, but limited, skills and interests of the practitioners ... the manager sees himself or herself as having "higher" imperatives above that of the organisation'. The Wild West represents a nightmare situation with every line manager free to develop his or her own style of relationship with employees: the potential for incoherence, inconsistency and a strong employee reaction is obvious. It is unlikely to exist in any organization with an effective human resource department.

The HR Department is involved strategically in the two upper quadrants, but in quite different ways. The top right-hand quadrant is where HRM is fully integrated and there is a high degree of devolved responsibility to the line: the senior personnel specialists operate as catalysts, facilitators and coordinators at the policy level of the organization. This is styled a Pivotal position since 'small, highly respected personnel departments at the policy-making level can exert a powerful disproportionate influence'. This offers a most attractive, if demanding, role for the department. The alternative position, the Guarded Strategist, occurs where devolvement is low. Although the HR specialists are powerful and have few problems (other than coping with an enormous workload), according to Brewster and Larsen this can be a situation of considerable inefficiency and frustration: 'the weaker managers will welcome the chance to slough off their responsibilities, while simultaneously having someone to blame for all failures; the better managers will be frustrated'.

The tensions involved in acting as a Guarded Strategist mean that such a position is likely to be untenable in practice, certainly for any sustained period. This underlines the need to pay careful attention to the management of effective devolution of responsibility.

The task facing the department, therefore, is to move from the role of Professional Mechanic to the influential Pivotal position. The attraction of the Brewster-Larsen model is that inspection of the two-by-two matrix illustrates that this can only be achieved by moving diagonally – both the link with strategy and devolution to line management must be promoted if progress is to be sustained. It is not enough simply to attempt to create a closer strategic matching of human resource activities. In applying the model in organizations where I have worked an intermediate position between the Professional Mechanic and the Pivotal role has been suggested. It has been called the Business Operative and defined on the following basis: 'The intermediate position between Professional Mechanic and Pivotal. It is characterized by a good relationship between the HR manager and the business area based on mutual trust and understanding. The main ambition of the HR manager is to give an effective service to the line – limited strategic ambitions are expressed beyond this.'

This analysis has proved useful in practice and I have devised an instrument to assess the position of the human resource function in the organization. This is reproduced as Figure 2.3. It is intended as a basis for clarification and discussion rather than a research tool. It can be particularly effective in promoting dialogue between human resource professionals and line management on the desired position of the HR function and the steps required to achieve this status.

Participants award three points for each Pivotal answer, two for Business Operative and one for Professional Mechanic. The maximum number of points is 30 and the minimum is 10. Compare marks and ask for comments on the how the organization might develop a more pivotal role.

P   Pivotal 'A small highly respected personnel department at the policy making level of the organization can exert a powerful, disproportionate influence. The problems that the organization faces in this model are concerned mainly with resourcing the department with high calibre specialists who understand the way the business operates; and with training and developing the managers to handle HRM effectively'.

PM   Professional Mechanic This is almost the classical model of the professional Human Resources manager: the manager sees himself or herself as having 'higher imperatives above those of the organization. Like other professionals, the specialist believes that there are many areas for specialism which are beyond the understanding of trained people and which only specialists can handle'.

BO   Business Operative This is the intermediate position between Pivotal and Professional Mechanic. It is characterized by a good relationship between the Human Resources manager and the business area based on mutual trust and understanding. The main ambition of the Human Resources manager is to give an effective service to the line – limited strategic ambitions are expressed beyond this.

I   Line managers within the organization:

    a   are generally not interested in human resources issues
    b   work with human resources issues function on recruitment, reward, development and related issues
    c   see the development of human resources as a key strategic issue

II   Human resources people think primarily in terms of:

    a   delivering a 'professional' human resource service
    b   the needs of their 'client' business units
    c   the needs of the organization as a whole

III   The human resources function is best known for:

    a   handling payroll, appointments and administering salary reviews
    b   working with business units on recruitment and retention issues
    c   devising and developing human resources policies

Figure 2.3   Models of HRM: a diagnostic instrument

IV What do you believe is the basis of legitimacy and credibility for the human resources function in your organization?

    a   administration of personnel rules and regulations
    b   knowledge of the business
    c   contribution to business development

V The business units and the human resources function within your organization:

    a   have a shared understanding of the strategic issues that affect the success of the organization
    b   do not engage in discussions on the strategic issues that affect the organization

VI The human resources function believes that one of the greatest threats to the future organizational survival is:

    a   a lack of appreciation of the resource implications of strategy
    b   'inappropriate' hiring/firing and misdirected remuneration

VII When thinking of human resources do the senior managers within your firm stress:

    a   the need to get the right staff with the right reward structure for their part of the organization
    b   people as a competitive resource
    c   the need to control costs and numbers

VIII Individuals are promoted to senior human resources positions in your organisation mainly because:

    a   they have a sound knowledge of procedures and practices
    b   they have gained the confidence of senior line management in the business units
    c   they are perceived to have the ability to help the business grow and develop

IX Information on human resources in the organization relates to:

    a   overall cost and headcount figures
    b   'people resourcing issues' affecting the future of the organization
    c   the staffing requirements of each individual business area and associated costs and statistics

X Do the human resources personnel within your organization normally talk in terms of:

    a   the needs of the organization
    b   the human resources problems faced by business units and their line managers
    c   the need to apply rules and procedures

Scoring Key

	I	II	III	IV	V	VI	VII	VIII	IX	X
a	PM	PM	PM	PM	P	P	BO	PM	PM	P
b	BO	BO	BO	P	PM	PM	P	BO	P	BO
c	P	P	P	BO			PM	P	BO	PM

Figure 2.3 Concluded

CAREERS AND THE PSYCHOLOGICAL CONTRACT

Summary: *An important debate is taking place on the relevance of the career in the modern organization. The psychological contract is a useful concept which helps us understand the underlying issues. The conclusion is that career management is still relevant but has taken a different, more complex form.*

In the Introduction to this book development was described as a more ambitious process than training. Development is concerned with the growth of the individual through a series of jobs, not just the current role, and with providing the organization with a workforce which will meet future requirements.

Development is more than advanced training or training concentrated on the potential winners. Development initiatives generally have the following characteristics:

- development activities (for example high-level courses at business schools) are more expensive than lower-level training events
- development activities are concentrated on a smaller proportion of the workforce
- development activities are seen as part of an integrated plan or systematic path for the individual.

This suggestion of an integrated plan or systematic path for the individual leads inevitably to the question of relevance of the career in the modern organization, and also leads to discussion of the underlying concept of the psychological contract.

As is well known, the current business environment and labour market have raised profound issues on the future of career planning. Reorganizations have led to job losses and 'downsizing', and 'delayering' (the elimination of a whole level of management control) has entered the business vocabulary. Large high-profile organizations – the high street banks, British Telecom (and, prominently, in the US, ATT) have at times instituted large-scale redundancies. The process was parodied by the Institute for Employment Studies in the following terms:

> companies are looking for highly committed, totally flexible and completely disposable employees.[10]

Given this background, it is reasonable to ask if there is any meaning for the term career in the current climate. Should employers restrict themselves to training in its narrowest sense – imparting the knowledge and skills required for the current role? Is there any value in providing staff with training for broader opportunities and in seeking to provide career opportunities? This debate has been shaped by new thinking on the psychological contract, which, in broad terms, concerns the undocumented understanding that exists between an organization and its employees.

The concept of the psychological contract has attracted considerable attention in recent years – it is one of the emerging topics of human resource management. Its impact extends way beyond the area of development and training. At its heart is a recognition that the employment relationship runs across a spectrum from the narrow legal terms (contained in the contract of employment) to the emotion and attitudes that are developed though never explicitly articulated. Spindler, writing in *Human Resource Management,*[11] has expressed the psychological contract simply in terms of 'what can I reasonably expect from the company, and what should I reasonably expect to contribute in return'.

The following definition emphasizes both the importance of the psychological contract and its informal unwritten nature:

> An individual's belief regarding the terms and conditions of a reciprocal exchange agreement between that focal person and another party … a belief that some form of a promise has been made and that the terms and conditions of the contract have been accepted by both parties.[12]

In this definition, what matters is what the individual believes. This is illustrated in career terms. Someone joins an organization attracted by the prospect of old-style career management. This involved advancement through a promotion structure, reinforced by supportive training and development. There is an expectation that if stardom is not achieved, he (this sort of pattern was generally assumed to apply to men!) would plateau at an appropriate level and lead a comfortable if not necessarily exciting life. In turn he would expect to be managed by someone who had plateaued. None of this finds its way into written terms of exchange. The new-style psychological contract is very different. Someone who joins is expected to demonstrate high levels of performance and to absorb the company culture. He or she (not all change is for the worse!) will be offered opportunities to advance, and will be managed by people who are seeking further advancement. Any signs of reaching a plateau will invite the risk of removal. This risk is in any event present in any downsizing or delayering exercise.

The implications for the organization's career management process (and more generally for training and development) are evident. People feel angry if the contract is not honoured. It is seen as a breach of trust: a concept that was an important part of Charles Handy's thinking on organizations (see Chapter 1, p. 17) and to the ethical dimensions of the new human resources. Moreover, times and organizations change. Individuals could join with one set of expectations and end up working under a completely different order. This can create resentment, which is compounded if the changes, and the underlying reasons for them, are never made clear. Insecurity as well as resentment will result. Although there may be disputes as the extent to which the employment market has changed, it is generally accepted that the 1990s were a period in which insecurity increased. Active career management is therefore essential.

The psychological contract is a powerful concept in today's human resource climate. It is, however, of theoretical rather than practical value. One illustration of how it can be used is shown in Figure 2.4. This is taken from an internal Ernst & Young document and shows that the concept of contract can establish a framework in which career progression can be mapped and subsequently, appropriate policies developed. This representation has proved particularly useful in structuring internal career discussions.[13]

The new organizational context, then, demands a new approach to career management.

The radical challenge to the concept of the career is based on an amplified extrapolation of current trends: crudely, if we are all to become self-employed knowledge workers, what is the point of an organization bothering about our careers? If, as has been argued, many large organizations have unilaterally broken the psychological contract (by undertaking extensive downsizing), the traditional career may have met its demise.

It should be evident by now that such a calamitous view of the prospect for career management is incorrect. Careers must be considered in the context of the new approach to competition and the consequent organizational climate. Most commentators, having reviewed the evidence and arguments, conclude that the concept of the career will be just as relevant. However, career management has become more complex and interventions will need to become more sophisticated to balance legitimate organizational and individual needs.

Consider this modern definition of the career offered by John Arnold of Loughborough Business School.

> A career is the sequence of employment-related positions, roles, activities and experiences encountered by a person.[14]

This definition positions the modern career very differently from the traditional bureaucratic career – to borrow a term used by Rosabeth Moss Kanter in her seminal work *When Giants Learn to Dance*.[15] Kanter described this form of career as defined by the 'logic of advancement' and involving a sequence of positions in a defined hierarchy of positions. John Arnold's definition sees the career as the property of the individual and based on their subjective experience. To Arnold careers are a sequence of experiences which unfold over time and are related, but not identical, with experiences in employment. Kanter, writing over a decade ago, saw the decline of the bureaucratic career pattern as inevitable and desirable. She foresaw and advocated the professional career structure (defined by craft or skill) and the entrepreneurial career (where growth occurs through the individual's ability to create a produce or service of value). In general, professional careers are

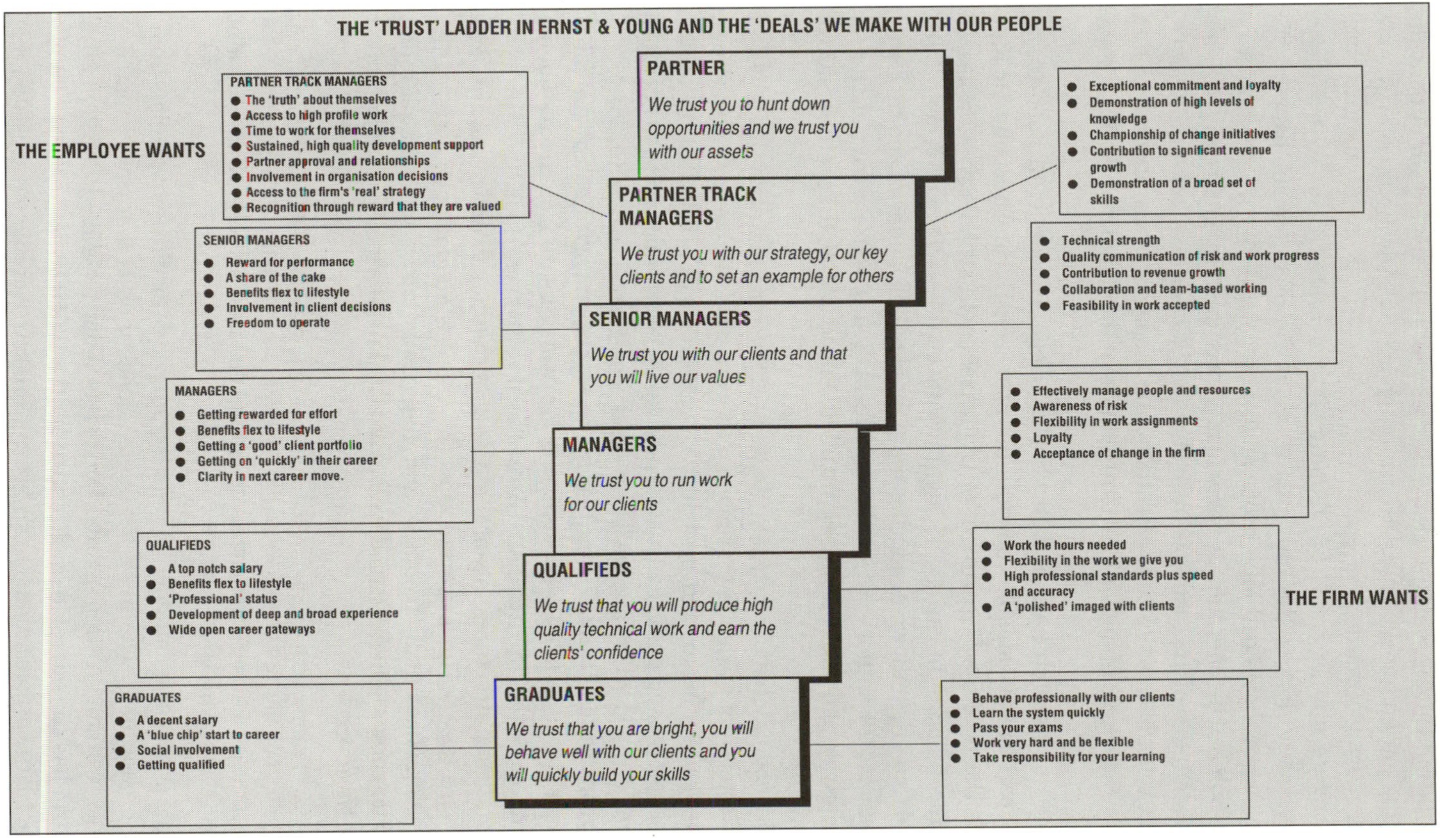
THE 'TRUST' LADDER IN ERNST & YOUNG AND THE 'DEALS' WE MAKE WITH OUR PEOPLE
THE EMPLOYEE WANTS
PARTNER TRACK MANAGERS
The 'truth' about themselves
Access to high profile work
Time to work for themselves
Sustained, high quality development support
Partner approval and relationships
Involvement in organisation decisions
Access to the firm's 'real' strategy
Recognition through reward that they are valued
SENIOR MANAGERS
Reward for performance
A share of the cake
Benefits flex to lifestyle
Involvement in client decisions
Freedom to operate
MANAGERS
Getting rewarded for effort
Benefits flex to lifestyle
Getting a 'good' client portfolio
Getting on 'quickly' in their career
Clarity in next career move.
QUALIFIEDS
A top notch salary
Benefits flex to lifestyle
'Professional' status
Development of deep and broad experience
Wide open career gateways
GRADUATES
A decent salary
A 'blue chip' start to career
Social involvement
Getting qualified
PARTNER
We trust you to hunt down opportunities and we trust you with our assets
PARTNER TRACK MANAGERS
We trust you with our strategy, our key clients and to set an example for others
SENIOR MANAGERS
We trust you with our clients and that you will live our values
MANAGERS
We trust you to run work for our clients
QUALIFIEDS
We trust that you will produce high quality technical work and earn the clients' confidence
GRADUATES
We trust that you are bright, you will behave well with our clients and you will quickly build your skills
Exceptional commitment and loyalty
Demonstration of high levels of knowledge
Championship of change initiatives
Contribution to significant revenue growth
Demonstration of a broad set of skills
Technical strength
Quality communication of risk and work progress
Contribution to revenue growth
Collaboration and team-based working
Feasibility in work accepted
Effectively manage people and resources
Awareness of risk
Flexibility in work assignments
Loyalty
Acceptance of change in the firm
Work the hours needed
Flexibility in the work we give you
High professional standards plus speed and accuracy
A 'polished' imaged with clients
THE FIRM WANTS
Behave professionally with our clients
Learn the system quickly
Pass your exams
Work very hard and be flexible
Take responsibility for your learning

(Reproduced with acknowledgement to Des Woods, Head of Learning and Development Ernst & Young.)

Figure 2.4 The psychological contract: an illustration

grown by the individual making a name for himself or herself inside or outside the organization; entrepreneurial careers are extended by growing territory below rather than moving upwards.

The literature on careers is burgeoning. It is accepted that the traditional bureaucratic is no longer the universal or even the predominant pattern. We need to move on beyond thinking of careers as an orderly progression up a hierarchy. Some of the literature is analytic and examines current trends to determine the extent to which practice is truly changing. Other texts offer guidance to individuals, organizations or to Governments on managing the transition to new forms of careers – or coping with the implication of the demise of the traditional career.

The Careers Research Forum at Birkbeck College, University of London has provided a particularly valuable contribution. Professor David Guest and Dr Kate Mackenzie Davey of the Department of Organizational Psychology summarized some of the findings in an article significantly entitled, 'Don't Write off the Traditional Career'.[16] After considering the possible implications of the new shift of organizations, the authors present the results of their research undertaken with 33 leading private and public sector companies who constitute the membership of the Forum.

The evidence on changing structures was patchy (or unavailable). However, there was consistent evidence that managers were working harder than before. One senior manager is reported as saying: 'What we actually practice is Taylorism, chaining people to their desks and just turning up the wick under them to get more out of them. It's hypocritical and we'll lose good people because of it' (p. 23).

Most organizations in the Forum had made extensive use of consultants, but very few had moved to fixed term contracts for managers. In fact 'the traditional organisation and with it the traditional career, is alive and well' (p. 23).

However, flatter structures meant that the opportunities to move onwards and upwards were fewer. The importance of the more traditional elements of the career system (succession planning and manpower flows, for example) had decreased and new elements (self-development and mentoring, for example) had increased. However:

> New forms of career management will only succeed in transformed organisational cultures, not as bolt-ons to existing systems. Concepts such as self-development and the learning organisation need time and space – things that are in short supply in a period of corporate anorexia (p. 24).

This volume is primarily intended to offer a framework for those managing training in the organization. The news for this audience then is that career management is alive, well and growing in importance. It is taking a radically different form and this form has considerable implications for the training manager. Moreover, best practice large organizations/firms are putting considerable emphasis on this issue and a new consensus is emerging, which is firmly part of the new approach to human resource development.

The new organizational context, then, demands a new approach to career management, which will be considered in this section, beginning by offering some practical definitions.

Andrew Mayo, the former Head of Personnel at ICL Europe, offered the following definition for career management:

> The design and implementation of processes that enable the careers of individuals to be planned and managed in a way that optimises both the needs of the organization and the preferences and capabilities of individuals (p. xii).[17]

This distinction recognizes the needs of both the organization and the individual. It is in the organization's interest to develop and promote work from within and to reduce turnover. Recruitment is expensive. Mayo estimates 'a year's remuneration is the cost of replacement – more if substantial training investment is needed'. In addition, career development communicates a strong expression of employer interest and fosters a positive image of recruitment. It improves motivation.

Appropriate policies must recognize that the needs of the individual and the organization are not one and the same. The following definition assists in highlighting that difference and in emphasizing the employee's responsibilities:

> an organized planned effort comprised of structured activities or processes involving both employees and the organization within this system. The employee is responsible for *career planning*, the organization is responsible for *career management.*[18]

It is also useful to review the term 'succession planning'. This is concerned with the identification of individuals who are possible successors for key senior posts in the organization.

Succession planning seeks to ensure:

- that the organization does not face a crisis brought about by the loss of key individuals – particularly unexpected defections to competitors
- that appropriate attention is given to the training and development needs of those who are destined for senior positions.

Traditional succession planning mechanisms have fallen from fashion. These had been based on capturing and maintaining data on current key post-holders and potential successors – often using computerised systems. The danger in putting too many resources behind such systems is that, in a fast-moving environment, key posts change as much as key individuals. Emphasis has shifted to developing a talent pool – identifying capable managers who are the leaders of the future and ensuring that their development needs are met.

A recognition of the need to approach career management and succession planning differently has led to two radically new suggestions for employers: the first has been articulated effectively by Peter Herriot of the Institute of Employment Studies and Carole Pemberton, Managing Consultant at Change Matters, and is based on contracting.[19] A second has been articulated in the United States by Robert Waterman and is based on covenanting.[20]

Herriot's and Pemberton's approach begins with a call for a review of the psychological contract. As the employment market has changed, so the contract has changed. Herriot argues that much of the frustration and demotivation that occurs in the workplace results from a one-sided reneging on the contract by the employer and can only be resolved by an explicit re-negotiation. Other frustrations can occur if unrealistic expectations are raised for the individual. Herriot therefore defines the new organizational career as a sequence of re-negotiations of the psychological contract during the period of employment.

From this perspective the traditional notion of a career is now redundant. If dignity is to be brought to the process of employment, it is necessary to engage in an explicit contract. This requires that:

- each party possesses something which the other needs (both employer and employee need each other)
- there is a mutual inter-dependence
- that a matching and bargaining process takes place
- there is a promissory element to this bargaining.

The renegotiation of a contract can be seen as a potentially liberating activity because it allows individuals to negotiate on the basis of their changing needs. Contracts can differ and vary over time. Indeed, Herriot argues that business success depends upon the co-existence of three different forms of psychological contract in the same organization. First, there will be part-time contracts with flexible hours to meet peak demands – he calls these 'lifestyle contracts'. Second, there will be project contracts with outcomes and completion dates specified but methods less prescribed – he describes these as 'autonomy contracts'. Third, there will be core contracts with learning flexibility to meet organization changes but some security in employability – he calls these 'development contracts'. If this approach is adopted within an organization the implications for the delivery of training and development are far reaching. At the extreme, there will be a series of explicit individual contracts with individuals which cover their development needs. Different categories of employee will require different training support ranging from minimal socialization through to maximum developmental support.

Even more radical is Waterman's proposal for a new covenant. Waterman and his co-authors suggest that employers should consider entering into a new covenant under which both employer and employee share responsibility for maintaining – even enhancing – the individual's employability *both inside and outside the company*.

Under the old covenant, employees always left major decisions affecting their careers to the organization. This in many ways is a paternalistic view of the organization and demanded a 'supremo in the sky' who would be all-knowing as far as organizational opportunities went and be prepared to intervene as appropriate for the individual. Under the new covenant, however:

- employers will give individuals the opportunity to enhance employability
- in exchange employers will receive better productivity and some degree of commitment to company purpose for as long as the employee works at the organization
- the employee will be responsible for managing his or her own career
- to assist the employee, the company will provide the tools, the environment and the opportunities for assessment and developing their skills.

The distinction made earlier in this section, between career planning and career management, is particularly relevant to this concept of covenanting. The responsibilities of both parties are made quite explicit. Waterman argues that the result of this process could be a group of self-reliant workers, which he calls a *career resilient workforce*. These are employees who are determined to update their skills and reinvent themselves to keep pace with change. They take responsibility for their own careers, but are committed to the company's success.

The approaches based on contracting and covenanting have much in common. Both assume a far more open exchange of information between employer and employee. Both are based on the premise that the employee is willing to take more responsibility for his or her development. The organization must ensure that the framework is in place. One of the problems with this approach is that it is far more attractive to the capable, self-resilient employee than to those who lack fundamental skills.

Much of the discussion on the new approach to careers is of value only to larger, highly structured organizations, which can give people opportunities to develop internally and can provide the supporting resources. For these organizations, a new consensus is emerging which can be labelled best practice. New best practice can be said, therefore, to embrace the following elements. A distinction is made between career planning (the responsibility of the individual) and career management (which is the responsibility of the firm). An employer who is concerned for staff will ensure that adequate career management mechanisms are in place and that they are publicized throughout the organization so there is no ambiguity or misunderstanding. What these career management processes are will depend on the nature and size and culture of the organization but they are likely to include the following:

- programmes for job movement and/or training; in particular, fast-track management development programmes may be instituted in larger organizations

CAREER MANAGEMENT INTERVENTIONS

Internal vacancy notification. Information about jobs available in the organization, normally in advance of any external advertising, and with some details of preferred experience, qualifications, and a job description.

Career paths. Information about the sequences of jobs that a person can do, or competencies he or she can acquire, in the organization. This should include details of how high in the organization any path goes, the kinds of inter-departmental transfers that are possible, and perhaps the skills/experience required to follow various paths.

Career workbooks. These consist of questions and exercises designed to guide individuals in determining their strengths and weaknesses, identifying job and career opportunities, and determining necessary steps for reaching their goals.

Career planning workshops. Cover some of the same ground as workbooks, but offer more change for discussion, feedback from others, information about organization-specific opportunities and policies. May include psychometric testing.

Computer-assisted career management. Various packages exist for helping employees to assess their skills, interests and values, and translate these into job options. Sometimes those options are customized to a particular organization. A few packages designed for personnel or manpower planning also include some career-relevant facilities.

Individual counselling. Can be done by specialists from inside or outside the organization, or by line managers who have received training. May include psychometric testing.

Training and educational opportunities. Information and financial support about, and possibly delivery of, sources in the organization or outside it. These can enable employees to update, retrain or deepen their knowledge in particular fields. In keeping with the notion of careers involving sequences, training in this contract is not solely to improve performance in a person's present job.

Personal development plans (PDPs). These often arise from the appraisal process and other sources such as development centres. PDPs are statements of how a person's skills and knowledge might appropriately develop, and how this development could occur, in a given timescale.

Career action centres. Resources such as literature, videos and CD ROMS, and perhaps more personal inputs such as counselling, available to employees on a drop-in basis.

Development Centres. Like assessment centres in that participants are assessed on the basis of their performance in a number of exercises and tests. However, development centres focus more on identifying a person's strengths, weaknesses and styles for the purpose of development, not selection.

Mentoring programmes. Attaching employees to more senior ones who act as advisers, and perhaps also as advocates, protectors and counsellors.

Succession planning. The identification of individuals who are expected to occupy key posts in the future, and who are exposed to experiences which prepare them appropriately.

Job assignments/rotation. Careful use of work tasks can help a person stay employable for the future, and an organization to benefit from the adaptability of staff.

Outplacement. This may involve several interventions listed above. Its purpose is to support people who are leaving the organization to clarify and implement plans for their future.

(Reproduced with permission from John Arnold, *Managing Careers into the 21st Century* (see Ref. 14).

Figure 2.5   **Career management interventions in organizations**

- job filling through open advertisement, which ensures that all individuals are well aware of opportunities
- a switch from Assessment Centres, where individuals are assessed for promotion, to Development Centres, where individuals will be given feedback on their skills for their own use (see Figure 2.5 for more details)
- specific resources will be made available for individual development and will not necessarily be rationed, for example, access to distance learning facilities – whether libraries or videos.

Underpinning all this, however, is a need to ensure that managers have the required skills to advise and support their staff and that staff have the understanding and knowledge to take advantage of the opportunities available. Many companies have set up coaching or mentoring programmes to ensure that line managers have the skill to advise their staff. This subject, like so many others, is evolving rapidly. John Arnold's book[14] is recommended, because of its practical tone. His comprehensive list of career management interventions is set out in Figure 2.5.

THE CONTRIBUTION OF TRAINING

Summary: *The new context in which training operates has redefined best practice. It has given rise to a number of key dilemmas for the training manager which are growing in importance. However these dilemmas are resolved, the training manager must become less isolated. Responsibility for training in organizations will become more diffuse.*

The first two chapters of this book have placed training in its new context. In Chapter 1 I considered the claim that training can play a new exciting role, based on a recognition that the key source for competitive advantage is now embedded in the skills and capabilities of knowledge workers. This second chapter has examined and developed three key elements that must be understood if competition though people is to be translated into training practice. First, I discussed the changing perspectives on strategy, especially the emergence of resource-based strategy. Second, I considered strategic human resources and defined the new human resources. This is not only about developing competitive advantage through people but also reinforcing it though appropriate policies on encouragement, involvement and commitment. Third, I reviewed one key element of the framework in which the new human resources must operate. This concerned the renewed interest in the psychological contract and its impact on thinking on careers.

The discussion to date suggests that not only are there new exciting opportunities for the training function, but also that there is a need for repositioning and redefinition of its role. In the next chapter a series of alternative models and perspectives on the role of training are considered. To be of practical value a model must not only define and clarify the role of training and development: it must offer a framework in which a number of potential dilemmas can be brought to light and resolved.

Corporate or organizational training and development, at its simplest, creates a framework in which employees can acquire relevant knowledge and skills. The changing organizational context has, however, given rise to three key dilemmas for those responsible for the creation of this framework and its management. These dilemmas are growing in importance.

The first dilemma concerns the requirement to maintain an appropriate balance between the needs of the organization and the needs of the individual. The knowledge and skills that the organization demands of its employees will be those required to deliver long-term competitive advantage. If the Hamel and Prahalad approach appeals, these will be seen as the knowledge and skills needed to nurture and protect the core competencies of the organization. The knowledge and the skills that the employees desire, however, could be those related to their personal employability. These allow them to build up an attractive personal portfolio of capability which will be valued both inside their current organization and by other potential employers. In practice the dilemma may be masked: the knowledge and skills desired by the organization and individual may be, to all intents and purposes, the same. However, the expectations of the individual may be raised as employability is increased but succession planning cannot deliver desired advancement. The dilemma is also important when considering the wider training arena and has implications for national training policy. For example, training which gives recognized portable qualifications (from a first level professional qualification through to an MBA) could hold disproportionate attractions for the individual.

The second dilemma concerns the focus of responsibility for the formulation of training policy and the management of its implementation. This is explored more fully in the final two chapters of this book. However, at this early stage it is evident that responsibility is becoming more diffuse in two respects. First, the new human resources requires a coordinated approach on developing and reinforcing competitive advantage though people. This means that training can no longer be regarded as a compartmentalized task for the training professional. An effective training infrastructure must be created and maintained by the human resource department as a whole. Second, all line managers in the organization must carry a responsibility for developing and motivating their staff if the new human resources are to take effect.

The third dilemma (which will be fully explored in Chapter 8) concerns the monitoring and recording of management information on training. It follows as an inevitable consequence of the second dilemma. If responsibility for training is becoming more diffuse, more people in the organization will be allowed, indeed expected, to initiate training activity. Unless the management information systems are operating to a very high standard, much of this training activity will not be recorded. Those activities that are unrecorded will not necessarily be monitored, nor their value to the organization measured. Not only does competition through people require a substantial resource commitment, but the targeting of this resource commitment becomes more difficult.

The main purpose of this summary overview of the arguments advanced to date is to set the scene for the analysis of the alternative models and perspectives on the role of training contained in the next chapter. The dilemmas identified were also used in the design of the survey of how best practice organizations in the UK are responding to current challenges (see Appendix IV, p. 267, particularly Figure AIV.1, p. 268). However, two key conclusions can be advanced at this stage. First, the training manager can no longer remain an isolated figure, staying within his or her functional zone and relying solely on a narrow-based expertise in training design and delivery. Second, since the resources that will be devoted to training are both greater and more diffuse the need to plan and monitor will become important. Both these points will be developed in the final section of the book when the role of the function and the task of the trainer are discussed. It is in this context, summarized in Figure 2.6, that the value of the models for training must now be considered.

BEST TRAINING PRACTICE INVOLVES:

- a significant and distinctive contribution to the development of an organization's competitive strategy, based on enhancing the skills and capabilities of employees
- giving individuals in the organizations appropriate opportunities to develop their own capability in both the short and long term.

Because responsibility for the 'new human resources' has become far more diffuse in making this contribution the training function will need to define its relationship with:

- the other human resource specialists
- line managers in the organization

And also ensure that management information on training activity is available to all who need it.

Figure 2.6   Features of best training practice

REFERENCES

1. Kay, J. (1996), *The Business of Economics*, Oxford: Oxford University Press.
2. Torrington, D. and Hall, L. (1991), *Personnel Management: A New Approach*, London: Prentice Hall.
3. The Price Waterhouse Cranfield Project (1990), *International Strategic Human Resource Management*, London: Price Waterhouse.
4. The Price Waterhouse Cranfield Project (1991), *International Strategic Human Resource Management*, London: Price Waterhouse.
5. Pfeffer, J. (1995), 'Producing Sustainable Advantage Through the Effective Management of People', *Academy of Management Executive*, **9** (1), pp. 55–72.
6. Pfeffer, J. (1994), *Competitive Advantage Through People*, Boston: Harvard Business School Press.
7. Pfeffer, J. (1998), *The Human Equation*, Boston: Harvard Business School Press.
8. Ulrich, D. (1998), 'A New Mandate for Human Resources', *Harvard Business Review*, **76** (1), pp. 125–34, January–February.
9. Brewster, C. and Larsen, H.H. (1992), 'Human Resource Management in Europe: Evidence from Ten Countries', *International Journal of Human Resource Management,* **3** (3), December.
10. Hirsh, W., Jackson, C. and Jackson C. (1995), *Careers in Organisations: Issues for the Future*, Sussex, Institute for Employment Studies Report 287, p. 15.
11. Spindler, G.S. (1994), 'Psychological Contracts in the Workplace – A Lawyer's View', *Human Resource Management*, **33**, pp. 325–33, Fall 1994.
12. Robinson, S.L. and Rousseau, D.M. (1994), 'Violating the Psychological Contract: Not the Exception but the Norm', *Journal of Organizational Behaviour*, **15**, p. 264.
13. My acknowledgements to my colleague, Des Woods of Ernst & Young, for this analysis and application of the psychogical contract.
14. Arnold, J. (1997), *Managing Careers into the 21st Century*, London: Paul Chapman Publishing, p. 16.
15. Kanter, R.M. (1989), *When Giants Learn to Dance*, New York: Simon & Schuster, pp. 298–319.
16. Guest, D. and Mackenzie Davey, K. (1996), 'Don't Write off the Traditional Career', *People Management*, 22 February 1996.
17. Mayo, A. (1992), *Managing Careers: Strategies for Organisations*, London: Institute of Personnel Management.
18. Gilley, J.W. (1989), 'Career Development as a Partnership', *Personnel Administrator*, **33** (4), April, pp. 62–8.
19. Herriot, P. and Pemberton, C. (1995), *New Deals: The Revolution in Managerial Careers*, London: Wiley.
20. Waterman, R.H., Waterman, J.A. and Collard, B.A. (1994), 'Toward a Career Resilient Workforce', *Harvard Business Review,* **72** (4).

3 Models for training

So far it has been argued that a number of factors have questioned the validity of the traditional model for the management of training. These factors were described in the previous chapters and, as a result, I defined some characteristics of best training practice. In this chapter a number of models are outlined and I consider how they can underpin the delivery of best practice: in this way the requirements of a model which reflects the changed context are identified.

A word of caution is necessary. Not all of the exemplars presented below were intended by those involved in their derivation to deal with the delivery of best training practice. Analysis of these models is valuable in so far as it highlights the additional features that need to be considered in defining new, more comprehensive, models. The text below should therefore not be construed as a criticism of previous contributions to the literature: they could not be fairly criticized for not achieving what they did not set out to achieve.

THE SYSTEMATIC TRAINING MODEL

Summary: *The systematic training model has shaped the approach to training since the 1960s. Although of considerable value in introducing discipline it is at a best a partial guide to what the training manager should do.*

The most important, and pervasive, model for the role of training in the organization can be labelled the systematic training model. A standard glossary of training terms defined systematic training as:

> training undertaken on a planned basis as a result of applying a logical series of steps. In practice, the number and description of these steps tends to vary, but in general terms they would cover such aspects as:
>
> ● Development of training policy
> ● Identification of training needs

- Development of training objectives and plans
- Implementation of planned training
- Validation, evaluation and review of training (p. 59).[1]

In the US, the approach has been derived from the work undertaken by the military on Instructional Systems Design. Characteristically such models have five stages: analysis of training needs, design of training curriculum, development of training curriculum, implementation (delivery) and evaluation (p. 30).[2]

In the UK, the model, and its many variations, received an immense stimulus with the creation of the Industrial Training Boards in the late 1960s; it accurately caught the move towards increased concern for rationality and efficiency under the competitive pressures of that time. Definitive works were later produced by Boydell,[3] who depicted ten stages of a cyclical process. Such models were simplified and restated in countless texts, most often in the simple diagrammatic form of Figure 3.1.

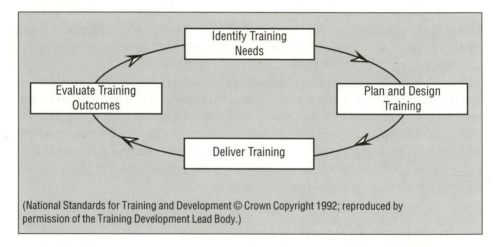

(National Standards for Training and Development © Crown Copyright 1992; reproduced by permission of the Training Development Lead Body.)

Figure 3.1   The systematic training model

A circular model is presented because it introduces a link from evaluation to the further identification of training needs. The process then becomes continuous. Indeed, most refinements of the model involve feedback loops in some form. The text recommended by the former Institute of Personnel Management (now the Institute of Personnel and Development (IPD)) by Kenney and Reid offered the version of planned training reproduced in Figure 3.2.[4] It can be seen that the Kenney and Reid version emphasizes the importance of considering the feedback from evaluation at all stages in the process.

Whatever the embellishments, the systematic model has two important characteristics. First, training can helpfully be perceived as a set of sequential steps;

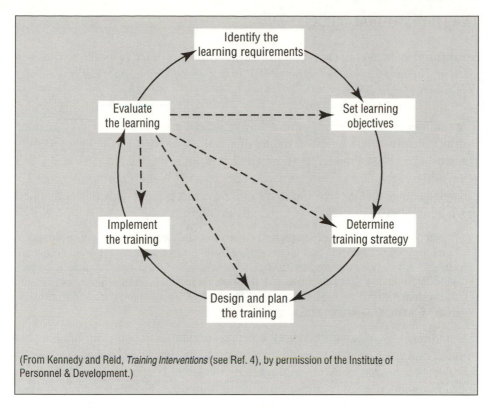

(From Kennedy and Reid, *Training Interventions* (see Ref. 4), by permission of the Institute of Personnel & Development.)

Figure 3.2   A model of planned training

second, the identification of needs is something that can be introduced into the training cycle at the appropriate stage. These are discovered through carrying out a thorough investigation of individual or group training requirements or by interpreting overall objectives set by the organization, or by a well-managed combination of the two.

The systematic training model is useful so far as it goes: it does centre the trainer's attention on the need to act in a structured and disciplined way and, most importantly, stresses the place of effective evaluation of the training activity and the benefits that it can bring to other parts of the training cycle.

However, it cannot be regarded as, nor indeed does it purport to be, a structured attempt to address the issues involved in delivering best training practice. In particular, it does not suggest that the training function should take a proactive role in developing capability, nor does it consider the need to embed the modern training function in the organization and define its relationship with the other parties involved in the delivery of training.

THE TRANSITIONAL MODEL

Summary: *A critique of the systematic training model has led to an interesting suggestion. The model could be improved if it were embedded in a mapping of the wider corporate strategic context.*

The traditional model is comprehensively criticized in an article by Harry Taylor,[5] in which he also offers a revised model that is intended to remedy one of its deficiencies; this revised model he styles the transitional model. His critique, which repays direct examination, is summarized below and his alternative is presented.

Taylor argues that the traditional systematic training model is firmly embedded in what he calls the strategic management paradigm:

> Based on an examination of the current environmental circumstances in terms of problems, threats or opportunities for the organisation, top management sets the overall objectives which are then broken down into manageable functional objectives to be pursued by functional specialists working through their own sequence of stages ... Thus the systematic training model is meant to be both a mirror of, and a contributor to, the general strategic management process (pp. 261–2).

He continues by arguing that three basic assumptions underly the model: that training is seen as an investment in the organization; that a mechanism is required for allocating resources between competing investment opportunities and that the appropriate mechanism is strategic planning; that there is a high degree of commonality between the interests of 'the organization' and the needs of individuals who may or may not receive training. In fact, there is a considerable divergence between theory and practice. Decisions on training are not always consciously made, but evolve; successive published reports have reflected only tenuous links between training and organizational objectives.

Taylor then offers two critiques of the model. The first attempts to refine, repair and rehabilitate the model and bring it closer to reality. For example, the profile of training in the organization can be raised, and evaluation techniques can be improved. The second, more radical, critique challenges all the underlying assumptions: training cannot be characterized as an investment, since an investment in human resources is quite different in character from other forms of investment; the strategic management paradigm is of limited application; in the training sphere there can be a marked divergence of interests between the organization and the individual.

Taylor's assessment is that the model has been developed as a means of professionalizing training and thus attempts to establish its credibility. It has been put forward to explain and predict training activities and has been used by practising trainers as a route map.

the overall assessment is that the systematic training model – despite its undoubted virtues of simplicity and its orientation to action – can no longer, on its own, be regarded as generally valid (p. 273).

Taylor offers a new model which he calls the transitional model, shown in Figure 3.3. This he describes as a double-loop of corporate strategy and learning.

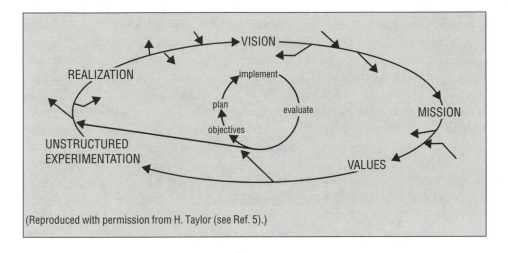

(Reproduced with permission from H. Taylor (see Ref. 5).)

Figure 3.3 **A transitional model of systematic training**

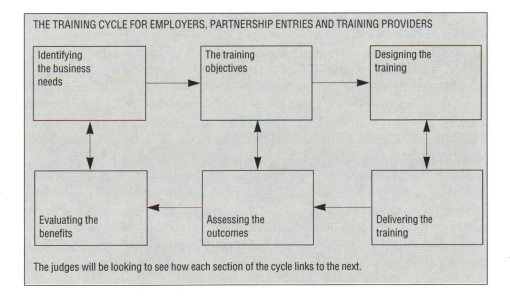

Figure 3.4 **The National Training Award model**

The inner loop is the systematic training model: the outer loop is described as 'crafted strategy' and learning. Vision (the desired scenario), mission (a statement of why the organization exists) and values (the translation of the first two into communicable ideals) must all precede specific attention to objectives.

Taylor is tentative in offering this new transitional model. His work, however, does offer insight. It retains the attractiveness of the systematic model as a route map; it embeds training strategy in the wider corporate context; it recognizes that the organization as a whole may be tentative in its approach to strategic development. The weaknesses are two-fold. First, his two loops differ in quality: the inner systematic training loop is robust and clear; the outer loop of crafted strategy and learning varies in its visibility and is exploratory. It is far less tangible and few organizations would be able to define its existence. Second, his model does not offer practical guidance for practitioners – a point which the author himself freely admits. He would argue that an alternative is required which is far more creative and intuitive and less specific, controlled and pre-programmed.

THE NATIONAL TRAINING AWARD MODEL

Summary: *The model that underpins the National Training Award is designed to fit the principles of the systematic training model. As a result it may fail to capture the uncertainty that can govern training decisions.*

The previous section concerned a reappraisal of the systematic training model which was tentative and exploratory in its approach. The next model to be considered is also a development of the systematic training model, but is far from tentative. This is the model that is made explicit in the National Training Awards introduced in 1987. It is important to note that the model does not purport to reflect best practice. It was created as a framework for securing evidence and judging entrants to a national competition. Entrants, moreover, were drawn from a wide variety of organizations of different sizes and sectors. Its strengths and weaknesses are assessed in the context of a review of models.

Entrants to the National Training Award programme are advised that the judges look for training which is exceptionally effective in meeting business needs and helping the organization to meet its goal. Additionally, entries are considered within a framework of features which demand the systematic marshalling of evidence and the effective evaluation of the training. The framework is presented diagramatically in Figure 3.4.

It is evident that the two-thirds of the framework on the right-hand side is a formal systematic training model. The link between training and broader organizational strategy is expressed in a way that implies that the training system could be

regarded as an isolated and independent sub-system of the organization. The ear.,
National Training Awards guidance notes took this to an extreme:

> Business Need is what prompted the training initiative ... Training Objectives describe
> what the individuals involved should be able to do, and to what standard, in order to
> meet the training need ... Training Design is the plan of what is to be done to achieve
> the Training Objectives ... Training Delivery is the implementation of the training plan
> ... Training Outcomes are the measure to what the training actually achieved for the
> business and trainees, and decide how fully the Objectives were achieved ...

The earlier guidance did, it is true, recognize that training outcomes could have
less tangible and predictable consequences arguing 'while it is important that
training outcomes lead to benefits for the organization – these may not necessarily
address the "original problems" but may include some unforeseen, yet valuable,
results'. Current (1998) guidance describes the training cycle in terms of the following components.

Why you need training
- What specific problems did you need to solve?
- What changes did you want to bring about?

The training objectives
- What improvements were you looking for, and to what standard?

Training design
- Show how you designed your training programme to achieve the targets you
  set.

Training delivery
- How did the delivery of the training programme match your original design?

Outcomes of the training
- Give the results of your training programme, showing how people benefited
  and the impact on behaviour and performance of learners.
- Explain how these results match the original objectives.

Benefits for your organisation
- Show how the training programme effectively met your organisation's needs –
  both immediately and in the long-term.

If this approach were taken to an extreme it could indicate a high confidence in the
precision of the systematic training model. In particular a belief that:

- the requirements of organizational strategy should be translated into training
  objectives
- that such a translation is feasible
- that training should take place in a systematic and sequential fashion

- that the results are capable of evaluation (quantifiable results are recommended).

Any criticism of the model must recognize that the National Training Awards are a valuable and laudable attempt to promote effective training throughout all organizations in many different sectors of the UK economy. Those companies that have won National Training Awards can be fairly said to epitomize best UK training. Moreover, the model and the approach to judging entrants, and the quality of entries, have all evolved and improved over time. Furthermore, there are a number of positive features to the model – it explicitly recognizes the need to link training objectives with the requirements of the organization; it does not assume that training activity is solely the preserve of training specialists.

However, at its most simplistic, the National Training Award model does not fully look at or recognize some other facets of training practice. In particular:

- it implicitly denies a proactive role for training in the organization, whereby the training function assists in generating and articulating organization needs as well as reacting to them
- by placing such a firm emphasis on quantifiable results it downgrades the importance of the other less quantifiable effects of training activity (for example, improved morale through team-building which, though not the prime objective of the activity, is a clear, if intangible, benefit)
- by concentrating on monitoring performance against pre-specified objectives, which are handed down to the trainer, it limits creativity.

As a framework for judging the competition it has proved its value. It has limitations as a model for expressing the aspirations of trainers in organizations that have a developed approach to training.

INVESTORS IN PEOPLE

Summary: *Investors in People (IiP) is Government endorsement of company training. It can provide a valuable framework for improving the focus and effectiveness of training in its wider context.*

One way of stimulating an improvement of the focus and effectiveness of training across the firm would be to commit to Investors in People.

The Investors in People (IiP) standard was introduced in 1991. IiP is based on the implementation of four key training principles: commitment, planning, action (delivery) and evaluation. To obtain IiP accreditation an organization has to satisfy an external assessor, nominated by the Local Training and Enterprise Council, that it meets 23 separate indicators divided across these four principles.

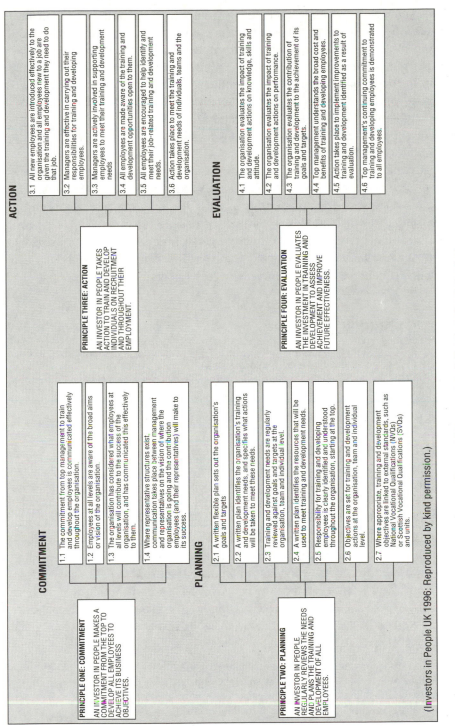

COMMITMENT

PRINCIPLE ONE: COMMITMENT

AN INVESTOR IN PEOPLE MAKES A COMMITMENT FROM THE TOP TO DEVELOP ALL EMPLOYEES TO ACHIEVE ITS BUSINESS OBJECTIVES.

1.1 The commitment from top management to train and develop employees is communicated effectively throughout the organisation.

1.2 Employees at all levels are aware of the broad aims or vision of the organisation.

1.3 The organisation has considered what employees at all levels will contribute to the success of the organisation, and has communicated this effectively to them.

1.4 Where representative structures exist, communication takes place between management and representatives on the vision of where the organisation is going and the contribution employees (and their representatives) will make to its success.

PLANNING

PRINCIPLE TWO: PLANNING

AN INVESTOR IN PEOPLE REGULARLY REVIEWS THE NEEDS AND PLANS THE TRAINING AND DEVELOPMENT OF ALL EMPLOYEES.

2.1 A written flexible plan sets out the organisation's goals and targets

2.2 A written plan identifies the organisation's training and development needs, and specifies what actions will be taken to meet these needs.

2.3 Training and development needs are regularly reviewed against goals and targets at the organisation, team and individual level.

2.4 A written plan identifies the resources that will be used to meet training and development needs.

2.5 Responsibility for training and developing employees is clearly identified and understood throughout the organisation, starting at the top.

2.6 Objectives are set for training and development actions at the organisation, team and individual level.

2.7 Where appropriate, training and development objectives are linked to external standards, such as National Vocational Qualifications (NVQs) or Scottish Vocational Qualifications (SVQs) and units.

ACTION

PRINCIPLE THREE: ACTION

AN INVESTOR IN PEOPLE TAKES ACTION TO TRAIN AND DEVELOP INDIVIDUALS ON RECRUITMENT AND THROUGHOUT THEIR EMPLOYMENT.

3.1 All new employees are introduced effectively to the organisation and all employees new to a job are given the training and development they need to do that job.

3.2 Managers are effective in carrying out their responsibilities for training and developing employees.

3.3 Managers are actively involved in supporting employees to meet their training and development needs.

3.4 All employees are made aware of the training and development opportunities open to them.

3.5 All employees are encouraged to help identify and meet their job-related training and development needs.

3.6 Action takes place to meet the training and development needs of individuals, teams and the organisation.

EVALUATION

PRINCIPLE FOUR: EVALUATION

AN INVESTOR IN PEOPLE EVALUATES THE INVESTMENT IN TRAINING AND DEVELOPMENT TO ASSESS ACHIEVEMENT AND IMPROVE FUTURE EFFECTIVENESS.

4.1 The organisation evaluates the impact of training and development actions on knowledge, skills and attitude.

4.2 The organisation evaluates the impact of training and development actions on performance.

4.3 The organisation evaluates the contribution of training and development to the achievement of its goals and targets.

4.4 Top management understands the broad cost and benefits of training and developing employees.

4.5 Action takes place to implement improvements to training and development identified as a result of evaluation.

4.6 Top management's continuing commitment to training and developing employees is demonstrated to all employees.

(Investors in People UK 1996: Reproduced by kind permission.)

Figure 3.5 Investors in People national standard

For most organizations the most difficult principles to satisfy will be the indicators on evaluation (an Investor in People evaluates the investment in training and development to assess achievement and improve future effectiveness). Other issues surround indicators on the need for regular reviews against goals and targets and the need for a written plan. The indicator which proposes (albeit where appropriate) linking training and development with external standards and qualifications might not always find favour. Meeting the Investors in People standards demands a considerable effort from employees and necessitates a review of the organization's entire training philosophy.

One advantage of IiP is that it is 'business strategy neutral'. Nothing specific is required of an organization's training effort beyond good practice. Providing the training effort supports the organization's goals, the goals can take any form. But IiP does require a considerable commitment, is paper-intensive and it takes about 18 months to meet the assessor's requirements. Moreover, there is growing evidence to suggest that, in national policy terms, IiP's main effect will be to focus training investment rather than to increase it (see Appendix III, p. 265).

TRAINING AS CONSULTANCY

Summary: *The consultancy model has attracted a number of advocates. It is important to distinguish between consultancy skills (which all human resource professionals need) and the consultancy model. The latter has limitations because, at the extreme, it could result in the isolation of the training function.*

It is questionable whether the perspective on training in the organization considered next should be called a model. Certainly the authors of the works cited did not intend their ideas to be interpreted as a comprehensive attempt to address the question of best training practice. What they presented was an articulation and examination of a major trend in training in the organization; they recognized a need to offer guidance to practitioners in facing the important new challenges thus presented.

Perhaps the strongest case made for the consultancy approach is that presented by Holdaway and Saunders, who focused on the attractiveness of the consultancy route: 'Consultancy can mean more control over what you do and how and where and when you do it' (p. 10).[6] Although this comment was meant to apply mainly to self-employed consultants outside the organization it was also applied to internal consultants:

> We are firmly convinced that the consultancy role is the way ahead for trainers, who should be able to work in this way despite the constraints of an established job. It can provide the flexibility and responsiveness required by the organization as well as personal satisfaction and growth for the individual (p. 10).

The authors argue that the organization will benefit because internal consultants offer more focused solutions and the 'knowledge, skills and experience normally deployed and gained by external consultants' remain within the organization. Problems are solved jointly by business operations and training services. Holdaway and Saunders go on to devote most of their analysis to the practical consequences of the trainer working in this way and offer some valuable insights.

The discussion of the consultancy model is in danger of being clouded if the role of the trainer as internal consultant is confused with two other features of the current training landscape. First, there are a growing number of training professionals who either through choice or force of circumstances have chosen to operate as consultants rather than in-house training managers. Much of the 'training as consultancy' literature is designed to meet their needs and, understandably, to justify the consultancy role.

The second feature is more subtle but more important. It is necessary to distinguish between the case for the in-house trainer or training managers formally developing the skills of the consultant and the need to manage the input of training consultants external to the organization. Very different processes are needed to deliver the internal consultancy service and to manage input from elsewhere.

In assessing the value of the consultancy model to the determination of best training practice it is also helpful to distinguish between the benefits of offering consultancy skills and the relevance of the consultancy relationship.

The new skills required of the training managers will be considered in Chapter 10. At this stage, however, it can be stated that all human resource professionals will need to acquire a new set of skills common to those deployed by external consultants. The survey of best practice outlined in Appendix IV shows that consultancy skills and the ability to undertake process interventions was identified as a critical capability for the training manager of the future. Consultancy classically proceeds through a series of stages: gaining entry, research and analysis, implementation and disengagement. A recognition of such stages can help the training manager clarify his or her route through the management of any project.

The labelling of the last stage of the process as disengagement does, however, force attention on the weakness of the consultancy model as a determinant of best training practice. In-house trainers do not disengage. The outline of best training practice presented at the end of Chapter 2 talks of continuous skills enhancement and a pivotal role which must necessarily be ongoing within the organization. To deliver at this level, training professionals must work in conjunction with other human resource professionals and must be seen, to the greatest extent possible, as equal partners with line management in running the business – though offering a specialist service based on a particular sort of expertise.

In summary, therefore, the consultancy model offers a useful perspective on the skills required by the training professional. The consultancy relationship, however, is not an appropriate paradigm for the delivery of effective training within the organization.

THE ASHRIDGE MODEL

Summary: *Researchers at Ashridge have developed a classification of training activity across three levels of sophistication. Although stronger on description than prescription, their work offers a useful ladder of progression for the training manager.*

The model discussed here is drawn from a substantial research project undertaken in 1986 by the Ashridge Management Research Group and jointly sponsored by Ashridge Management College and the Foundation for Management Education. Basically, the researchers undertook a study of leading-edge companies in the UK and proceeded through a literature search and detailed interviews with a cross-section of managers. The results were published as 'Management for the Future'.[7]

An important section of the report concerned the role of training and development. Here it was suggested that such activity within an organization can be considered at three levels of sophistication:

- a fragmented approach
- a formalized approach
- a focused approach.

Because of the importance of the model to the arguments advanced in this book, these stages are summarized in Figure 3.6 on page 57.

At the lowest level, education, training and development are peripheral to the organization and are seen as a cost rather than an investment: 'The organization takes little responsibility for training and expects little in return' (p .46).

As the sophistication of the delivery of training and development increases, organizations adopt a more formalized approach. Training and development become more structured and linked into organizational processes such as appraisal systems.

The Ashridge report suggests, however, that the full potential of training and development is released in those organizations adopting a focused approach. Training and development are then intrinsic to the organization and occur continuously. The emphasis moves from formal training to personal development, driven both by the goals of the organization and the needs of the individual. Line managers and individuals assume the main responsibility for development, while trainers adopt wider roles as advisers, facilitators and agents of change. Organizations achieving this level of sophistication are described in the report as learning organizations – a term which will be considered more fully later in this chapter.

THE ROLE OF TRAINING AND DEVELOPMENT

1. **The Fragmented Approach**
   - Training is not linked to organizational goals
   - Training is perceived as a luxury or a waste of time
   - Approach to training is non-systematic
   - Training is directive
   - Training is carried out by trainers
   - Training takes place in the Training Department
   - Emphasis on knowledge-based courses
   - The focus on training (a discontinuous process) rather than development (a continuous process).

2. **The Formalized Approach**
   - Training becomes linked to human resource (HR) needs
   - Training becomes systematic by linking it to an appraisal system
   - The emphasis is still on knowledge-based courses but the focus of the course broadens, with greater emphasis on skill-based courses
   - The link which is made between training and HR needs encourages organizations to adopt a more developmental approach
   - Training is carried out by trainers, but the range of skill demands placed on a trainer develops with the new breadth of courses offered
   - Line managers become involved in training and development through their role as appraisers
   - Pre- and post-course activities attempt to facilitate the transfer of off-the-job learning
   - Training is carried out off-the-job, but through career development the value of on-the-job learning gains formal recognition
   - There is more concern to link a programme of training to individual needs.

3. **The Focused Approach**
   - Training and development and continuous learning by individuals is perceived as a necessity for organizational survival in a rapidly changing business environment
   - Training is regarded as a competitive weapon
   - Learning is linked to organizational strategy and to individual goals
   - The emphasis is on on-the-job development so that learning becomes a totally continuous activity
   - Specialist training courses are available across the knowledge/skill/value spectrum
   - Self-selection for training courses
   - Training is generally non-directive, unless knowledge-based
   - New forms of training activity are utilized e.g. open and distance learning packages, self-development programmes, etc
   - More concern to measure effectiveness of training and development
   - Main responsibility for training rests with line management
   - Trainers adopt a wider role
   - New emphasis on learning as a process
   - Tolerance of some failure as part of the learning process.

(Source: *Management for the Future*)

Figure 3.6   Features of the Ashridge model

The Ashridge report offers an important piece of research. It recognizes – unlike any of the other models previously discussed – that training is delivered at a number of different levels of sophistication in the UK. It offers a clear ladder of progression through stages to the focused approach which it regards as the way of the future. The three-phase description is offered as a basis for a model of training and development against which organizations could plot progress.

The Ashridge model describes an ideal state for training and development in the organization and offers a useful set of indicators which could be used to measure progress. It does not, however, address the detailed mechanics involved in securing such progress. In particular, it does not offer directions for the training manager in an organization which is fundamentally unreceptive.

THE LEARNING ORGANIZATION

Summary: *The creation of a 'learning organization' has emerged as an important objective for trainers. However, the term is often used imprecisely and needs critical examination if it is to be regarded as a practical model.*

One perspective on training that has attracted particular support in recent years has been the concept of the 'learning organization'. The term has achieved a currency and prominence among the training and management development community and has gained wide acceptance as an expression of the desired or ideal state for training in the organization. Inevitably, given the circumstances of its rapid rise in popularity, the term 'learning organization' has been used in a variety of different ways – and on occasions with imprecision.

Much of the early impetus came from the organizational psychologist Chris Argyris, whose work has centred on developing individual potential within the company. In a book written jointly with Donald Schon,[8] he developed the concept of single- and double-loop organizational learning. The authors argued that organizational learning involves the detection of errors and their subsequent correction. If this detection and correction allows current policies and objectives to continue, the process is described as single-loop organizational learning. If, however, the detection and correction activities modify and change fundamental behaviour, the organization can be said to have undergone double-loop learning; this involves learning from others, through discussion and a willingness to accept change. Organizations learn through the agency of individuals, and the appropriate climate must be encouraged to develop the synergy that can be gained through shared experience.

Argyris and Schon's work is a contribution to our perception of learning: they wrote on organizational learning rather than the learning organization but in so doing helped to develop the latter concept. Another important contribution to learning theory which particularly influenced the development of the learning organization was the work of David Kolb, an American academic and consultant.[9] Kolb introduced the concept of the learning cycle: at stage one a person starts off with an experience; stage two of the cycle is to observe and reflect on that experience; stage three is to develop certain principles and concepts from that reflection; stage four is to test these principles and concepts either by replicating the initial experience or by trying out the principles in new circumstances. This will produce a new experience (stage one again), and the cycle continues. Some advocates of the learning organization would suggest that the individual's experience of the learning cycle can also be paralleled in the organization. In this case it is particularly important that the organization ensures that there is adequate opportunity for stages two and three of the cycle (respectively called 'systematic reflection' and 'abstract conceptualization') to take place.

A conceptual leap from individual to corporate learning is central to the notion of the learning organization; it is a form of anthropomorphism, defined as the ascription of a human attribute to anything impersonal. This leap was evidently accepted by Peters and Waterman in the early 1980s, who, in *In Search of Excellence*,[10] wrote of the learning company as a truly adaptive organization evolving in a Darwinian fashion.

> the company is trying lots of things, experimenting, making the right sorts of mistakes; that is to say, it is fostering its own mutations. The adaptive corporation has learned quickly to kill off the dumb mutations and invest heavily in the ones that work (p. 114).

Is the learning organization simply two linked concepts: that it is a good idea for individuals to learn and thus contribute to the development of the organization; and that this process can be facilitated if the correct environment is put in place? If so, it adds little new to the training manager's agenda and certainly does not deserve to be described as a new model of training management. However, a number of commentators have developed the underlying concept and placed it in a broader organizational context; when this is done the 'learning organization' can be regarded as a practical model.

An extension of the concept has found expression in the work of Peter Senge. His important work *The Fifth Discipline*[11] has the subsidiary title, *The Art and Practice of the Learning Organization*. It is a conceptually difficult work, which is frequently misunderstood: the fifth discipline of the title does not, for example, refer to organizational learning but to the need for a systems approach.

Senge differentiates learning organizations from traditional authoritarian 'controlling organizations'. The former are achieved by the mastery of certain disciplines, using the word in a broader sense: to Senge a discipline is a body of practice based in some underlying theory of the world. He argues that five new 'component technologies' or disciplines are gradually converging to innovate learning organizations. They are:

- personal mastery, the capacity to clarify what is most important to the individual
- team learning, based on a dialogue in which assumptions are suspended so that a genuine thinking together occurs
- mental models, the capacity to reflect on internal pictures of the world to see how they shape actions
- shared vision, the ability to build a sense of commitment in a group based on what people would really like to create
- systems thinking, the capacity for putting things together and seeking holistic solutions.

Systems thinking is the fifth discipline because it is the one that integrates the others, fusing them into a coherent body of theory and practice. In Senge's words: 'It keeps them [the other disciplines] from being separate gimmicks or the latest organizational change fads' (p. 12).

Senge's comments on team learning are of considerable value but his fundamental message is that such activity must not be seen in isolation: it must be underpinned by the fifth discipline. Ironically, therefore, someone who is revered as a guru of the learning organization should more properly be treated as a major critic of the concept as advocated, since it is frequently viewed in isolation from other corporate activities. In a sense, therefore, the organization's leadership must buy into the total concept before Senge's learning organization can be implemented. This makes an important theoretical construct but a demanding idea in practice.

A further practical extension of the concept was briefly outlined in the previous section: the suggestion by the Ashridge academics that the learning organization is the focused approach to training and development at its most sophisticated. To quote from *Management for the Future*:

> The learning organization may be defined as one in which learning is not restricted to discrete 'chunks' of training activity, either fragmented or systematic, but is one where it has become a continuous process, and where on-the-job learning has become a way of life (p. 50).[7]

Two members of the Ashridge faculty, Valerie Hammond and Edgar Wille, have extended this underlying concept in an important way. They argue that the learning organization becomes of value when, instead of developing in an arbitrary fashion, deliberate attempts are made to create conditions fundamental to its growth. This demands the development of proper frameworks so that systematic reflection takes place, and greater responsibility is given to the individual operating with a collegiate spirit. They offer the following elaboration of the concept:

The phrase 'the learning organization' is being used to describe the bringing
of people to achieve some objective, great or small, in conditions where they are
searching, all the time, for ways of doing whatever needs to be done in a better way. In
learning organizations people are alert all the time for signals which show whether or
not they are on the path to success in achieving their objectives. Learning organizations
are continuously looking at the detail of their actions in the light of the whole, informed
by a vision which they share with each other (p. 129).[12]

The use of the words 'all the time' and 'continuously' offers a significant
extension of the concept. They suggest that a learning organization is much more
than a high-level training organization; it views learning as a necessary part of its
day-to-day activity over and above what is needed for narrow business requirements.

With the exception of those commentators listed above, attempts to develop
the learning concept as a coherent whole are few and far between. In general,
there is acceptance among the training and development community that learning
organizations are 'good things'. More valuable discussions on the learning organization are generally those which do not dwell on its philosophical aspects, but
which offer practical advice on actions which should be taken to implement the
concept.

In general, however, the term 'learning organization' lacks precision. It
certainly describes an organization which exhibits the characteristics set out in
Figure 3.7. These are admittedly drawn from various commentaries, but they
do not constitute a dramatic sea change in thinking about the place of training in
the organization. The concept is of value when it is applied, and it needs be
applied in organizations where training is less well accepted. One can readily
share the frustration felt by Peter Honey, a leading writer on learning theory, who
offered a simple recipe for creating your own learning organization and concluded

you cannot wait for Utopian conditions otherwise you'd wait forever. If top management
are out of sympathy with the notion of the Learning Organisation that is unfortunate but
not the end of the matter. Simply use the steps to create a mini-learning organisation in
the parts you *can* influence. Small incremental changes, *if sustained*, have the habit of
gaining momentum to be point where they become transformational.[13]

A LEARNING ORGANIZATION IS ONE:

- where the importance of individual learning to corporate development is recognized
- where team learning is promoted through interaction and feedback
- where experimentation is encouraged and hence failure is tolerated
- where there is an effort to devolve responsibility in a supportive environment in a way that allows the
  individual to develop and grow.

Figure 3.7 **Characteristics of a learning organization**

This seems sound advice, but is a far cry from the total concept offered by Senge.

THE NEW LEARNING PARTNERSHIP

Summary: *A radical new model is represented by the concept of learning contracts. These follow from a recognition that a new psychological contract needs shared responsibility for learning. Both employers and employees must recognize their obligations and responsibilities if these are to be effective.*

In the previous chapter, I considered some aspects of the relationship changes between the organization and the individual. The changing psychological contract and new perceptions of the career led to the ideas that valued long-term staff should be offered training and development that promotes their employability. This could shift the focus of training and development to an individual-centered approach. As a result a new model is emerging and this was well articulated by David Finegold in a publication from the Centre for Effective Organizations.[14]

Finegold starts with a recognition that the major changes in the global market place in organizations have undermined the old psychological contract. As a result a new learning contract is needed which centres on the concept of shared responsibility for ongoing development. Most importantly, to fulfil their side of the bargain 'companies must shift from the old training paradigm to a new learning paradigm for building competencies' (p. 232).

This shift is necessary because the traditional paths to skill development have been closed or narrowed. In addition, there are:

- few job levels, so individuals cannot advance through hierarchies
- fewer mentoring relationships because senior people now have greater responsibilities and less time
- fewer internal personnel dedicated to training and development as firms place responsibilities on line managers

And there is:

- less incentive for individuals to invest in company-specific competencies
- less time off to participate in training.

For a fuller discussion on the concept of competencies see Chapter 5, p. 101. At this stage, however, it is sufficient to interpret the term in its everyday usage – as a synonym for skills.

Finegold writes from a US perspective and not all the forces listed above will have the same resonance in a UK context. However, the argument that the pressure on training and development has become more intense will gain general acceptance.

He makes a case for a new employment bargain or psychological contract, suited to these new realities. Thus far his argument is not unusual. However, he is at his most powerful when he advocates:

> A mutual commitment to ongoing competency development, or a learning contract ... The organization, although not able to offer employment security, pledges to increase the employability of its workers and managers by investing in their continuous skill development and by providing them with opportunities (including lateral career paths) (p. 234).

The link with Waterman's concept of the career-resilient workforce discussed in Chapter 2 (p. 39) is obvious.

The key elements of Finegold's learning contract are reproduced as Figure 3.8. Not every organization should adopt this approach. Employment circumstances may vary or the nature of market competition may not make such a high commitment of resources appropriate. It is important for an employer to consider the response and to avoid unrealistic commitments. However,

> If a company sees the creation and use of knowledge as a source of competitive advantage, and if it requires skills that cannot easily be hired from outside, then that company needs a new way of fostering the development of both individual and organizational competencies (pp. 236–7).

Learning contracts potentially represent a radical shift. All contributing employees need to be trained. There is a move from developing technical and managerial skills for effective performance to developing cross-functional capabilities to create competitive advantage. The ways in which leading companies are coping with this transaction suggest that there is a shift in focus from 'training and development' to 'development and learning'.

THE EMPLOYER MUST COMMIT TO:

- providing ongoing opportunities and support for education and training
- structuring daily work and career paths to use existing competencies and build new individual capabilities
- encouraging and rewarding individuals who use competencies effectively
- helping individuals find new work opportunities, either internal or external, if demand for existing competencies decreases

THE EMPLOYEE MUST COMMIT TO:

- investing in own development of competencies
- using competencies to help achieve organizational objectives
- helping build competencies of co-workers
- contributing to organizational learning

(Reproduced with permission from D. Finegold (1998) *The New Learning Partnership*, San Francisco: Jossey-Bass.)

Figure 3.8   Elements of the new learning contract

DEVELOPING A NEW TRAINING MODEL

Summary: *Whatever the limitations, deriving a training model for the organization is worthwhile. Drawing on the perspective given by the models considered earlier in this chapter, some characteristics of best practice are presented.*

The analysis of the alternative models can now be brought together and some conclusions advanced. These implications are then explored in the course of the next two parts of this book.

First, however, there is an important issue to be addressed: do we need training models at all? Two linked arguments can be advanced which suggest that the results from the effort needed to produce effective models may not be worth the investment.

The first argument is pragmatic. Given the diverse nature of organizations in which trainers work, no model of general applicability can be derived. Training must be delivered in organizations of varying size, with centralized or decentralized structures, with different patterns of ownership and with different traditions. The Ashridge model, for example, distinguishes three separate phases of the training development. Can the same approach be applied sensibly to organizations which are in different phases? The second argument proceeds from an acceptance of these difficulties and suggests that to impose a model could be damaging to the achievement of objectives. To some extent this perspective is reflected in the consultancy model already considered. By operating as internal consultants, it is suggested, trainers will have the opportunity to enter into different contracts with appropriate line managers; the combination of internal requests from line managers and the initiative of the trainer will be sufficient to produce the flexibility and responsiveness that best serves the organization's interests. No model is required beyond this.

Neither argument should be dismissed out of hand. At the end of the book the reader may well decide that attempts to develop a new model have been of limited value – though I hope some useful insights on the place of training in the organization will have emerged in the course of the investigation.

At this stage, however, I suggest that an attempt to formulate such a model is worthwhile, and will assist in the articulation of best practice. First, it will provide a route map for the trainer in determining his or her next steps, particularly in fulfilling a higher strategic role. Second, it will add to the professionalism of the function and its credibility within the organization. Third, it will define the appropriate relationships with the other human resource professionals and with line managers.

Moreover, the new context and pressures mean that the training is at a pivotal phase. This will be seen to be a major conclusion to emerge from the survey of best practice organizations undertaken for this book and outlined in Appendix IV. The training function is wrestling with some important change issues. For some issues the way forward is clear; for others the future direction is uncertain. Thinking through the implications of a model, and formulating a robust and coherent model, will assist in clarifying the trainer's role and communicating it within the organization.

Accordingly the outline of an effective model of training practice is shown in Figure 3.9. This outline has been derived largely from an analysis of the models considered earlier in this chapter.

FEATURES OF AN EFFECTIVE MODEL OF TRAINING PRACTICE RETAIN THE BEST ELEMENTS OF THE SYSTEMATIC TRAINING MODEL AND:

- offer the trainer a structured and disciplined framework in which to work
- ensure that an effective loop from evaluation is in operation
- emphasize the importance of quantifiable results, even though the feasibility of this varies

THEY TAKE INTO ACCOUNT

- the need to embed training activity firmly in the organization, thus securing links to strategic objectives and permitting training to operate in a corporate context
- that the training function has a role in articulating training needs as well as reacting to them
- that different organizations are at different stages in terms of training sophistication and that different approaches may therefore be necessary.

Moreover, given the diversity of organizations and different business objectives, one size may not fit all. The search must be for general principles.

Figure 3.9   Features of an effective model of training practice

The more authoritative features of the systematic training model have been retained: the importance of working within a framework is stressed. Although this view can only be supported anecdotally, few criticisms are more pertinent and more damaging to trainers than the implication that they are working without any clear strategy and to an agenda that is totally self-determined. The importance of the loop from evaluation is underlined, but it should be recognized that much of what the trainer does, and the organization regards as important, cannot readily be quantified – a topic that will be discussed more fully in Chapter 8.

Additionally, the outline in Figure 3.9 explicitly endorses the strategic role for the training function and demands that the training professional accepts responsibility for articulating needs as well as reacting to them.

Most importantly it endorses the requirement that an organization moves through a series of different levels of responses to and acceptance of training initiatives – henceforth this will be described as the level of training culture within the organization. This follows from a consideration of the Ashridge model and the desire to move towards a learning organization (however defined). It is clear, however, that the relationships implied in the consultancy model have been explicitly rejected, even though the needs for consultancy skills are accepted and will be looked at further.

In addition, it is suggested that the activities of the training cycle must, to have maximum effectiveness, be conducted with the following objectives in mind:

- in almost all cases the training culture of the organization will need to be developed, line managers and human resource professionals will need to be made more aware of the importance of training and their role in its management – they will need to be taken up a learning curve
- the trainer should therefore actively develop the responsibility and responsiveness of line management
- the trainer will need to take part in the articulation of the strategic contribution that training can make, rather than relying on the organization to identify this.

So far Figure 3.9 has been deliberately described as an outline for a new model of training practice – it clearly is too imprecise to be described as a model. A fuller discussion will be presented and discussed in Part III, Chapter 9. Since one of the main arguments of this book is that models should be determined by practical realities, further examination of these realities is needed before the model can be fully developed. The discussion so far has, however, given some useful indications on how that examination should proceed.

Because value has been found in the systematic training model, its underlying structure will be used as a framework for that examination. In Part II of this book the identification of training needs, the design and delivery of training and the evaluation of training programmes (in their broader sense) will be discussed in turn.

REFERENCES

1. Manpower Services Commission (1981), *Glossary of Training Terms*, London: HMSO.
2. Carnevale, A.P, Gainer, L.J. and Villet, J. (1990), *Training in America: The Organization and Strategic Role of Training*, San Francisco: Jossey-Bass.
3. Boydell, T. (1970), *Job Analysis*, London: BACIE and (1971), *A Guide to the Identification of Training Needs*, London: BACIE.
4. Kenney, J. and Reid, M. (1992), *Training Interventions*, London: Institute of Personnel Management.
5. Taylor, H. (1991), 'The Systematic Training Model: Corn Circles in Search of a Spaceship?', *Management Education and Development*, **22** (4).
6. Holdaway, K. and Saunders, M. (1992), *The In-House Trainer as Consultant*, London: Kogan Page.
7. Barham, K., Fraser, J. and Heath, L. (1988), *Management for the Future*, Berkhamstead: Ashridge Management Research Group.
8. Argyris, C. and Schon, D. A. (1978), *Organizational Learning: A Theory of Action Perspective*, Wokingham: Addison-Wesley.

9. Kolb, D. (1984), *Experiential Learning*, Englewood Cliffs: Prentice-Hall.
10. Peters, T. J. and Waterman, R. H., (1982), *In Search of Excellence: Lessons from America's Best-Run Companies*, New York: Harper Row.
11. Senge, P. M. (1990), *The Fifth Discipline: The Art and Practice of the Learning Organization*, New York: Doubleday.
12. Hammond, V. and Wille, E. (1991). 'The Learning Organization' in Prior, J. (ed.), *Gower Handbook of Training and Development*, Second Edition, Aldershot: Gower.
13. Honey, P. (1991), 'The Learning Organization Simplified', *Training and Development*, **9** (7), July.
14. Finegold, D. (1998), The New Learning Partnership' in Mohrman, S., Galbraith, J.A. and Lawler, E., III, *Tomorrow's Organizations*, San Francisco: Jossey Bass/Centre for Effective Organization, pp. 231–61.

Part II
The Process of Training

Introduction to Part II

In this second part of the book I consider in turn the identification of training needs, the design and delivery of training, and its evaluation (the components of the systematic training model). They are reviewed in the new context outlined in Part I. Given the importance of performance appraisal, it is the subject of a separate chapter. I have therefore divided needs identification into three areas: identifying needs at the organizational level (Chapter 4) and at the individual level (Chapter 5), and improving the effectiveness of performance appraisal (Chapter 6). Design and delivery are then considered together (Chapter 7). To reflect the importance of the value of training being demonstrated to the organization, the consideration of evaluation is extended into a broader discussion of measurement systems (Chapter 8).

Best practice demands that the training manager and trainer play a proactive role. This is nothing new: it has been universally accepted in the profession and is developed in almost all the literature. The shifting role of the function, however, demands a changed emphasis in two respects:

- needs identification, design, delivery and evaluation must all take place in a broader context, reflecting the contribution that training must play in supporting competition though people
- line managers must be encouraged to develop their role and extend their participation in the process.

Few would disagree with these statements. In practice, however, considerable problems arise in translating them into operational procedures. First, the broader context in which training must be delivered is itself amorphous. As I discuss in Chapter 4, it is not easy to express strategic human resource objectives in terms of practical training delivery. Second, there is a need to increase line managers' awareness of the options involved at all stages of the training cycle.

These problems are considered in this second part of the book and some solutions suggested. One additional point should be made at the outset. Meeting training needs is classically a demand-led activity, but, paradoxically, it can be made more successful if the training manager also engages in supply-side activity. Part of the job is to suggest training events that will reinforce the business objectives and the line manager's operational needs – events that, without this prompting, would not have been given any consideration by those managers who do not possess a high degree of training awareness.

4   Training and the organization

The identification of training needs must begin with a recognition that the training manager is functioning in the broader context: that there are both corporate and individual training requirements. In the first two sections of this chapter this broader context is explored by examining two important areas: the link with strategic planning and the link with corporate culture. This is followed by a review of a topic that is rapidly advancing up the agenda: the particular issues raised by the international company – discussed as training for the global workforce.

The conclusions on training at this macro-level are somewhat depressing: human resource professionals have a long way to go before they can say with confidence that they are fully equipped to determine and implement training at this level. There is work to be done here. This is important since it is in these areas that training activity is about more than narrow skills enhancement; it can capture broader human resource benefits. In Chapter 5, where the identification of training needs is undertaken at the micro-level, the trainer is on much safer and well-researched ground. In all three chapters on training needs, I present some practical instruments which have proved of value.

THE LINK WITH STRATEGIC PLANNING

Summary: *Forging an effective link between training and strategic planning is one of the most important challenges facing the training manager. Mutual consistency and a clear fit of human resource activities is recommended, as is gaining an understanding of the process of strategy formation. The importance of human resource planning itself is underlined.*

No one would dispute that training programmes should reflect (or, according to taste, be a product of, be aligned with, be consistent with) a company's business strategy. The survey of best practice organizations undertaken for this book (see

Appendix IV, p. 269) reinforces this view. Market competition and organizational change are identified as the two most powerful influences on training. What is at issue is what this means in operational terms.

In Chapter 2 I discussed the concept of strategic human resources. This followed from the acceptance of competition through people and the recognition that human resources must develop and motivate the workforce to achieve this objective. A more strategic role for the human resource function, and for training and development in particular, is an inevitable consequence of that movement. Another consequence is the need for coherence of personnel practices with one another and their consistency with the organization's strategic planning process. This leads on to the concept of alignment – put simply, the idea that the elements of a human resource system should fit together.

In an important book, *Strategic Human Resource Management*, Fombrun, Tichy and Devanna[1] argue that the critical managerial task is to align the formal structure and the human resources system so that they drive the strategic objectives of the organization. Fombrun *et al*'s. four key components of HRM are selection, appraisal, development and rewards, and the link with performance is presented diagrammatically at Figure 4.1.

Mutual consistency of human resource activities and goodness of fit with the company's strategic objectives are laudable aims. No one would advocate discordance and inconsistency. Securing alignment, however defined, does presuppose an ability to translate the corporate strategy into practical human resource procedures. This demands an understanding of the strategic planning process in the organization and also raises questions on human resource planning. Inevitably,

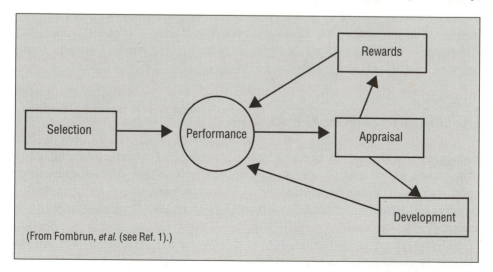

(From Fombrun, *et al.* (see Ref. 1).)

Figure 4.1   The human resource management cycle

but unfortunately, this area is blurred. In part, this is because business strategy is itself evolving as the implications of resource-based strategy are explored. Identifying and nurturing an organization's core competencies is a compelling theoretical concept. However, there is a dearth of practical literature on how this can be accomplished – though one volume by Campbell and Luchs of the Ashridge Strategic Management Research Centre is recommended .[2]

The fact that the approach to strategy is changing does not excuse inaction. It is still vitally important to ask 'what practical steps should be taken by the training manager in the organization?'. Within the context of the determination of best training practice, it is possible to offer some guidance on steps that can be taken. These are summarized in Figure 4.2. The first step for those responsible for training in the organization is to obtain a broad overview of the strategic management and planning process. This does not mean they should become strategic planning experts, merely that they should appreciate the difference between alternative approaches.

LINKING TRAINING WITH STRATEGIC MANAGEMENT NECESSITATES

- trainers or training managers having a broad theoretical understanding of the strategic management and planning process
- trainers or training managers ascertaining the methods used in their organization

And, distinguishing between strategy formation and formulation,

- the HRM implications of strategic options should be expressed coherently and developed using a proactive rather than a reactive approach, and as part of the broader human resource management activities.

Figure 4.2   **Linking training with strategic management**

As strategic planning became fashionable the early emphasis was placed on prescriptive strategy. Planning was seen as methodical, rational and sequential actions, with formulation preceding implementation. Subsequently there has been a movement to a more descriptive, adaptive strategy, with far more flexibility between formulation and implementation.

An important contribution in the latter development has come from Henry Mintzberg, who distinguishes between strategy formulation and strategy formation. Formulation implies a formal planning process in which decision-making precedes relatively unproblematic implementation.[3] Mintzberg suggested that strategy may also be a far less structured but evolving process: it may emerge in a process of formation. He distinguishes between intended, emergent and realized strategy – presented in Figure 4.3 on page 77.

A key task for the training manager, then, is to adopt a proactive approach and to provide an input to strategy formation. This must be achieved by presenting the human resource implications of the intended strategy and also by generating options which assist competition through people.

The best immediate advice, therefore, to anyone undertaking such activity would be to ascertain the methods used to determine strategy in their organization and, quite simply, to forge working relationships with those responsible for the activity.

Other useful guidance is in the work of Carnevale, Gainer and Villet for the American Society for Training and Development (ASTD). Their investigations of the organization and strategic role of training in the US were published in *Training in America* (see Reference 2, Chapter 3). In their book they present the findings of a three-year study of how training in the workplace is structured, managed, financed and coordinated with organizational strategy.

The three chapters of the book that consider building the strategic role of training probably make up its weakest part. It is a measure of the state of the art that in a volume full of the results of practical fieldwork, it is found necessary to include a large section simply describing the textbook alternatives for the strategic process. It does, however, offer considerable practical advice and the section on gathering strategic information is helpful. Figure 4.4 reproduces a series of questions that the trainer should ask regardless of the strategy. The authors then present an additional list of questions that are in turn specific to one of four 'umbrella' strategies: concentration, internal growth, external growth and disinvestment.

In summary, the development of an appropriate training response to the strategic management and planning process demands an exploratory and contingent approach. It depends on the nature and location of the strategic planning process adopted in the organization.

So far the assumption has been that the training manager's initiatives should be determined by the strategic planning process. It is by no means inconsistent to argue that the training manager's initiatives should also be determined by the human resource planning process. The strategic and human resource planning processes should be mutually consistent, it is not a matter of choosing between the two. The training manager must seize the opportunity to ensure that the strategic role of training is discussed and understood, and high-level plans offer such a vehicle.

Again, effective human resource planning depends on the detailed circumstances that are present in a particular organization. However, there are general lessons that can be gained from a review of current and best practice. One particularly significant analysis has been undertaken by Professor Shaun Tyson, Director of the Human Resource Management Centre at Cranfield School of Management.

Tyson is a leading commentator on trends in human resource practice, who has examined current thinking on human resource strategies as a response to new business strategies and to changes in the planning environment.[4]

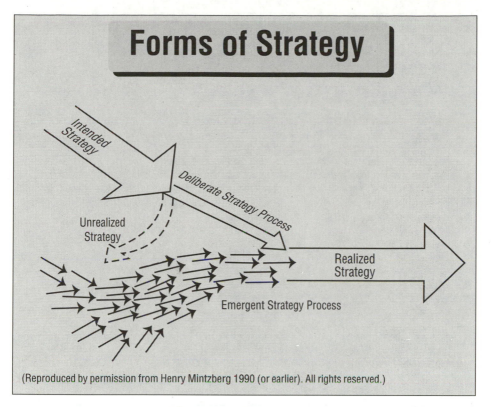

Figure 4.3   Forms of strategy

Broad Issues

- The training advocate needs to understand the environment in which her or his organization operates. Is the organization's current industry evolving or stable? What do the growth trends in the industry look like? Who are the main domestic and foreign competitors, and what is the organization's competitive advantage over those competitors? How can or will the organization capitalize on competitors' strategic vulnerabilities? (For example, is the organization capable of widening the competitive gap in its favour?)
- Why has the organization been successful in the past? What strategies has it successfully employed? What was learned during that time that can be applied under the new strategy? What forces have driven the organization to select a new strategy?
- What technology does the organization plan to use? If the organization plans to use new technology, when will it come on line? Any new processes? When will they be instituted?
- Are innovations anticipated in the industry that could change the competitive playing field? Will these be radical breakthroughs or modifications to existing products or technologies? What effect would there be on the organization's product and its competitive position?
- What new management philosophies or procedures, such as constant quality pursuit (*kaizen*), working through teams and participative management will be instituted by the organization? When?

Figure 4.4   Questions to ask in gathering strategic information (Continued)

- Are there any regulatory issues - current, pending, or anticipated - that could influence strategic considerations?
- What functional strategies will be employed by the various divisions or operating units to effect the overarching strategy? Why? How?

Human Resource Issues

- The training advocate needs to understand the workplace profile of the organization. What are the current strengths and weaknesses of the workforce? In the aggregate, is the workforce technical? Is it skilled? What kind of education or training have most employees received to enter their positions? What do they need to stay current? It is a flexible and adaptable workforce?
- What changes, if any, must occur in the job(s), organizational culture and skill levels of the workforce?
- Is the organization's decision to pursue an umbrella strategy likely to result in layoffs or other turnover? How much is anticipated?
- How will union contract agreements be affected? What is the strategic role of the union?
- What human resource management policies should be reviewed or modified in the light of the organization's strategic emphasis (such as selection, hiring, appraisal, rewards or career development)?
- What are the training implications of the overarching strategy? Of each functional/operational strategy and its companion tactics? How could training help the organization reach any or all of its strategic goals?
- What kind of specific training programs are needed? Are they needed in basic workplace, technical, product knowledge, managerial/supervisory, or motivational skills? Does the organization have in-house capability to implement the necessary programs? Are there outside experts who can assist? Who are they?
- How has training been regarded by the workforce in the past? By management? How credible are the programs and the trainers? How will these views affect future training efforts?
- What delivery mechanisms are most cost-effective and practical for each training program?
- Does the organization have an employee educational assistance plan (tuition reimbursement)? Do many employees take advantage of it? If so, how can it be used to enhance worker skills?
- What kind of training evaluation process is currently being used? Does it provide information on return on investment? If not, would such a process contribute to the strategic information flow?
- Is there a formal procedure to ascertain if current training is appropriate in the light of a new strategy or, alternatively, to identify training needs that will be dictated by the new strategy?
- Do human resource management functions other than training (such as selection, hiring, appraisal, rewards or career development) need to be reviewed? Should they be modified?

(Reproduced with permission from (1990) Carnevale, A.P., Gainer, L.J. and Villet, J., *Training in America*, San Francisco: Jossey Bass (pp. 202–5).

Figure 4.4 Concluded

He notes that researchers often find it difficult to apply business strategy classifications to real companies. In practice there is often a mixture of strategies with companies trying to compete on the basis of both cost and quality. The pace of change (shorter product life cycles, instant communication and international competition) means that different products and services have to be sold in many different markets.

The consequent demise of long-range corporate planning, however, should not lead to the rejection of the concept of business strategy. There is ample evidence that managers do strive for agreed corporate goals – which are formulated by the most senior managers. He therefore offers a social scientist's definition of business strategy:

> the attempt by those who control an organisation to find ways to position their business/organisation objectives so that they can exploit the planning environment, and make optimum use of capital and human assets (p. 5).

Strategy incorporates both the need to respond to the environment and the need to make use of the strengths of the organization in exploiting available opportunities. In practice, however, an organization's strategy does not reside in a single accessible document – certainly not one which is metaphorically cast in stone.

Tyson draws on earlier research to suggest that human resource strategies do not exist in all organizations – one survey suggests that around 50 per cent of UK companies have a written human resource strategy. This he describes as follows:

> human resource strategy can be defined as a set of ideas, policies and practices that management adopts in order to achieve a people management objective. (p. 6).

In his earlier study of 30 high-performing organizations,[5] Tyson identified three distinct approaches to strategy formation:

a) a *flexible approach* to strategy formulation, where companies create flexible, responsive structures and policies so they could respond to future challenges. This was the most common approach
b) *formal* long-range planning, which was evident in capital intensive business or where there was a technical need for long-term horizons
c) *attributional* strategies, which were really after the event rationalizations of a stream of managerial decisions.

Quite often, where they existed, human resource strategy documents were seen as drafts, constantly up for revision, 'framed to reinterpret organisational or business/corporate strategies into people management objectives'. More formal planning processes were most likely to be in place in respect of succession planning and management development. In a review of the human resource strategy documents that did exist, certain common elements were identified and these are shown in Figure 4.5.

In addition, the strategy often has a flavour reflecting the organization's philosophy of management. Human resource plans often state what the organization's values are and how they should be reflected in the management process.

COMMON ELEMENTS OF HUMAN RESOURCE STRATEGY DOCUMENTS INCLUDE:

a) a review of external influences, including the political (e.g. what the effects of a government change will be, or European institutional arrangements); the economic (inflation, interest rate, unemployment, pay prospects); and the social (demographic, marital, crime and other trends)

b) technical and social (the impact of new technology on work, communications etc.) and any specific legislative trends or changes anticipated – for example the Employment Rights and Disability Act or the European directive on atypical workers may be cited

c) an examination of the main business trends as they are likely to affect human resources in particular – expansion, contraction, and any collaborative arrangements

d) the examination in turn of each main policy area, in order to analyse the impact of external and business change on, for example:

- employee resourcing
- employee relations
- rewards
- health and safety
- training and development
- performance management.

e) a description of the prospects for the type of service from the specialist human resource function. Relationships with line management, the expertise required in the function, and the way in which the function should operate in the future are dealt with here.

(From Tyson (see Ref. 4, pp. 7–8).)

Figure 4.5   Common elements of human resource strategy documents

THE LINK WITH CORPORATE CULTURE

Summary: *The concept of corporate culture has achieved prominence in human resources in recent years. Some definitions are offered and a practical approach to determining the organizational culture is outlined. Culture is seen as something that can be managed within an organization and change management programmes are receiving attention. An illustrative programme that shows the importance of training will be presented.*

One of the most important developments in human resource management over the last three decades has been a recognition of the importance of culture. In particular, the need to identify the corporate culture that exists in the organization and to nurture the desired culture has been widely accepted. Nowadays, the following statements are accepted as true:

- an organization has a corporate culture which can be investigated and categorized

- management can determine whether the existing corporate cu
priate to the organization that they desire; in other words, a mat
is possible
- structuring a desired corporate culture is important because it can be a key
determinant in the achievement of corporate objectives; more importantly an
inappropriate culture can prevent the achievement of corporate objectives
- that by a combination of well-identified organizational and personnel procedures such a structuring of corporate culture is possible; crudely, corporate
culture can be manipulated by management through change management
programmes
- organizations with strong corporate cultures that are well aligned with the
desired corporate objectives are more likely to succeed than those with weak
corporate cultures.

If these statements are correct they are clearly of fundamental importance to training practice. Training programmes will figure prominently on the list of personnel
procedures which can be used to restructure corporate cultures.

Training managers must therefore have an appreciation of the debate on corporate culture and realize the potential implications for the way in which they do
their job. Culture and change management programmes have generated large-
scale opportunities for external consultants – particularly those who wish to act as
change agents for the client organization. Problems can arise with this relationship. If cultural change is initiated by the board and senior management and is
guided by external consultants, human resources management must attempt, at
the outset, to ensure that the process is translated into hard recommendations that
can be expressed as training programmes or other personnel activities. If this does
not occur there is a danger of high-profile transient programmes, ephemeral in
their impact. The training department will be taking all staff through a sheep-dip –
a quick programme designed to reinforce a policy that is perceived as imposed
from above.

The training manager must therefore understand corporate culture, and a starting point must be a consideration of how the concept has come to prominence.
There is underlying confusion, arising in part from the fact that the concept has
been borrowed from social anthropology. Given this uncertainty, it is not surprising that there is confusion over practical definitions. A 1989 Institute of Personnel
Management's (IPM) publication on corporate culture[6] refers to a text containing
164 definitions of culture itself and of some perceptions of culture as an entity,
which, by definition, is almost impossible to measure, study or change. The simplest definition that can be offered – 'the way we do things round here' – is limited
in scope: most commentators would argue that culture is about the underlying
beliefs and values that pervade an organization as well as the things that are done –

the visible manifestations of the culture. The IPM therefore gave the following definition, that 'Culture is the commonly held and relatively stable beliefs, attitudes and values that exist within the organization' (p. 11).

Harrison and Stokes put forward the following alternative definition:

> Organization culture is those aspects of an organization which give it a particular climate or 'feel'. 'Culture' is to an organization what 'personality' is to an individual person. It is that distinctive constellation of beliefs, values, work styles, and relationships which distinguish one organization from another (p. 9).[7]

Other commentators have spoken of strategy as the key god of the organization in recent years, norms as dealing with the 'how to' achieve things in the organization, and values as the 'why' we do things in the organization. Norms and values determine culture.

The questions 'How do we determine our organization's culture?' and 'How do we manage it?' are therefore of considerable importance to the training profession – not least because senior management will ask them. Edgar H. Schein, an important US writer on culture, has argued that culture is difficult to study and 'the problem of deciphering a particular organization's culture, then, is more a matter of surfacing assumptions, which will be recognizable once uncovered' (p. 249).[8] He recommends four approaches to data collection:

● analyse the process and content of the socialization of new members, particularly by interviewing those who undertake such tasks
● analyse the responses to critical incidents in the organization's history, since these are often significant periods of culture formation
● analyse the beliefs, values and assumptions of 'culture creators or carriers', through detailed interviews
● jointly explore and analyse with insiders the anomalies or puzzling features observed or uncovered in interviews.

Schein suggests some diagnostic tools but offers less of immediate value for prescriptive change.

Another valuable approach is offered by Harrison and Stokes,[7] who have created a useful instrument for assessing organization culture. By examining how people treat one another, what values people live by, how people are motivated to produce and how people use power, they claim to have uncovered the core of what most people mean by their organization's culture.

Harrison and Stokes argue that all organizations have a combination of four basic cultural orientations: power, role, achievement and support. These are described more fully in Figure 4.6, which reproduces two sample questions from their user-friendly questionnaire. Completion of the questionnaire enables participants to compare their perceptions of the culture pertaining in their organization with their views on the desired culture. All organizations must have some combination of all four basic cultural orientations; what is at issue is the optimum balance between the four, and increased emphasis on one can only be achieved at the expense of some of the others. The instrument also permits participants to calculate a culture index for the organization – derived by adding the achievement and support scores and subtracting the power and role scores. This culture index, the authors argue, is a measure which reflects the general level of 'empowerment, trust and co-operation within the organization': their declared bias is towards the release of the human spirit in work.

Harrison and Stokes have produced a helpful tool for the training manager, especially in promoting structured discussion of the desired directions of organizational change. However, this is but the first step towards dealing with the process of cultural change since, in their own words, what is required is:

> A consensus about what kind of culture is most likely to satisfy the interests and needs of the organization's various stakeholders. A well-designed long-term strategy for reaching the desired state (p. 18).

Generally, given the problems in identifying, let alone managing, culture, it is not surprising that the practical emphasis has been placed on its more tangible aspects. Particular attention has been given to taking the temperature through employee surveys and articulating intentions by means of mission statements. This emphasis on the practical aspects has found its most powerful expression in change management programmes. These have achieved particular prominence in many of the former public sector industries that were privatized in the late 1980s and early 1990s.

Many of these organizations have embraced change as a positive step. They have addressed a number of major cultural issues which would have inevitably been faced if the organization was to maintain credibility. The case study outlined below, which describes how Anglia Railways adjusted to privatization, offers a particularly interesting example.[9]

The 1993 Railways Act marked a traumatic shift in the industry. Until April 1994 British Rail was a nationalized industry employing 128 000 people. It was a vertically integrated railway business: it owned, built and maintained the track and other infrastructure, building land and rolling stock. It serviced the customer both on and off the train. The 1993 Act split the centralized structure into eighty separate companies, which came into existence in less than 12 months from Royal Assent. One of these companies was Anglia Railways, a train operating unit. It was established to manage both the InterCity route to East Anglia and local lines. Although small, it had the advantage of a clear regional identity.

Changing ownership and size was, however, only one aspect. Many cultural issues needed to be dealt with. Historically the industry was engineering-oriented and overlaid by a command and control management structure. There were clearly defined ranks, complex terms and conditions, and clear lines of promotion.

POWER
- based on inequality of access to resources
- leadership rests in ability and willingness to administer rewards and punishment
- at best based on strength, justice and paternalistic benevolence
- at worst tends towards rule by fear.

ROLE
- substitutes a system of structures and procedures for the naked power of leaders
- values order, dependability, rationality and consistency
- at best provides stability, justice and efficient performance
- at worst inhibits individual autonomy and discretion.

ACHIEVEMENT
- members are expected to contribute their personal energy in return for rewards
- develops 'high energy' work situations
- at best attracts and releases the personal energy of its members in pursuit of common goals
- at worst produces burnout, disillusionment, lack of coordination.

SUPPORT
- based on mutual trust between individual and organization
- people believe they are valued as human beings not just cogs in machines or contributors to a task
- at best fosters warmth as well as driving enthusiasm
- at worst, lack of results orientation means the business is uncompetitive.

Typical example used in the Harrison and Stokes instrument for assessing organization culture is:

EXISTING   PREFERRED
CULTURE   CULTURE

1. Members of the organization are expected to give first priority to

———   ———   a. meeting the needs and demands on their supervisor and other high-level people in the organization.

———   ———   b. carrying out the duties of their own job; staying within the policies and procedures related to it.

———   ———   c. meeting the challenges of the task, finding a better way to do things.

———   ———   d. co-operating with the people they work with, to solve work and personal problems.

2. People who do well in the organization tend to be those who

———   ———   a. know how to please their supervisor, and are able and willing to use power and politics to get ahead.

———   ———   b. play by the rules, work within the system, and strive to do things correctly.

———   ———   c. are technically competent and effective, with a strong commitment to getting the job done.

———   ———   d. build close working relationships with others by being co-operative, responsive and caring.

(Reproduced from Harrison and Stokes (see Ref. 7) by permission of Pfeiffer & Co. 1992.)

Figure 4.6   **Four basic culture orientations**

Many of the predominantly male staff were long-serving and a job-for-life mentality was endemic.

Anglia Railways therefore faced a significant problem of cultural transformation on many levels. Three aspects of the transformation make it an interesting case study:

- the link between human resources and culture change was recognized as vital at the outset
- a clear model of transformational change was adopted
- the role of training was clearly considered in advance and formed a key part of the process.

Each of these aspects will be considered in turn.

The link between human resources and culture followed from the business vision and key strategy. In early 1994 this was given in the following terms:

> To be a respected and successful East Anglia business, recognised for its standards of customer service.

This marked a departure from the traditional engineering focus of British Rail. Five key areas were identified as fundamental to supporting this vision: business growth, more effective supplier management, regional identity, resource management, and individual and team performance. Before these could be addressed, however, individuals needed to work through the trauma of the change. Staff were brought together in small multi-functional groups. Subsequently, staff conferences were held and focused on the new business.

The human resources policies and programmes that were implemented to support this change were underpinned by the Burke-Litwin model of personal and organizational performance.[10] This model had been used in British Airways, which had experienced a similar change: public to private, engineering focus to customer focus. The model involves interventions using a series of interrelated variables that affect performance. Most importantly it clearly identifies two key sets of factors: those which are transformational and those which are transactional. Anglia Railways identified three transformational factors as the primary focus of efforts. These three factors were Mission and Strategy, Leadership and Organisational Culture. The formulation and implementation of effective policies for these factors was crucial to success.

The human resources function in Anglia Railways therefore needed to interpret and translate this model into practice and reality on a day-to-day basis. Cultural changes to support the vision were ongoing. Effective training was an essential part of the process. Training in Anglia Railways needed to be redefined. The training initiatives concerned management development, service management and performance management. In addition, a number of ongoing requirements had to be met.

The first component in the new approach to training was a substantial emphasis on management development. Many managers in the middle level and first line had previously experienced little or no personal development training. Meeting this requirement involved a number of different processes, including support for the Certificate in Management Studies. All the processes had common themes:

- the ability to be clear about expectations and give feedback
- the ability to engender trust
- the skills for motivation and involvement
- the confidence to act as mentor and advocate
- a focus on development and teamwork.

This list offers a good categorization of the required soft skills for the modern people manager. In Anglia Railways this form of training was seen as a way of giving managers confidence in the organizational change.

A second significant use of training to support organizational change was an emphasis on service management. This followed directly from the vision and a need for a multi-level programme that would focus on customer service. Five key factors were identified: reliability, assurance (people believing that the organization does what it says), tangibles (meals, the appearance of trains, etc.), empathy (the soft skills of customer management) and responsiveness. One hundred and twenty staff attended a three-day event. Most importantly, to encourage ownership, this programme was delivered by trainers within the business.

The third component was an important move towards a new style of performance management. Initiatives were taken to ensure that performance management processes were understandable throughout the organization. Encouraging responses from an annual staff survey indicated a willingness to buy in at all levels.

While undergoing these significant changes, Anglia Railways needed to undertake ongoing training across the following areas.

- the introduction of National Vocational Qualifications, particularly for critical safety work
- training for catering staff, involving hygiene and customer concern
- sales training for tele-centre staff
- training initiatives dealing with handling aggression and harassment, and IT training on new systems
- technical training required to meet safety and electrical regulations.

Inevitably the organization has faced further cultural change in the years since privatization and encountered and managed new challenges.

Perhaps the most important lesson from Anglia Railways, however, was the deliberate attempt to see training as an integral part of change, reinforced by initiatives designed to support the achievement of the vision and cultural change. A high degree of involvement was sought from staff at all levels.

Not all organizations have such a clear opportunity for forging a link between strategy and training as Anglia Railways did in the early 1990s. Not all organizations have a clear strategy. However, all organizations, whether consciously or unconsciously, are making and implementing decisions to ensure their survival, and this implies some form of strategy.

TRAINING FOR THE GLOBAL WORKFORCE

Summary: *Few, if any, organizations will be untouched by the growing trend towards international business. The problems of training for the global firm differ in degree and emphasis from the problems of training for the domestic market. In formulating a training intervention it is necessary to understand the nature of the business response and to determine the skills required. The design and delivery of training in an international context may require special consideration.*

The first two elements of the new competitive model, identified in Chapter 1 (see Figure 1:1, p. 6) reflected the growing trend towards international business. It was argued that this new global economy, reinforced by the information/telecommunications revolution and by deregulation, has changed the nature of competition. The removal of barriers to international trade has – because developed countries cannot compete through costs – changed the strategic response of many companies: it has been a primary driver of the attempt to compete through the development of a sophisticated workforce.

If the above is accepted, few companies will be untouched by the impact of internationalization. Even the most insular domestic organization will be affected at some stage by ideas and influences generated elsewhere in the world. For many firms, however, international competition in a global market is a reality. The training function must be proactive in its response and ensure that training and development is aligned with the new strategic demands. This section explores how this can be achieved in practice.

One question should be considered at the outset: are the problems of training for the global firm fundamentally different from those that arise when managing training domestically? It will be seen from the following discussion that the differences are of degree and emphasis, rather than ones which require a new approach. As in the formulation and management of domestic training, what is required is an understanding of the business, the nature of its market, and the ability to design and deliver an appropriate training response that is effective in the culture.

In 1997 the Institute of Personnel and Development (IPD) published a guide which offers a useful framework for considering the training manager's response. It began by arguing that:

> the world is becoming a smaller, yet more complex place. Reasons for the accelerating internationalization of corporate activity, increased pace of technological change and organisational innovation as well as the rapid globalization of markets include:
>
> - growth of foreign direct investment
> - increase in the number, size and importance of multinational companies
> - globalisation of market competition
> - increased number of mergers & acquisitions and joint ventures
>
> The work of managers has become more international. Increasingly they have to plan their strategies on policies for more than one country, communicate more frequently across cultural boundaries, and travel or live abroad more often. (p. 5).[11]

International management development is therefore growing in importance and this was defined as:

> an activity that comprises all methods of internationalising key personnel which leaves them better prepared for their cross-national tasks. From an organisational perspective, international management development can also be used to support business strategy and corporate structure: shaping cross-border co-operation and communication (p. 5).

The need then is two-fold: it is to support the business at the strategic level and to equip individuals with the knowledge and skills required to perform their current and future functions. How this is delivered must, again, depend on the precise circumstances facing the training manager in his or her organization. To help develop an appropriate response, the following three questions should be answered:

- how has the business responded to the global challenge; what organizational structure has it adopted?
- what skills are required of the international manager of the future and how may they be developed?
- what special considerations or issues should apply to the design and delivery of training in the international context?

By appreciating the importance of these three questions the training manager will have taken many steps towards understanding and meeting the needs of the organization. Each question will now be considered in turn.

THE ORGANIZATIONAL RESPONSE

Different organizations have adopted different approaches to the demands of competition in the international market place and this determines the extent to which they can be regarded as 'international firms'. For example, in *Transnational Management*, published in 1995, Bartlett and Ghoshal identified and distinguished the following different strategic orientations:

- *Multinational* Building flexibility to respond to national differences, through strong resourceful and entrepreneurial national operations.
- *International* Exploiting parent-company knowledge and capabilities through worldwide diffusion and adaptations.
- *Global* Building cost advantages through centralization and global-scale operations.
- *Transnational* Developing global efficiency, flexibility and worldwide learning capability simultaneously (p. 251).[12]

Bartlett and Ghoshal's argument is that many firms have been transformed from multinational, international or global forms towards a transnational form.

Bartlett and Ghoshal's perspective has developed over time, and their terminology has varied. What is important to recognize, however, is that organizations which superficially could be described as 'international' may be seeking competitive advantage in very different ways. Moreover, organizational forms may be evolving and adapting. The strategic orientation will determine the management of assets and capabilities; it therefore must shape the desired approach to training. At one extreme, a firm may be competing by adapting a product to different consumer tastes and preferences in different national markets. At the other, the firm may be seeking to operate as a full-blown transnational company.

One company that has attracted considerable attention (so much so that for some commentators it almost serves as a model for the organization of the future) is the electrical engineering giant ABB. It was created in 1987 through a merger of the Swedish Asea and the Swiss Brown Boveri. Its company motto is 'the art of being local worldwide'. It has developed a complex transnational matrix structure to balance global and local pressures. It describes itself as a 'multi-domestic' federation of national companies with a small Zurich-based global coordination centre.[13] The former President and Chief Executive Percy Barnevik has described the company's organizing philosophy as follows:

> You want to be able to optimize a business globally – to specialize in the production of components, to drive economies of scale as far as you can, to rotate managers and technologists around the world to share expertise and solve problems. But you also want to have deep local roots everywhere you operate – building products in the countries where you sell them, recruiting the best local talent from the universities, working with the local government to increase exports (p. 92).[14]

Formulating and implementing the appropriate training and development response for such an organization is a demanding process. It requires effort to maintain and develop the culture, to equip individuals to manage the complex matrix and to facilitate and support results through the operation of international teams.

The purpose of this discussion is to emphasize the importance of organizational structure in determining training in the international firm. One approach to the analysis of international firms leading to a consideration of the consequences for training has been formulated by Dowling, Schuler and Welch. As part of their examination of international human resource management they offer a framework based on four types of international operations. Each type calls for different training and development needs. They are:

- *Limited relationships* This operation achieves international sales through export offices, representatives and joint ventures. Businesses in this category generally limit their management development efforts to their own managers but may offer some help to their partners or associates.
- *Subsidiaries* If an organization has national subsidiaries, training and development opportunities need to be provided to local managers to enable them to learn how the subsidiary operates and to develop the skills to fulfil their managerial roles.
- *Regional business* Here senior managers should be aware of the cultural and geographic differences that must be balanced in arriving at overall strategies and business plans for the region. Expatriate managers will require preparatory development assignments. All managers, whether host or third country, will need training in strategic leadership skills and financial analysis.
- *Global businesses* For the world-class company with several global businesses 'management development programs need to emphasize worldwide information sharing on economic, social, political, technological and market trends and to focus on building teamwork across related business lines as well as across functional and country-regional lines'.[15]

Training and development for the global business is particularly challenging. There is a need to develop a cadre of career international managers – succession planning becomes more important and more complicated. There is also the difficult issue of how many levels of managers require international experience.

All this analysis serves to emphasize some straightforward points. First, the nature of the response to international competition, expressed through the organizational structure, is the main starting point for determining the training and development framework. Second, this response will vary and the more the organization has moved towards the transnational model, the more complex the challenge becomes. Effective international human resource management can involve the management of cultural issues, succession planning and the development of an international cadre of managers, as well as the formulation and delivery of appropriate shared training programmes. This last topic will be determined by the organization's view on the skills required of the international managers: these will be considered next.

THE SKILLS OF THE INTERNATIONAL MANAGER

Irrespective of the organizational strategy that a company chooses to adopt, it is fair to assume that the international company will be operating in a more complex, and potentially demanding, environment. One of the groups of writers already considered, Dowling et al., have argued that the shift to a global market place has given rise to a new set of demands. To compete, companies must maintain growth and profitability and tackle the following issues:

● which business to operate in, and which competitive strategies must be followed to compete successfully in these businesses
● the formulation of detailed competitive strategies and viable implementation plans for these businesses
● the need to be aware of and responsive to changing markets and technologies all over the world
● the need to be more flexible and resilient dealing with unexpected political, economic and competitive challenges and opportunities (p. 122).[15]

This list can be summarized as a need for a strong strategic and commercial awareness, coupled with adaptability.

> The demands of managing a business internationally call for different perspectives and skills and a much greater tolerance for ambiguity and uncertainty (p. 123).

Not only are skills needed but also a different mindset must be nurtured. Much of Dowling et al.'s subsequent analysis concentrates on the management system required to reinforce these changes. Reflecting the discussion of the previous subsection, these involve acting in an environment where decision-making responsibilities are widely distributed, where information gathering and sharing is essential and close teamworking is needed.

C.K. Prahalad, in a work published in 1990, covered similar territory in considering the emerging world of the manager in a diversified multi-national corporation (DMNC). He argued that, although the impact of the international competitive challenge may vary:

> All firms (and managers) will be forced to re-examine their approaches to management, audit their skill base, recalibrate their performance, and learn new behaviours. Managers must:
>
> ● Develop an ability to conceive of and execute complex strategies.
> ● Cope with decreasing degrees of strategic freedom.
> ● Protect and nurture invisible assets – intellectual property, commitment of people, brands, multicultural workforce, longstanding relationships with host governments, etc.
> ● Cope with an increasingly complex interface between public and private policy
> ● Integrate totally new technologies – learn to operate outside their comfort zone.

91

- Provide administrative and intellectual leadership.
- Become fast and flexible without losing clarity and consistency to direction (p. 34).[16]

Prahalad's analysis, like Dowling's, seems to suggest a need for a super-manager displaying the skills of a capable domestic manager reinforced by the flexibility needed to recognize and react in a changing environment.

Again there is an implicit distinction between the skills that an individual can demonstrate and the underlying mindset. Kevin Barham and Stefan Wills took this distinction a stage further. In their study, which specifically set out to identify the competencies of the international manager, they distinguish between 'doing' competencies and a 'being' competence (note the use of the singular).

> We believe that there are two sides to international management competence. Many competency frameworks focus only on the active or 'doing' competencies needed by managers. Such competencies largely reveal themselves in observable activities and change in accordance with changes in the business environment. The active competencies, however, are only half the picture. Our discussions have struck us most forcibly that international managers underpin their active competencies with a less changing spiritual or moral competence. They have what seems to us 'a philosophy of life' or 'being' that sustains the active side of their job. Furthermore international managers are great learners. For them, 'doing' and 'being' are wrapped up together in the lifelong process of 'becoming' international (p. 2).[13]

A more general discussion of the value of competencies in determining training needs is considered more fully in Chapter 5. At this stage, however, it should be noted that Barham and Wills' 'doing' competencies mainly describe the role of the international manager; the competence involved in 'being' takes us into the psychology of the international manager. The determination of an appropriate outline competency framework is of particular merit when considering what is required of the international manager, and how to select, develop and equip individuals for this task. Accordingly Barham and Wills' valuable list of 'doing' competencies is reproduced in Figure 4.7. They consider whether these competencies are generically different from those required of any other manager and argue that it is the context in which managers operate that gives life and meaning to any competency framework. The most important factors, which distinguish the context in which the international manager operates, include culture, language, geography, time and organization.

The psychological or 'being' competence is much less tangible. Barham and Wills analyse it in terms of three interlinked parts: cognitive complexity (thinking), emotional energy (feeling) and psychological maturity (willing). Their work is of sufficient value to any training manager in an international arena to demand reading the original. It is thoroughly recommended. For example, in considering the development of the cognitive complicity aspect of being, they identified four

ACTIVE COMPETENCIES OF THE INTERNATIONAL MANAGER INCLUDE

Championing international strategy, which involves:
- visioning the future
- setting up forums for crafting international strategy
- exploiting learning from other markets
- ensuring corporate centre support for international activities
- maintaining global awareness

Operating as cross-border coach and co-ordinator, which involves:
- providing clear guidelines and targets
- setting up early warning systems
- 'managing by travelling the globe'
- giving and receiving feedback
- coaching the customer contacts
- building multinational teams
- managing in the transnational matrix
- rotating people internationally

Acting as intercultural mediator and charge agent, which involves:
- cultivating empathy and self-awareness
- digging below surface explanations
- working with important stakeholders
- addressing ethical dilemmas
- understanding pressures of local management
- signalling the need for action
- balancing speed and sensitivity
- acting decisively

Managing personal effectiveness for international business, which involves:
- managing time
- handling stress
- managing the balance between work and family life

(With permission from Barham and Wills, *Management Across Frontiers* (see Ref. 13).)

Figure 4.7   Active competencies of the international manager

development stages: language fluency, cultural immersion (involving the historical and socio-political background of the country), business systems understanding, and performing inter-culturally (testing the boundaries and creating a new inter-cultural framework).

DESIGN AND DELIVERY

It is now appropriate to turn to the third key question introduced at the beginning of this section and ask what special considerations should apply to the design and delivery of training in the international context. The discussion to date should have indicated that there are a number of interrelated subsidiary components to this question. Two of the most important are: who is being trained and for what?; are the approaches required in training for an international audience fundamentally different?

An intermediary issue, and one that is of particular concern to the training manager, concerns the identification of the components of a training programme targeted at developing an international business. The intermediary issue can only be properly considered once the first two questions have been considered – and, moreover, reviewed in the context of the training managers' own organization. Nevertheless, an outline checklist for determining the elements of such a training programme is set out in Figure 4.8.

Strategic/structural/organizational
- how is the firm organized to meet international competition?
- how does it wish to be organized?

Management development
- to what extent has the organization sought to build an international management cadre?
- have such people been identified and are they aware of this process?

Elements of the programme
Which of the following should take priority? To what extent is such training in place? Who has received it and how successful has it been?
- understanding global business/strategy
- managing the global matrix
- cultural awareness/immersion (starting with familiarization and language training)
- international/cross-cultural teamworking.

Figure 4.8 Checklist for producing a training programme for developing the international business

Broadly, the objective of an international training and development programme is to provide a high calibre staff to compete successfully in the global market. The interdependence of training and development with the other aspects of human resources, an important theme throughout this book, is arguably more fundamental here than for any other training activity. Selection of those capable of developing an international mindset (Barham and Wills' 'being' competence) could be crucial for the organization. So could the deliberate planned use of international secondments. Training will only be one component of the process. At the highest level, the successful international manager must understand the international business environment inside and outside the company. He or she must be able to manage and negotiate across different cultures, lead cross-cultural teams and understand the different environments in which they operate. A quick training fix cannot remedy deficiencies in selection, development and retention.

The checklist in Figure 4.8 offers a useful starting point. If considered properly and an effective training plan is produced, the training manager will at least avoid a temptation to arbitrary *ad hoc* intervention in training in the international firm.

Before concluding this section the two important questions should be considered. The first is 'who is to be trained?' To a large extent this must reflect intentions and progress on building an international cadre. If a group of managers has been identified as the potential leaders of the future, much of the training effect will concentrate on their development. This suggests a narrow focusing of all training resources. However, although such managers may be the driving forces of the organization they are only part of it. In recent literature there has been a discernible shift towards recognition of the importance of non-managerial employees in the process of successful internationalization. This means moving beyond giving younger high-potential managers international exposure and training support. International firms are recognizing more and more that it is important to invest in all staff, including host country and third country nationals. Many such firms are developing larger pools of employees through increasing use of short-term assignments.

This diffusion of training effort is an observed tendency rather than a well-documented fact. It is hard to be certain about the extent to which employees outside the international management elite are currently involved in the internationalization process. The challenge for the training manager, when interpreting the organization's global strategy, is to decide on the extent to which non-managerial employees are part of the desired globalization process and what specific training they should be given.

The final question concerns the design and delivery of training: is a fundamentally different approach required for the international organization? Once again, Barham and Wills (pp. 80–81)[13] offer a useful starting point: they include a section in which they suggest that management developers:

- have an important role to play in providing international perspectives across the range of general management and functional disciplines.
- have to make international managers ever more aware of their own cultural roots and the way these affect how they think and behave.
- could make more use of action learning approaches which bring managers together in multicultural groups in situations where managers are forced to question their own values and assumptions and to develop new perspectives.
- should incorporate more moral/value/ethical dilemmas in their portfolio of experiential exercises.
- must realize the wealth of international experience, knowledge and insight that many managers bring with them on programmes, and find ways to capitalize on it.

Finally, management developers must refrain from taking a fragmented approach to their learners' lives. They should, for example, make students more aware of the work/home dilemmas and balance of life issues involved in international careers.

This useful framework is of particular value in designing training interventions for managing in the international arena. A related, but different, issue, concerns training for an international audience. Undoubtedly cross-cultural differences will present a major challenge. Trainers will need to be aware of the implications of differing beliefs, values and expectations held by participants from different backgrounds. Fortunately, there are advice and suggestions available on the practicalities of cross-cultural training. Adrian Thornhill, writing in the *Journal of European Industrial Training*,[17] identifies a number of issues. Trainers must recognize the work-related values held by participants from other countries and identify the implications of these for the context of training programmes. This will in turn be affected by the differing job roles and context between those who hold apparently similar roles in different countries. There will be a need to meet expectations about the extent and nature of training which third country nationals hold from their own previous experience. A fourth issue concerns the competencies which trainers will themselves require in order to function effectively in such training events – they must consider their own communication and presentational skills for this cross-cultural stage.

More generally, trainers may need to begin by understanding how their own culture affects their behaviour and attitudes. They must, in delivery, stay flexible, be aware of the different attitudes to hierarchy and be careful of humour – which often does not translate across national cultural barriers.

REFERENCES

1. Fombrun, C.J., Tichy, N.M. and Devanna, M.A. (1984), *Strategic Human Resource Management*, Chichester: Wiley.
2. Campbell, A. and Luchs, K.S. (eds) (1997), *Core Competency-Based Strategy*, London: International Thomson Business Press.
3. Mintzberg, H. (1978), 'Patterns in Strategy Formation', *Management Science*, **24** (9), May.
4. Tyson, S. (1995), *Strategic Prospects for HRM*, London: IPD.
5. Tyson, S. (1995), *Human Resources Strategy: Towards a General Theory of Human Resource Management*, London: Pitman
6. Williams, A., Dobson, P. and Walters, M. (1989), *Changing Culture*, London: Institute of Personnel Management.
7. Harrison, R. and Stokes, H. (1992), *Diagnosing Organizational Culture*, San Diego, CA: Pfeiffer and Co. The instrument, from which extracts appear in Figure 4.6 on p. 84 is distributed by Pfeiffer and Company, London and San Diego.
8. Schein, E.H. (1984), 'Coming to a New Awareness of Organizational Culture', *Sloan Management Review*, **25** (2), Winter, reproduced in Salaman, G. (ed., 1992), *Human Resource Strategies*, London: Sage

9. I am grateful to Anglia Railways and to Zoe van Zwanenberg, formerly Director of Personnel, for permission to reproduce this case study, which first appeared in Croners' *Training and Development*.

10. Burke, W.W. and Litwin, G.H. (1992), 'A Causal Model of Organizational Performance and Change', *Journal of Management*, **18** (3).

11. Institute of Personnel and Development (1997), *The IPD Guide on International Management Development*, London: Institute of Personnel and Development.

12. Bartlett, C.A. and Ghoshal, S., (1995), *Transnational Management*, Second Edition, Illinois: Irwin.

13. Barham, K. and Wills, S. (1992), *Management Across Frontiers*, Ashridge: Ashridge Management Research Group, pp. 7–9.

14. Taylor, W. (1991), 'The Logic of Global Business: An interview with ABB's Percy Barnevik', *Harvard Business Review*, **69** (2), March–April, pp. 91–105.

15. Dowling, P.J., Schuler, R.S. and Welch, D.E. (1993), *International Dimensions of Human Resource Management*, Second Edition, Belmont, California: Wadsworth, pp. 123–5. (Third Edition now available, *International Human Resource Management*, 1998.)

16. Prahalad, C.K. (1990), 'Globalization: The Intellectual and Managerial Challenges', *Human Resource Management*, **29** (1), Spring, pp. 27–37.

17. Thornhill, A.R. (1993), 'Managing Training Across Cultures: The Challenge for Trainers', *Journal of European Industrial Training*, **17** (10), pp. 43–51.

5 Training and the individual

This part of the book is about new processes. It is not my intention to duplicate approaches or perspectives that are well-documented elsewhere; methods of identifying individual needs are discussed extensively in the literature.

For readers who are not familiar with generic methods of identifying training needs, Figure 5.1, which has been supplied by a consultancy specializing in this topic, contains a brief overview of the more important techniques.

Despite the confidence which comes from habitual use, today's training manager must review his or her approach. Because of the new context outlined in Part I, techniques must be used in a way that promotes best training practice in the organization. Emphasis must be given to the need to work within a structured and disciplined framework, to embed training activity firmly in the organization, and to develop the responsibility and responsiveness of line management. The aim

---

ANALYSING TRAINING NEEDS

There are many approaches to establishing training needs. Conventional methods include repertory grid, job analysis and critical incident interviews. An outline of these approaches can be found in many training texts.

Alternative methods include the use of 360° feedback tools (see Chapter 6, p. 132), the introduction of development reviews, self-managed learning and the growth of development centres, which are outlined below, together with the use of the structured interview as a sampling tool.

360° feedback

Many organizations have now introduced 360° feedback tools into their human resource processes. Individuals invite feedback on their performance against known competencies from colleagues, peers, managers, senior managers, and in some cases clients and consultants. The feedback is summarized and used to highlight strengths and development needs. An individual development plan can then be drawn up. For senior executives the development plan can often be facilitated through one-to-one coaching with either an external or internal coach. Alternatively, in larger organizations, in-company norm groups are established and group training and development needs can be identified.

Figure 5.1   Analysing training needs (Continued)

Development reviews

Historically, training and development needs were highlighted as part of an annual appraisal process. This system had two main problems. First, managers struggled to achieve a thorough review of past performance, an accurate assessment of present performance, objective setting and the assessment of training needs in one interview. Second, an annual process was not sufficient to keep skills up to date and to identify 'just in time' training needs.

Some organisations have countered these problems by introducing development reviews every six months. This process, conducted by the line manager, is divorced from the annual appraisal, and seeks to identify training needs and solutions, for the short and medium term. The output is a personal development plan containing personal development objectives.

Development Centres

Development Centres are a derivative of assessment centres. Organizations that regularly use Development Centres have typically developed a set of competencies for their management population. The Development Centre provides a realistic environment where participants can demonstrate their performance measured against these competencies. Participants are asked to assess themselves against the competencies using structured behavioural rating scales. Trained facilitators, using the same behavioural indicators, provide feedback on their performance. Participants, assisted by the facilitators, prepare an individual development plan, which is discussed with their line manager on their return to work.

Structured interviews

Organizations that need to review all their employees' training needs, as part of a drive towards Investors in People or as part of a major culture change, tend to favour the use of structured interviews and questionnaires to gather a broad range of views across all levels. Typically all directors are interviewed face-to-face to determine the major changes and influences on current and future skill levels. The results of these discussions focus the content of a questionnaire used either for telephone interviews, further face-to-face discussions or postal questionnaires. Alternatively a series of focus group discussions can be held where groups of employees attend facilitated sessions to identify common training needs. Typically, using a combination of any or all of these methods, between 10 and 15 per cent of employees are sampled. The success of such large-scale training needs analysis depends upon ensuring that a truly representative sample of employees is consulted and the design of the questionnaire, which provides the correct quantitative and qualitative information to enable training needs and solutions to be identified and prioritized.

Self-managed learning

The increasing fluidity and flexibility of organizations has led to a changing development contract between the employer and employee. Some organizations that are preaching the self-managed learning message are clarifying the respective roles and responsibilities in the process. These organizations believe that their role is to provide the framework for learning and development, and it is the individual's responsibility to manage their career and their development. The individual is tasked with identifying:

- where they are now – skills, abilities, motivations, development needs
- where they want to be – promotion, new roles
- how they will get there – training, development, job moves, transfers, secondments.

The identification of training needs is therefore the responsibility of the individual. The organization may provide a number of tools to help them assess their training and development needs such as psychometric tools and feedback, development discussions, role skill grids (which identify skills required for current, future or alternative roles), self-managed learning groups (where groups come together to support each other in achieving agreed learning objectives), personal development workshops, coaching and in-house career counselling.

(Reproduced by kind permission of Cedar International.)

Figure 5.1   Concluded

should be to use methods of identifying training needs which require the training manager to work closely with line management for joint solutions, and encourage the latter's shared ownership of the resulting product. Later in this chapter I present some practical instruments designed to help in managing the devolution of responsibility. First, however, the use of management competencies will be considered.

COMPETENCY ANALYSIS

Summary: *Competencies (or competences, the spelling varies) provide a useful tool for needs analysis. Potentially competency analysis can assist in communicating and agreeing training requirements with managers. However, there is a danger of muddled thinking unless the training professional is precise in his or her definitions. The term competency has been used to describe three distinct concepts and it is important to distinguish between these uses. Illustrative generic and tailored competency lists are presented.*

David McClelland, the Harvard Professor, did much to promote the current interest in competencies as a tool for the human resource profession. In his work he describes a competency 'as an underlying characteristic of a person that causes effective or superior performance in a job. Competencies can be motives, traits, skills, aspects of one's self image or social role or a body of knowledge which one uses. A competency is an ability in that it describes what someone can do, not necessarily what he or she does all the time'. This, however, is descriptive of only one of three ways in which the term competencies are currently used in human resource management. All are quite different and a failure to appreciate the distinction will inevitably lead to muddled thinking.

The use introduced in the paragraph above – which can be described as behavioural competency – is the most valuable and important and as such will be described and developed after the other two have been considered. Industrial Relations Services, the UK research organization, produce an Annual Survey of competency developments, and a review article by Katherine Adams in the 1996 edition is commended for its clarity of analysis on this difficult area.[1] It is the source of the definition offered at the beginning of the previous paragraph.

The first use of the term competency has already been introduced in Chapter 1 where I considered the work of Gary Hamel and C.K. Prahalad (p. 13). They focused on the core competencies and capabilities of organizations as the main source of competitive advantage. From this perspective, a competency is a bundle of skills and technologies rather than a single discrete skill or technology. An example is Motorola's competence in fast cycle time production (minimizing the time between an order and the fulfilment of that order), which rests upon a broad range of underlying skills including design disciplines that maximize commonality across a production line, flexible manufacturing, sophisticated order entry systems, inventory management and supplier management. The core competence Federal Express possesses in package routing and delivery rests on the integration of bar code technology, wireless communication and linear programming (pp. 202–3).[2] As Hamel and Prahalad argue, a core competence is unlikely to reside in an individual or a team, but must extend across the organization.

A useful analysis of this concept of organizational competencies is contained in the 1998 publication by the Center for Effective Organizations.[3] The authors begin by identifying some key characteristics of core competencies: they represent a complex bundle of skills and technologies that span multiple businesses and products; they are more stable and evolve more slowly than products; they are difficult to imitate. They then cite the work of Lado and Wilson (1994)[4] who distinguish four types of competencies:

- managerial competencies, including the articulation of the strategic vision and (enacting) managing the environment
- input-based competencies including exploiting imperfections in the labour market, creating an internal labour market and investing in firm specific capital
- transformational competencies, including harnessing innovation and entrepreneurship, fostering organizational learning and promoting organizational culture
- output-based competencies, including building a corporate reputation, building product or service quality and building customer loyalty.

Other US commentators use the term organizational capabilities: quality, speed, low-cost operations, learning, innovation and customer focus are examples of these capabilities. What is important to emphasize is they reside, not with individuals, but are properties of the systems, structures, cumulative knowledge and mindset of the organization. 'In essence, they are the key to allowing organizations to turn their important technological and operational core competencies into products and services that are superior to those offered by competing organizations' (p. 136); see reference 3.

Organizational capabilities, then, are what translate core competencies into products and services that the market wants.

The other two uses of the term competency are firmly identified with the individual rather than the organization. One of these two underpins the UK's national and occupational standards programme, and the National Vocational Qualifications structure (see Chapter 10, p. 250 and Appendix II, p. 261, for an outline). The approach here is based on an examination of what is required to undertake a job. This job-related competency is identified in a fundamentally different way from the behavioural competency defined at the beginning of this section. Job-related competencies are derived using a technique called functional analysis: a domain of work (for example, hairdressing) is identified; experts try to define the activities undertaken in that field in terms of outcomes; standards are set for these outcomes (which may lead to qualifications).

As I have noted, it is competencies in the third behavioural sense of the term that are the most useful to the training professional. These are the traits of the high performer. If they can be identified, communicated and reinforced they can improve the success of the organization by raising the level of other employees to that of the higher achievers. Their potential value to the trainer is evident. These (behavioural) competencies are derived from a process known as behavioural analysis, which looks at the actions, activities or outcomes of successful performers, and seek to classify the underlying characteristics. Figure 5.2 below summarizes the differences between the second and third use of the term competency.

Job-related	Behavioural
Focus on job/tasks	Focus on people/job holder
Aim to set (minimum) standards for job actions	Aim to identify superior performance
Examine actions or outcomes	Seek characteristics that cause successful actions

Figure 5.2   Differences between job-related and behavioural competencies

Are behavioural competencies, which are characteristic of superior performance, specific to an individual organizational situation, or are they generic? Are behavioural competencies common across different sectors? These questions have important implications and are not as straightforward as they may appear. On the one hand there are organizations, particularly consultancies, that have created generic models of competency for particular roles – especially management. One example is the Hay/McBer list, which derives in part from the original work of David McClelland. Another list based on extensive research is the Schroder/Cockerill list of eleven high-performance managerial competencies.[5]

In general, higher level managerial competencies can be clustered under the following headings:

- cognitive/intellectual
- personal/motivational
- interpersonal
- leadership/managerial
- business/technical.

On the other hand, many organizations derive their own lists and in their annual survey of competencies undertaken in 1996,[1] Industrial Relations Services listed the following as the six most frequently occurring competencies:

- communication
- achievement/results orientation
- customer focus
- teamwork
- leadership
- planning and organization.

Given the possibility of customizing generic lists available through a consultant or gaining access to published lists, why do so many organizations produce their own lists? In practice the process involved in developing such a list can be an important part of the communication of expectations between line management and the human resource department. Involvement in identifying and classifying the characteristics of the high performer, particularly using a pre-prepared competency menu, is seen by many line managers as a sensible and worthwhile use of their time. The resulting competency list becomes jointly owned, not part of a process imposed by human resources. This can lead to a consistent and common approach to human resource management across a variety of areas. It is this, more than anything else, that makes a competency framework such a valuable tool.

Two illustrative competency lists are set out in Figures 5.3 and 5.4. The first is a list of the competencies derived for an effective Director of an Investment Bank. These were prepared by Dr Charles Woodruffe of Human Assets Limited, a leading consultant and writer on competencies.

The second is the behavioural competency list (called Senior Management Attributes) used for senior staff at the Victoria and Albert Museum. These were developed by the senior managers themselves, though a series of facilitated discussions. These competencies link into performance management and pay systems.

Finally, it is helpful to ask what use can be made of competency (the micro application) and what are the potential pitfalls. The 1996 IRS survey (p.7)[1] listed the following as the six key reasons for introducing competencies:

- performance
- cultural change

- training and development
- recruitment and selection
- business objectives/competitiveness
- career/succession planning.

Intellectual Competencies

Awareness: Develops and maintains high-level networks and formal channels of communication within company and with the outside world: maintains an awareness of what should be happening and what progress is being made; keeps abreast of relevant political and economic developments; monitors competitor activity; informed on range of current and economic affairs and cultural issues.

Analysis: Highly incisive; gets a clear overview of a complex issue; grasps information quickly and accurately; gets to the heart of a problem; identifies the most productive lines of enquiry; adapts thinking in light of new information; tolerates and handles conflicting/ambiguous information and ideas.

Prescription: Generates options; produces novel solutions that gain others' respect; evaluates options by examining the positive and negative aspects of them if they were put into effect; anticipates effects of options on others; specifies strategic direction.

Adaptability: Sympathetic to change; challenges status quo; open to new ideas.

Work Style Competencies

Organization: Thoroughly prepares before meetings to ensure impact; identifies priorities; thinks back from deadline; schedules elements of tasks; anticipates resource needs; sets objectives for staff; manages own and others' time; delegates areas of personal interest.

Commitment: Installs solution within time-frame; takes on problems; suffers personal inconvenience to ensure problems are solved; comes forward with ideas; sets challenging targets; sets out to win new business; sets own objectives; recognizes areas for self-development; acquires new skills and capabilities; accepts new challenges; takes the initiative.

Focus: Sticks to a plan; does not get sidetracked; sacrifices the present for the future; bides time when conditions are not favourable; takes a long-term view; evaluates options against long-term goals; waits for right moment to strike.

Corporatism: Accepts collective responsibility; has a corporate perspective; looks for business opportunities for other parts of the company.

Interpersonal Competencies

Self-confidence: Expresses and conveys a strong belief in own ability; comfortable operating at and able to hold own ground at chief executive level; prepared to take and support decisions; stands up to seniors; willing to take calculated risks; admits to areas of inexpertise; open to feedback; stands up for own interests; faces up to conflicts; gives feedback to others; communicates directly and openly; speaks up if something is wrong.

Receptivity: Listens to others' viewpoint; takes account of others' needs; sees situation from others' viewpoint; shows empathy in communications; aware of others' expectations; aware of impact of own behaviour on others; identifies others' motives; judges others' vantage point.

Team playing: Involves others in own area and ideas; keeps others informed; shares contacts and networks; prepared to use available support services; utilizes skills of team members; open to others' ideas and suggestions; gives others support.

Influence: Has presence; behaves strategically to persuade others; uses understanding of others to win; communicates in client's language; conveys to client that his/her needs have been met; conveys energy; enthuses others; walks the floor; communicates decisions and direction; provides leadership.

(Reproduced by kind permission of Dr Charles Woodruffe, Human Assets Ltd.)

Figure 5.3 Director competencies for an investment bank

It is easiest to see the application of competencies in performance review and appraisal, recruitment selection and training than in other areas. An agreed competency framework can determine the focus of an assessment or selection process and can assist in framing the objectives of a training course. Some assessment processes make use of behaviourally-anchored rating scales (BARs) where graded levels of output are specified and performance judged against those levels. Inevitably this can cause difficulties of judgement and is not without controversy. These problems explain the limited growth of competency-based pay systems. In using competencies as a framework for training and development it is also important to be clear that the desired competencies are indeed trainable. Is resilience under pressure, which may be characteristic of the superior performer, a trainable trait?

Generally, a good competency framework has high face validity, is seen to be aligned to the business and its processes, is easy to use and is adaptable to change. Such a framework should promote a common development language and thus underpin any organizational change – particularly when this is conditional on cultural or behavioural attributes. Moreover, an effective competency framework is a useful tool in the development of an integrated human resource strategy.[6]

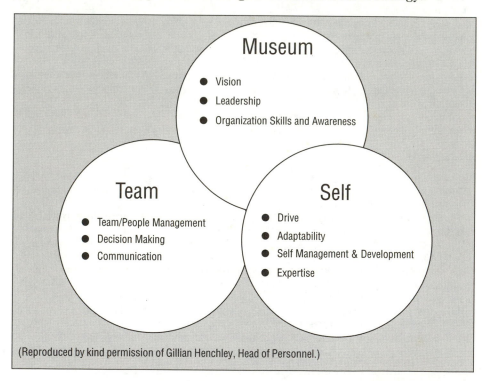

(Reproduced by kind permission of Gillian Henchley, Head of Personnel.)

Figure 5.4   **Senior management attributes: Victoria and Albert Museum**

DEVELOPING LINE MANAGEMENT RESPONSIVENESS

Summary: *One of the key tasks for the training professional is to ensure that the inevitable devolution of responsibility is managed effectively. This is assisted by the development of a categorization of skills and also requires the provision of training for line managers in their new responsibilities.*

By this stage the need to develop the responsiveness of line management should have been accepted. A devolution of responsibility to the line is inevitable; it is the trainer's job to ensure that the devolution is managed effectively, so that the organization's training objectives are met. One of the strongest conclusions of the survey undertaken for this book is that best practice organizations place considerable emphasis on improving line management's contribution to corporate training (see Appendix IV, p. 267).

Generally, a well-managed devolution requires:

- an increase in the line management's awareness of available training options
- design and delivery of training modules which increase the effectiveness of line management's role in identifying their own training needs and those of their staff.

Figure 5.5 illustrates, in practical terms, the way in which responsibility is devolving. At the entry end of the training cycle where needs are identified, the highest level of business and line manager involvement is required. Only they can know the needs of staff; their ownership is essential if training is to be effective. The training manager's role is one of specialist advice – almost the consultancy model (see Chapter 3, pp. 54–5). As the cycle progresses, so the training manager accepts more ownership and responsibility – though this will inevitably depend on the circumstances of the organization. Generally, however, it is unreasonable to expect busy line managers to initiate evaluation activities.

Increasing the awareness of line management by presenting options may be an anathema to the training professional. One of the implicit premises of the systematic training model was that training should be demand-led: the needs of the business should determine training requirements, rather than products being offered around the organization regardless of their contribution to the business objectives.

There is some justification in this viewpoint, and the 'menu' system, whereby the training department offers courses on a take it or leave it basis, has rightly been condemned. However, unless the organization is at a high level of training sophistication, managers will need assistance in drawing up training requirements.

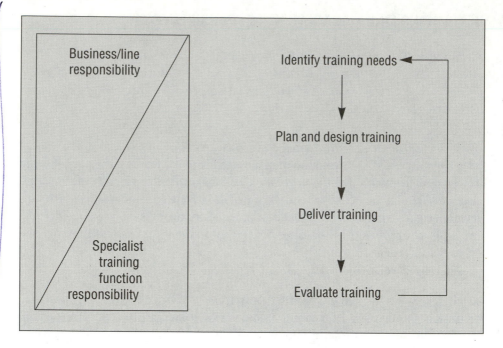

Figure 5.5   Responsibility for the systematic training model

It is therefore helpful for the training manager to have a broad categorization of skills that can be developed through training. He or she needs a conceptual map of what training can deliver to the line manager in the business area; such a map can assist in designing and shaping training events.

Surprisingly, such categorizations are rarely presented in the training literature – even though there is considerable discussion of the principles and techniques involved in identifying training needs. Most of the current interest in this area has been subsumed by the debate on competency analysis.

One useful source is to consider the classification used to present information in the National Training Index, a subscription service providing to its members information on the availability and quality of training. The Course Content Guide, although properly restricted to off-the-job training events, does offer the following listing by subject class:

- information technology
- finance
- general management
- industrial management
- management techniques
- marketing

- safety and health
- personnel and training
- specialized industries and professions.

Each of these categories is subdivided appropriately. 'Information technology', for example, is broken down into appreciation, operation, various programming languages and word processing. 'Finance' is broken down into auditing, banking, book-keeping, through to taxation and treasury management.

A more broad-brush categorization emerged from the work undertaken by the management consultants, Deloitte Haskins and Sells in the late 1980s. This divided training needs as follows:

- *functional skills*
    marketing
    accounting
    computing
    others
- *interpersonal skills*
    presentational
    counselling
    others
- *organizational skills*
    managing process
    managing change.

Alternative conceptual maps can be derived from the work undertaken by Amin Rajan for the London Human Resource Group. In a detailed analysis of the likely requirements for skilled staff for the City of London, and the strategies required to recruit, train and retrain them, Professor Rajan offered several useful models. In particular, he presented two separate approaches leading to different categorizations.

The first identified three attributes:

- job-specific skills (intellectual, practical, physical and vocational skills leading to effective performance)
- wider knowledge of work and business
- appropriate attitudes and behaviour (facilitating teamwork, effective interpersonal communication and staff management).

The second approach identified generic skills in the following areas:

- procedural skills
- technology skills
- interpersonal skills
- knowledge-based skills.

In his book *Capital People*,[7] Professor Rajan used both approaches to identify the skills required by various occupational groups in the City of London. He also gave a valuable representation of continuous learning, reproduced in Figure 5.6. The model represents the sequential phases through which anyone who aspires to be a professional worker must pass; it is unusual in illustrating the conceptual links between education, training and development. It assists the training professional in articulating the link between training and development.

Structuring a discussion with line management around a categorization will lead to a sharper focus on requirements. Such a categorization will also help in making the distinction between those attributes that can be improved by training and those that cannot. The importance of distinguishing between those skills that individuals can acquire through training and those that are innate is well accepted by the training community but less apparent to those outside it.

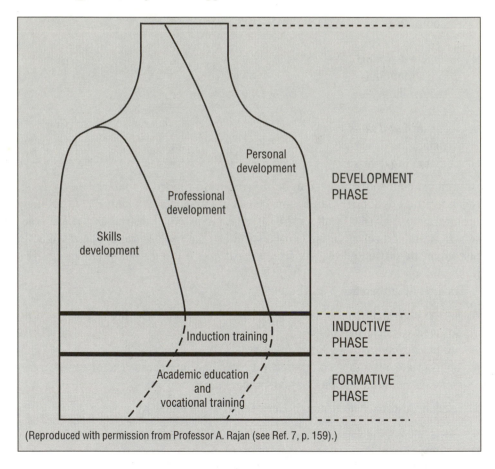

(Reproduced with permission from Professor A. Rajan (see Ref. 7, p. 159).)

Figure 5.6   A model of continuous learning

This emerged as a near universal activity undertaken by the best practice organizations surveyed for this book (see Appendix IV, p. 267). The second main aspect of developing line management responsiveness involves the design and delivery of training modules aimed at increasing the line manager's role. Best practice organizations had introduced train the trainer courses, coaching courses and courses in feedback skills. Course design is a routine activity to the trainer. However, for illustration, two comparatively sophisticated outlines are presented in Figures 5.7 and 5.8.

The first outline is a design for a two-day workshop – an off-the-job training event aimed at reinforcing the line manager's role in developing staff and focusing on the skills required. The second is a briefing document (which could be the basis of an appropriate training module) on the underlying concept of self-directed learning.

A two-day workshop designed to reinforce a manager's role in supporting the development of their staff. This workshop is run alongside a 'Managing my development' workshop which their staff may have attended.

Prework   Participants are asked to bring a live case with them to discuss on the workshop.

WORKSHOP OVERVIEW

Day One

Introductions and objectives   Participants, in pairs or trios, are asked to prepare and briefly introduce: what they are looking for from the workshop, what they bring to the workshop which may help others, success measures for the process.

Tutor introduces ground rules e.g. confidentiality, openness, etc.

The changing world of careers   Tutor discusses important concepts such as the move towards self-managed development, the changing world of careers, promotion versus portfolio careers.

Introduction to the development process   Tutor introduces the 3-step model for facilitating development discussions, which will be used throughout the two days:

where am I now?
where do I want to be?
how do I get there?

Tutor introduces the principles of the workshop, i.e. managers will learn by doing, using a range of tools on themselves, which they can then use with their staff during a development discussion.

Where am I now?   Participants individually conduct a personal skills audit and prepare a 'skills portfolio'. Participants prepare individual career summary and achievements statements which 'sell' their experience

General discussion, assessing skills and selling them, difficulties and issues. Application to their staff.

How have I got here?   Participants prepare a CareerLine, which tracks how they have developed their skills and their career up to the present date. General discussion of career patterns, catalysts in development. Application to their staff.

Figure 5.7   Skills in developing others: a two-day workshop for line managers (Continued)

Where do I want to go?   Participants continue their CareerLine into the future, highlighting the route to development they would like to take. General discussion and brainstorm of options and opportunities.

Participants complete the Career Drivers survey to identify what is driving their career and their development. Application to their staff.

Application   Participants discuss how they might apply these tools when discussing development with their own people, the benefits and disadvantages, barriers and constraints.

Day Two

Defining the support contract   Participants debate the respective roles of the employing organization, the line manager, and the individual in development. Tutor uses discussion to highlight the many options available for development to broaden thinking away from 'training courses'. Delegates discuss how many of these are available and working within their own organization.

Skills of a developing manager   Tutor leads a discussion around the skills required to support development in the individual. Depending upon the knowledge of the group, either an overview or refresher or detailed input on giving feedback, coaching, counselling and guiding. Use of GROW model in development discussion.

The development discussion   Input on how to structure and manage a development discussion.

Skills practice   Participants, in trios, practise conducting a development discussion using their live case. Observers, acting as peer coaches, help the participants to identify what worked well and what could be improved.

Development planning   Participants produce a personal development plan utilizing different approaches to development including mentors, secondments, coaching, etc.

Tutor leads a discussion on the use of personal development plans and alternative career planning tools.

Workshop review   Participants review the workshop, their own personal learning and how they will measure their own success in supporting development.

(Reproduced by kind permission of Cedar International.)

Figure 5.7   Concluded

FOCUS GROUPS AND THE CORE CURRICULUM

Summary: *Two practical approaches designed to encourage a joint approach to training needs identification are outlined. Both have been used successfully in an investment bank. These are followed by a case study on identifying training themes in a smaller city institution.*

In the remaining section of this chapter I describe two methods of identifying training needs: both promote the concept of joint ownership between line management and the training department. The first method, the focus group, is no more than an adaptation of a standard technique commonly used by management

Benefits of self-directed learning:
- A move away from a paternalistic and generic approach to learning and development
- Consistent with an enabling management philosophy
- Focused on individual needs
- Given at a pace and time to suit the needs of the individual
- Higher levels of commitment due to ownership and responsibility being passed to the individual
- Stimulates self assessment
- More holistic, life and career goals

Potential issues:
- Time commitment
- Mismatch between individual and company needs
- Perceived loss of a benefit from the employing organisation 'they used to care'
- Measurement and recognition of self-directed learning
- Integration into work practices

The move towards self-directed learning affects would touch most aspects of the organisational culture. Adapting McKinsey's 7-s model we can see that the organisation needs to address six key areas: the seventh, of shared values, should underpin all aspects of training design.

Strategy   How does self-directed learning fit into achieving our organisational objectives such as changing the skill base, accelerating our managers, developing global leaders? How does self-directed learning sit alongside other learning approaches? What is the organisational commitment to making self-directed learning part of the culture?

Structure   Discussion of the roles and responsibilities of line manager, internal and external coaches, mentors, HR, role models.

Systems   What organisational processes exist which can aid self-directed learning, e.g. learning resource centres, training directories, role/skill grid analyses, promotion criteria, appraisal and development processes? How will self-directed learning be supported and reinforced by practice at work?

Style   How to create a relationship of trust, support and honesty between individuals and managers to facilitate development. How open are we in confronting issues and giving feedback, both positive and negative?

Skills   What are the skills required if individuals are to direct their own learning and if managers are to support self-directed learning? Analysis of skills gaps and potential training needs if self-directed learning is to be effective.

Staff   How many of our staff will take up self-directed learning. What are the characteristics of our workforce? How can we help them make the transition to becoming self-directed learners? If this is to be a major culture shock or change to accepted ways of doing things, how can we help our staff through the change curve?

(Reproduced by kind permission of Cedar International.)

Figure 5.8   Self-directed learning : The line manager's role – a briefing

consultants and throughout the social sciences. As the name implies, a group of people are brought together to focus on a certain issue – in this case their training needs.

The key to a successful focus group is the quality of the stimulus material used. It is easy to facilitate a discussion by middle managers on their training needs; the event will run itself and all the unambitious trainer will need is a flip chart and pens. There is a danger, however, of unstructured results emerging that prove of little value in terms of carrying the project forward. Good stimulus material is needed to shape and steer the discussion and to accumulate results for meaningful analysis.

As has already been observed, any experienced trainer would have no problems in designing his or her own stimulus material and would indeed wish to undertake this task. The stimulus material used in the investment bank and reproduced in Figures 5.9 and 5.10 is therefore intended solely for illustrative purposes.

The questionnaires are designed for a one-hour session involving between five and ten participants. Although focus groups were used at all levels in the bank, experience indicated that the best results were produced when:

- the participants were first-line managers or above (though convening clerical and secretarial groups proved worthwhile in promoting involvement throughout the organization)
- group participants had roughly the same status in the organization; mixed groups involving senior managers and junior managers, or managers and clerical staff, inhibited the contribution from participants at both levels.

Different considerations could, of course, apply in other organizations. Turning to the use of questionnaires, Focus Group Questionnaire – Part 1 (Figure 5.9) is intended simply to get the participants to concentrate on the subject under discussion. They are given the questionnaire to complete on arrival with only minimal briefing. This is one way of managing the problem caused by the inevitable latecomers; waiting until everyone has assembled tests the patience of the punctual and is not conducive to creating an appropriate atmosphere.

The more important instrument is Part 2 (Figure 5.10), and the following questions are of value and receive particular attention in the discussion phase of the Focus Group:

- Question 1, which introduces the distinction between off-the-job and on-the-job training and emphasizes the value and also the neglect of the latter form of training. The number of days' training in both categories can be recorded and retained to produce comparative statistics across the organization. High levels of off-the-job training can be related to question 2, which in turn becomes the object of discussion.

Section 1 - About You

1. Age _____
2. Sex _____
3. What is your current position?
   Manager ☐
   Assistant Manager ☐
   Executive ☐
   Trainee ☐
   (Please tick one)
4. What is your job title? _____
5. How many years have you been at your current level? _____
6. How many years have you been with the Company? _____

Session 2 – Training

Please tick the box that most closely corresponds to your view:

	Strongly Agree	Agree	Neither Agree nor Disagree	Disagree	Strongly Disagree
Training is important in helping me to do my job well.	☐	☐	☐	☐	☐
Training is a good way of keeping up to date with recent developments in my work area.	☐	☐	☐	☐	☐
In general, I do not receive enough training.	☐	☐	☐	☐	☐
I would be more interested in training if it was linked to a qualification.	☐	☐	☐	☐	☐
Training is important in helping me develop as an employee.	☐	☐	☐	☐	☐

Figure 5.9   Focus group questionnaire – Part 1

● Questions 5 and 7, taken together, which invite the participant to recognize the challenges that arise in the job. Responses here permit the trainer to direct attention to the potential value of training as a solution, which hopefully the participants will have recognized in questions 6 and 8.

The next stage is for the training manager to introduce his or her categorization of training activities – based on an approach outlined earlier in this chapter. The resulting input can be used to identify training and to design training events; the process used should lead to the resultant events being viewed as a joint product.

An additional, and possibly complementary, instrument has been reproduced. Figure 5.11 is an example of some stimulus material which is designed for use in a one-to-one interview or as an element in a focus group. It can be seen that the first set of items broadly relate to interpersonal skills and the second to organizational skills.

1. How many days training have you received in the last year
    off-the-job (i.e. away from your normal workplace)
        in your employer's time in an employer's training facility?   _____
        in your employer's time, but not in an employer's training facility?   _____
    on-the-job (i.e. <u>supervised</u> learning to develop new skills at your workplace)?   _____

2. Please specify the training you have received last year

    _____
    _____
    _____

3. Was this training*
    a) at your own initiative with you bearing the cost?   ☐
    b) at your initiative with the Company bearing the cost?   ☐
    c) at the Company's initiative with the Company bearing the cost?   ☐

4. Which of this training, if any, was for a qualification?*

    _____
    _____

5. Think back over the work you have done during the last six months.
    What have been the most significant events/issues/achievements/or problems?
    a)_____

    b)_____

    c)_____

6. How has the training you have received helped you cope with these events, if at all?

    _____
    _____
    _____

7. What do you anticipate are going to be particularly demanding aspects of your job in the next two
    years?

    _____
    _____
    _____

8. What training, if any, would you like to receive to help you deal with these aspects of your job most
    effectively?

    _____
    _____
    _____

*   Please indicate if any of this training took place when you were with a previous employer

Figure 5.10   Focus group questionnaire – Part 2

Please tick the box which rates your view of the importance of the following skill areas:

	Essential	Very Important	Fairly Important	Not very Important	Not Necessary
Good listening skills	☐	☐	☐	☐	☐
Giving/receiving criticism/feedback	☐	☐	☐	☐	☐
Dealing with difficult people	☐	☐	☐	☐	☐
Influencing skills	☐	☐	☐	☐	☐
Asking effective questions	☐	☐	☐	☐	☐
One-to-one training	☐	☐	☐	☐	☐
Coaching skills	☐	☐	☐	☐	☐
Appraisal skills	☐	☐	☐	☐	☐
Analysis training requirements	☐	☐	☐	☐	☐
Selection interviewing skills	☐	☐	☐	☐	☐
Disciplinary interviewing skills	☐	☐	☐	☐	☐
Knowledge of employment law	☐	☐	☐	☐	☐
Counselling skills	☐	☐	☐	☐	☐
Team leadership skills	☐	☐	☐	☐	☐
Delegation skills	☐	☐	☐	☐	☐
Motivating staff	☐	☐	☐	☐	☐
Creative problem solving	☐	☐	☐	☐	☐
Strategy development	☐	☐	☐	☐	☐
Management of change	☐	☐	☐	☐	☐
Decision-making	☐	☐	☐	☐	☐
Time management	☐	☐	☐	☐	☐
Understanding organizational politics	☐	☐	☐	☐	☐
Knowledge of wider aspects of the commercial world	☐	☐	☐	☐	☐
Information finding/search	☐	☐	☐	☐	☐

Figure 5.11   Stimulus material for interpersonal and organizational skills identification

The second method of promoting joint ownership illustrated is the core curriculum, which has been used with considerable success in the investment bank. As is true of most training initiatives it is derivative rather than original. Due recognition should be given to the impressive work undertaken at the computer company ICL, which introduced a core training programme based on a set of four interlocking training modules.

The core curriculum is a variant on the concept of the core training programme. A core curriculum is defined as 'a programme of training activity for a business area targeted at an individual at various stages of his or her development'. Each business area reviews the central programme of training events and adapts and enhances it accordingly.

Three examples of core curricula are shown in Figures 5.12, 5.13 and 5.14: one for the human resources department, one for information technology and one for the financial control function. The difference in presentation is deliberate and encouraged: a standard package designed by the training department would remain just that – a product of the training department.

The process of drawing up the core curriculum is as important as the product. Experience has shown that senior managers are sympathetic to the idea and will delegate the task to an appropriate person in their team who will then work with the training professional. This person will rapidly become a member of the informal grouping of 'friends of training' that exists in every organization.

The declared intention with the core curriculum is that it should not account for more than a proportion of total training spend – about two-thirds seems the optimum. It should offer a guideline, not act as a strait-jacket. It is important for it to be linked with appropriate management information on training activity that is made available to line managers (see Chapter 8 for a fuller discussion of this issue).

The core curriculum approach can be criticized for being mechanistic. Such criticism is to some extent justified. It is a concept that is appropriate to the formalized stage of the Ashridge model (see Chapter 3) rather than the focused stage. It has, however, proved to be of considerable value in taking the organization up the learning curve and buying line management into the training process. It lies at the interface between individual and corporate training needs.

CASE STUDY: IDENTIFYING TRAINING THEMES

This case study describes how training needs were determined and a plan formulated for the London headquarters of a smaller city institution.[8]

LGT is a fund management group and a subsidiary of the Bank in Lichtenstein. In London and the Republic of Ireland it employed some 300 hundred people, split

Course Name	CLER 1–4	SEC 4–6	CLER 5–7	SEC 7	EXECUTIVE	MANAGER	ASST DIR	ASSOC DIR	DIRECTOR
Secretaries' Workshop		X							
Telephone Techniques	X	X	X						
Written Communications I (Letters)		X	X	X	X				
Written Communications II (Reports)			X	X	X	X			
Introduction to Bookkeeping & Accounts		X	X	X	X				
Introduction to the Securities Industry		X	X	X	X	X	X	X	X
The Regulatory Environment		X	X	X	X	X	X	X	X
Support Staff & Client Management Process	X	X	X	X	X	X	X		
Supervisory Skills Training			X	X	X	X			
Management Development Workshop				X	X	X			
Management Development I						X	X	X	X
Management Development II						X	X	X	X
Presentation Skills					X	X	X	X	
Advanced Presentation Skills							X	X	X
Assertiveness Workshop	AS APPROPRIATE								
Time Management	AS APPROPRIATE								
Induction Seminar	ALL NEW STARTERS								

Figure 5.12   Core curriculum – human resources

119

(a) **Courses for Personal Skills Development**

For new entrants (all):	Induction seminar
T/C Grades:	Supervisory skills
	Verbal/written communication skills (basic) including letter writing
For Executives:	Written skills II – report writing
	Management Development Workshops
	Presentation skills
	Introduction to bookkeeping and accounts
For Managers:	Management Development I – 1 week
Asst Directors:	Management Development II – 1 week
	Selling and negotiation skills
Directors:	Directors' development centre

The above are the basic skills courses appropriate to the duties of Central IT. Where individuals need additional training for their personal needs, suitable internal or external courses will be considered and used.

(b) **Internal Seminars (Business Activities Overview)**

Business area presentations. (This is going to be addressed with Development Training during the coming year.)

(c) **External Seminars/Courses – Technical Training**

The changing nature of technology necessitates an ever changing technical development programme. However, external courses can be categorized into the following areas:

Computer operations
Telecom operations
User support
Technical skills host processors
Technical skills voice/data communications
Technical skills networks
Application support and development

Figure 5.13   Core curriculum – information technology

between front office (sales, portfolio managers, investment analysts and dealers) and back office (settlements, information technology and other support functions). A new Head of European Human Resources was appointed in the mid-1990s and one of his most urgent tasks was that of reviewing training activity. He recognized that the level of ongoing training activity was not negligible; it was, however, comparatively unstructured. He therefore established a project, using external consultants, with the following terms of reference:

> The aim is to produce a clear training plan, covering the next two to three years and embracing both technical and managerial/supervisory needs. Given the necessity of securing early progress within resource constraints this may be best expressed in terms of a number of clear 'training themes'. Account must be taken of the different requirements across the different business areas but there is a need for training to be seen as a company-wide activity. At the highest level there should be compatibility with the senior staff initiatives introduced by the parent group.

METHOD AND APPROACH

The following were agreed to be the key elements in establishing training requirements.

- detailed interviews with key business managers to identify the essential skills required to drive the business; these were based on a pre-prepared list of competencies. In addition, the views of these key managers were sought on the current state of training in the organization
- an identification of the training obligations that followed from the requirements of the financial regulator – in this case the Investment Management Regulatory Organisation (IMRO)
- a review of the training records held by the Human Resources Department
- a series of Focus Groups, using structured questionnaires and designed to identify training priorities for staff at levels below the most senior.

It can be seen that this process combined:

- mapping – establishing the realities of the existing training
- clarifying objectives – determining the desired level of training in the organization.

In addition, perceptions on the most appropriate training management processes would be uncovered.

FINDINGS

A key finding to emerge, from both the senior management interviews and the Focus Groups, was that recent training activity had been very limited. It was

MANAGEMENT INTERPERSONAL SKILLS

MANAGEMENT INTERPERSONAL SKILLS		SECRETARY	CLERICAL JUNIOR	CLERICAL SENIOR	EXECUTIVE JUNIOR	EXECUTIVE SENIOR	ASST MGER / MANAGER	ASST DIR +
Assertiveness Workshop	**	X	X	X	X	X		X
Induction Seminar		X	X	X	X	X	X	X
Interviewing Skills I (Selection)							X	X
Interviewing Skills II (Appraisal)							X	X
Letter Writing	#		X	X	X	X	X	
Management Development I								
Management Development II						X	X	X
Management Development Workshop	**							
Minute Taking and Agendas	#			X	X	X	X	X
Presentation Skills I	**						X	X
Presentation Skills II	**						X	X
Report Writing	#		X	X	X	X		
Secretaries' Workshop		X						
Supervisory Skills	#			X	X	X		
Telephone Techniques	**	X	X	X	X		X	
Time Management	**				X	X	X	

WANG COURSES

WANG COURSES		SECRETARY	CLERICAL JUNIOR	CLERICAL SENIOR	EXECUTIVE JUNIOR	EXECUTIVE SENIOR	ASST MGER / MANAGER	ASST DIR +
Advanced Wang Word Processing		X	X	X	X	X		
Electronic Mail – Office II		X		X	X	X	X	X
Lotus 123 – Introduction	#		X	X	X	X		
Lotus 123 – Intermediate	#		X	X	X	X		
Word Processing Revision		X						

TECHNICAL AND FINANCIAL TRAINING

TECHNICAL AND FINANCIAL TRAINING		SECRETARY	CLERICAL JUNIOR	CLERICAL SENIOR	EXECUTIVE JUNIOR	EXECUTIVE SENIOR	ASST MGER MANAGER	ASST DIR + (SHEET TWO)
Advance Corporate Analysis – Module B	#/*						X	X
Aspects of Analysis of Accounts	#/*							X
Conceptual Corporate Finance – Module C	#/*					X		X
Financial Risk Analysis – Module A	#/*			X	X		X	
Fundamentals of Corporation Tax	#/*					X		
International Dimensions to Analysis	#/*				X	X	X	X
Introduction to the Regulatory Environment	#				X	X		
Introduction to the Securities Industry	#			X	X			

NOTES

* Credit Risk Group and Risk Secretariat only   # Job specific   ** As appropriate to individual needs

- Specialized system courses will be attended where appropriate eg. Texas Instrument System training.
- Graduates will additionally attend the Graduate Induction Course.
- Additional technical training programmes will be run where deficiencies become apparent.
- Directors will attend the Directors' Development Centre by invitation.
- On occasions staff may attend courses run by the Industrial Society.

Staff from Company Secretary's Office will attend the following courses:

COURSE	Co Sec	Co Set Asst	DATE	DURATION
Tolley Conferences Company Secretary Update	X		October annually	1 day
European Study Conferences Company Secretarial Administration – 3 part course	X	X	Choice of dates	3 days in total
Finborough Seminars Company Secretarial Administration		X		1 day each

Figure 5.14   Core curriculum – financial control

felt that some impetus had developed several years ago, but that this had not been maintained.

Participants within Focus Groups were asked to detail the amount of off- and on-the-job training they had received in the previous year. The average figure for off-the-job training, at just under three days per annum per head, was far from inconsequential. *However, the fact that this training was not delivered as part of a structured approach to staff development led recipients to understate its incidence.* This was accentuated by the high proportion of recorded training that related to technology systems (for example Microsoft Excel) and the relatively high level of training received by the information technology staff themselves. A related point was that on-the-job training was not recognized. Very few Focus Group participants recorded anything beyond a minimal incidence of this form of training. In addition, there was a recognized need to improve the quality of training records in the organization.

On the positive side, one of the most encouraging results of the survey was the clarity with which senior members of staff were able to voice their priorities. Much of the detail must remain confidential, but the broad priorities are set out in the table below.

Business Area	Training Requirement
Investment	Financial analysis Product knowledge Communication/presentation skills
Sales/Marketing	Selling skills More efficient use of technology Product knowledge
Information Technology and other support functions	Specific training in new technology systems Project management Professional training

The organization's Managing Director separately underlined the importance of sales training and improved project management.

The general perception that the organization had not given sufficient importance to training meant that the main input from the Focus Group was a general demand for more training. The detailed requirements were not well defined. However, the most common training needs identified were:

- information technology
- management/leadership
- marketing/presentation skills.

Other needs mentioned were product knowledge training, languages, internal seminars and time management. In addition there was a general desire to have greater awareness of the Company as a whole and its products.

CONCLUSIONS

The study showed that, at all levels, there was genuine interest and enthusiasm for increased training in the organization. Any initiative, however, needed to be handled carefully to prevent unreasonable expectations. It was therefore decided to institute a staged approach over two years. The aim was to improve the training culture in the organization. This was unlikely to require a significant increase in resources. It was felt that approximately three days average off-the-job training per head would be the right level.

The key training themes for each of the following two years are set out below:

Year 1

BUSINESS AREA	SPECIALIST COURSES	COMMON THEMES Technical	COMMON THEMES Management/ Interpersonal
Sales/Marketing)) Investment)	A joint approach to customer relations/ selling skills	Product awareness Technology training	Training for performance appraisal
			Delivering on-the-job training
Operations	Project management	Technology training	Time management

Each of the above training courses was then set out in more detail and the choice between delivery in-house and through external consultants analysed.

Year 2

In the second year the intention would be for each identified business area to draw up a core curriculum (defined as a programme of training activity for a business area targeted at an individual at various stages of his or her development).

This process would be established before the start of individual appraisal interviews and managers should use the core curriculum as a guide in determining training needs during the interview. It could be appropriate to set assigned training budgets for each business area at this stage.

The aim of this two-stage approach was to improve the training culture over a period. In the first stage the emphasis was on deliverable visible training events which met expressed needs. Thereafter the intention was designed to create a more sophisticated, mature approach to training. In particular it was designed:

- to identify the resources available for training
- to establish a process for the regular review of the training and development needs of all employees by appropriate managers
- to set clear targets, clear control and accountability.

It was recognized that progress would be incremental – as an immediate jump to a learning organization was not feasible.

REFERENCES

1. Adams, K, (1996), 'Competency Comes of Age in Industrial Relations Services', *Annual Survey of Competency Frameworks: Competency,* **4** (1), Autumn, pp. 25–33.
2. Hamel, G. and Prahalad, C.K. (1994), *Competing for the Future,* Boston: Harvard Business School Press (also referenced in Chapter 1).
3. Mohrman, S., Galbraith, J.R. and Lawler, E.E. (1998), *Tomorrow's Organization: Crafting Winning Capabilities in a Dynamic World,* San Francisco: Center for Effective Organizations: Jossey-Bass; see Chapter 5 by Finegold, D., Lawler, E.E. III and Ledford, G.E. Jnr., pp.133–6.
4. Lado, A.A. and Wilson, M.C. (1994), 'Human Resource Systems and Sustained Competitive Advantage: A Competency-Based Perspective', *Academy of Management Review,* **19**, pp. 699–727.
5. Cockerill, T. (1989), 'The Kind of Competence for Rapid Change', *Personnel Management,* **21** (9), September, pp. 52–6.
6. My acknowledgements to my colleague Andrew Wright of Ernst & Young for his ideas which assisted in this analysis.
7. Rajan, A., (1990), *Capital People,* London : Industrial Society/London Human Resources Group.
8. My acknowledgements to Tim Doyle, formerly Head of European HR LGT, for permission to reproduce this case study, which first appeared in Croners' *Training and Development.*

6 Performance appraisal

All available evidence suggests that, for many organizations, performance appraisal is an essential feature of best training practice and the most important means of identifying individual training needs. A well-structured and controlled performance appraisal system provides part of the framework in which the trainer must work. As performance appraisal lies at the interface between the trainer and the line manager, it also offers a valuable means of developing the latter's responsiveness and responsibility to training. Credible performance appraisal can thus assist significantly in taking the organization up the learning curve.

To appreciate its importance, performance appraisal must be placed in its human resource context. I consider the place of performance appraisal in performance management and define the latter term in the section immediately following. This is followed by a review of the ways of ensuring that performance appraisal is delivered and managed effectively. The process of 360° feedback is becoming increasingly popular and a brief discussion of some of the issues are included.

Given the importance of performance appraisal, it is essential that the system operates effectively. This chapter provides some practical ways of improving the impact of performance appraisal – drawing on experience in an investment bank.[1] One of the fundamental themes of the book is the need to develop models that are rooted in practice. Resistance to attempts to introduce effective personnel procedures is common as these may be perceived as mattering more to the human resource professional than to the line manager. It is in the training manager's interest to identify and implement ways of overcoming such resistance. How this may be achieved by training and by quality control will be discussed in the context of the case study.

PERFORMANCE APPRAISAL AND PERFORMANCE MANAGEMENT

Summary: *Performance management is an important theme in human resources today. Hard and soft definitions of performance management can be offered and both emphasize the centrality of performance appraisal. Performance management gives the training manager an attractive framework in which to operate: it is compatible with other major cultural change initiatives.*

Performance management can be regarded as one of the conceptual themes underpinning approaches to training management today. It is, moreover, particularly useful in the context of the central themes of this book: it is more cohesive and tangible than many alternatives and hence provides a clearer agenda for action.

The most useful analysis of the concept was in a 1992 two-stage study undertaken by the then Institute of Personnel Management (now the Institute for Personnel and Development), *Performance Management in the UK.*[2] This gave an overview of policy and practice, involving a larger-scale mapping exercise, followed by a detailed examination of the experiences of a number of organizations. Together the findings afforded both a theoretical analysis and a perspective on what was happening in practice. In the first section of the study, undertaken by staff from the Institute of Manpower Studies, performance management systems were considered to be operating when the following conditions were met by the organization:

- a vision of objectives is communicated to employees
- departmental and individual performance targets which are related to wider objectives are set
- a formal review of progress towards targets is conducted
- the whole process is evaluated to improve effectiveness.

Performance management is therefore an attempt to bring some coherence to driving the organization towards the realization of its goals. This involves setting and meeting objectives by business units and individuals; the goals set must be related to business objectives communicated through a shared vision.

> all factors must be geared towards creating a shared vision of performance, generating commitment from employees to the concepts of improving performance and creating an environment where it is 'OK to perform'. The shared vision is vital to the achievement of performance improvement and means that organizational objectives must be communicated to all employees clearly and in terms which they can relate to their own work role and tasks, to understand how their efforts are of importance of the organisation. Finally, the model must be rooted in the business plan of the organisation (p. 137).

The literature survey outlined in *Performance Management in the UK* identified a variety of approaches to the definition of performance. At one extreme the literature concentrates on matching appraisal systems with rewards, and does not identify with broader organizational goals; at the other extreme is the more integrated, holistic approach already described. The Institute of Manpower Studies mapping exercise highlighted the absence of a consistent definition of performance management in practice. Somewhat depressingly, no evidence was found to connect the pursuit of formal performance management with improved organizational performance – though the parameters of the exercise and sample size were unlikely to produce a definitive result. However, the looser conclusion offered in the second part of the study suggests that performance management does have something to offer.

> organisations that were taking performance management most seriously and which were closest to the general principles and ideas ... did seem to be those that produced the best results ... where employees report high commitment, job satisfaction, clarity of goals, good feedback and so on, it is difficult to imagine that this has no effect at all on performance at the individual level (p. 115).

In a successor study, published by the Institute of Personnel and Development in 1998,[3] Michael Armstrong and Angela Baron defined performance management as follows:

> a strategic and integrated approach to increasing the effectiveness of the organisations by improving the performance of the people who work in them and by developing the capabilities of teams and individual contributors (p. 7).

The 1998 study involved a survey of 550 personnel practitioners, visits to 35 organizations and 12 focus groups of line managers and staff in six organizations. Additionally, attitude surveys, telephone surveys and expert interviews were undertaken. The study could be fairly said to have gathered a fair and thorough picture of the current state of appraisal practice.

It was recognized that performance management processes can take many forms. These will depend on the context of the organization and its culture. However, clear trends have emerged over the six-year period. Most important, the emphasis has shifted from objective-setting and the appraisal of results against goals. There has been a move to a more rounded view of performance which includes how people get things done as well as what they get done.

Armstrong and Baron reported that there had been a shift away from an approach centred on objective-setting. There has also been a reaction against tick the box ratings. In addition there was greater emphasis on development and a best practice organization treats appraisal as a joint approach, requiring managers (and team leaders) to identify with individuals what support they need. Generally, systems are becoming less bureaucratic with more emphasis on the quality of the feedback interview and less on the form.

In terms of techniques, Armstrong and Baron found that personnel development plans (an action plan for individuals with the support of their managers and the organization) are now becoming common among those organizations that operate performance management systems. A third of the organizations in the survey used competency assessment. Interest in 360° feedback, considered in a later section of this chapter, is growing.

The growing devolution of ownership from human resources to the line manager also emerged as a strong conclusion of good practice among the organizations contacted. These should properly be read in the original text and this is thoroughly recommended. Design of the process must depend on the situation and organization of the business.

Whatever the process used, performance management is a powerful and compelling concept, of considerable importance to the modern human resource professional. Turning to the 1992 IPM definition: the need to communicate a vision within an organization is widely advocated; the setting and review of targets appears to have gained acceptance; evaluation and monitoring of progress is a natural consequence of the other components of the definition. The model has nothing to say about the nature of the vision to be communicated – hence it is consistent with any approach to securing competitive advantage and desired change in cultural direction. In short, the concept has stood the rest of time. Performance management therefore offers the training manager a sensible framework in which to fulfil his or her organizational function.

EFFECTIVE APPRAISAL

Summary: *Appraisal is concerned with effective feedback on performance delivered in a structured framework. The focus of appraisal and the processes used are changing over time. However, there are powerful ethical reasons for making appraisal effective and equitable and this has important implications for the training manager.*

By now the importance of the new human resources has been thoroughly underlined. To reiterate, this is about both developing competitive advantage through people and reinforcing it through appropriate policies on encouragement, involvement and commitment. Appraisal is an fundamental component of this reinforcement. At its most simple it is an occasion when the manager gives feedback on performance. This is of growing importance in the new forms of organization with their flatter and less hierarchical structures.

Managers need to ensure that staff know what is required of them and also need to tackle substandard performance effectively. Managers must use the opportunity to recognize and acknowledge good performance (whatever the reward system) and to communicate future priorities. Staff need to know what is expected of them. They should also be given the opportunity to seek support and training and development opportunities.

For an appraisal system to achieve the above requires a considerable amount of commitment, planning and reinforcement. Whatever the process adopted, the discussion/appraisal interview will be delivered though the diffuse platform of line managers across the organization. Some will be rigorous, thorough and capable; others will be more casual and may lack the skills. At the heart of whatever process is used is the need for staff to be trained in effective feedback skills.

For appraisal to be effective, it is important to be clear about the purpose of the system. Within the broad description of the need to 'give effective feedback on performance', the focus and requirements of appraisal activity can vary considerably.

A fundamental distinction can be made between two outcomes of an appraisal process: judging and coaching. The former looks at aspects ranging from comparative performance (and inputs to reward) and succession planning through disciplinary measures; the latter identifies means of personnel development including training requirements. In practice it can be difficult to accommodate such diverse outcomes in a single process.

Clive Fletcher, Professor of Occupational Psychology at Goldsmiths College, University of London, builds on this distinction to suggest a dual approach to appraisal. In *Appraisal: Routes to Improved Performance*, published as part of the IPD's Developing Practice series,[4] he notes that:

> the traditional model of a centrally devised and run appraisal system, with an emphasis on assessment and overall ratings of performance, applied to all staff in the same manner, is no longer appropriate to a high proportion of advanced companies, and is likely to be decreasingly suitable for many more in the next few years. The fact is that it is no longer clear in many organisations as to who is the most appropriate person to be the appraiser for an individual is enough in itself to indicate how things have changed (p. 161).

This leads Fletcher to argue that:

> The only way for practice in this field to make any sense is to break appraisal down in two parts:
>
> 1. A performance planning session that involves reviewing the achievement of objectives over the period in question and setting objectives for the period ahead ...
> 2. A development review, probably based on competencies or skills dimensions, that looks at the training and development needs of the individual, and which can feed into the assessment of potential (where the latter is done by other, more effective methods) (p. 163).

Whether splitting the function of appraisal is feasible must depend on the culture of the particular organization. Certainly this dual process could not have been implemented effectively in the investment bank which is the subject of the case study later in this chapter. However, this does not detract from the strength of Fletcher's argument and the importance of recognizing that the focus of appraisal is changing – this last point is emphasized by a comparison between the 1992 and 1998 IPM/IPD studies already cited.

However, as the emphasis and design changes, it is likely that performance appraisal will grow in importance. Figure 6.1 brings together a number of points which have been implicit in the discussion to date. They provide a simple summary agenda for the training manager. In this summary it is recognized that the design and management of the system will not necessarily reside with the training manager. Training in feedback skills and in the understanding of the system is properly his or her responsibility. Clive Fletcher's book contains much useful, practical advice on the role of training in improving the effectiveness of the system.

Performance appraisal is of vital importance to the training professional. It is a significant component of the new human resources.

The training manager must put training in place to ensure that:

- feedback skills are adequate to ensure that appraisal is conducted efficiently and fairly
- the process adopted is understood at all levels in the organisation.

The training manager must ensure that development needs identified in the process are considered appropriately and advanced accordingly and that specific training requests are captured

- irrespective of the responsibility for the design and management and general ownership of the system.

Figure 6.1 Performance appraisal: the role of the training manager

360° FEEDBACK

Summary: *360° feedback is growing in importance. It provides additional information for the individual and is a valuable tool in performance management. However, managing the process is particularly demanding.*

The survey undertaken by Armstrong and Baron[3] indicated that, although the proportion of organizations sampled using 360° feedback stood at only 11 per cent, interest is growing as the value of feedback from a variety of sources is recognized. Certainly leading-edge organizations are using 360° feedback as part of performance management, but implementation is not for the faint-hearted. Much thought and planning is needed if the pitfalls are to be avoided. Fletcher[4] again offers useful advice, as does a specific text on the subject in the IPD's developing practice series, Peter Ward's *360 Degree Feedback*.[5]

Potentially, 360° feedback offers an improvement on traditional top-down sources of feedback and appraisal. These top-down approaches increasingly appear to fit uneasily with current developments in management and motivation. So the development of 360° feedback can be said to be consistent with the movement towards participation and empowerment of staff. Clive Fletcher observed (see p. 131) that in many organizations it is no longer clear who is the most appropriate appraiser; equally, feedback on performance is unlikely to come from one source.

At its most basic, 360° feedback involves generating input on performance from multiple sources. David Bracken, in his contribution to a text on organizational surveys, uses the term 'multi-source feedback' (MSF),[6] describing this as designed to assist the recipient (he uses the term 'ratee') and to:

> maximize the quality of feedback from managers, peers and subordinates, and it expands the rater domain to include such other potentially valuable sources as team members, internal customers, and external customers. Feedback is collected systematically, and (often) anonymously from each relevant rating source to give ratees a 360° view of their behaviour as it relates to successful job performance (p. 118).

The above description is of multi-source feedback, or full-circle feedback. Less total variants include versions where only subordinates participate (upward feedback), or peer review, where colleagues at the same level provide input.

Several important points are evident from the above description. First, 360° feedback is not necessarily organizationally linked with performance appraisal. The multi-source information can be assembled for other reasons of personal development – some business schools insist on completion of feedback forms for participants on their courses, for example. Similar information can be collected as input to development centres (see Figure 2.5, p. 40). Second, the process of managing the process is critical. If feedback is anonymous, it may not be gentle. The way in which it is delivered to the individual may affect its acceptance significantly.

In 1998, for example, Ernst and Young instituted an extended feedback process for each of some 450 partners. The first part of the form is shown in Figure 6.2. It is more properly described as multi-source feedback rather than 360° feedback. Input was not required outside the practice, but partners needed to dispatch copies of the form to at least six people. Returns were anonymous and sent to a designated administrator who collated the information. Thereafter, although practices varied, the process was at its most effective when a trained human resource professional worked with the recipient in assessing the development implications of the feedback.

The main value of 360° feedback, judging by the literature, is that it is a method for improving individual effectiveness. Properly analysed and delivered, multiple

Partner Group 1998-1999

Performance Contribution *and Measurement Indicators*

Identify the level of performance from the four choices provided. Put an "X" in the box to the left of that description. At times, you might want to identify the 'average' level of performance. **Add specific comments** to support your choice using the lines provided beneath each question.

Person being assessed:...

Completed by:...

Date:...

I. Excelling at Client Service

Client Care*

| ☐ Clarifies/responds to client needs: quality of responsiveness and communication is 'uneven' | ☐ Clarifies/responds 'acceptably' to client needs: uses the firm's best practice | ☐ Response 'above average' to client needs: proactively and consistently uses best team/firm knowledge and best practice | ☐ 'Outstanding' response to client needs; Established as a key opinion former with client; regularly exceeds client expectations |

....
....
....

Account Management

| ☐ No 'significant' relationships with key clients | ☐ Good relationships with traditional sources of business in key clients | ☐ Has developed key relationships with a range of business decision makers within the client organisation | ☐ Has an influential relationship with a wide range of business decisions makers (including direct sources of business) |

....
....
....

Fast (Speed of Response)

| ☐ Timeliness of response to clients (others) not seen as a priority | ☐ Actions demonstrate concern for timely response to clients' (others') needs | ☐ Anticipates clients' (others') needs; emphasises speed of response | ☐ Sets targets to meet/exceed clients' (others') expectation for response time. Holds others to high standards |

....
....
....

* Primary measure for this criterion

ERNST & YOUNG

Figure 6.2   A multi-source feedback form

perspectives on an individual's capabilities are of considerable value: much rich learning can take place when different sources express their view. There is also potential value in simply giving all relevant parties an opportunity to express their point of view. The uncontentious rationale is that to improve performance an individual needs insight on his or her weaknesses in job performance. Two assumptions lead from this rationale to 360° feedback; both are explored fully in an article by Walter Borman, of the University of South Florida.[7] The first is that the multiple sources of each of the ratings offer at least some perspectives on the recipient's performance. The second is that having these additional sources yields greater validity than a single source. Both these assumptions are the subject of ongoing research.

On a more immediate and practical level, it is possible to identify the steps needed to improve the effectiveness of 360° feedback. Fletcher,[4] Ward[5] and Bracken[6] offer guidance. Effective design and communication in advance and high-quality administration and feedback arrangements are critical to success. The growing popularity of the technique should not blind training managers from the dangers. An ill-planned and ill-received 360° process could do immense damage. As Fletcher puts it:

> The enthusiasm and the speed with which 360 degree feedback has been embraced is remarkable. The concept of multi-source, multi-level feedback makes a lot of sense and, if used well, should have a great deal to offer. It seems to suit the move towards a less hierarchical, more flexibly structured, and knowledge-based organisations of the future. But the parallels with psychometric testing are striking... The rush to use tests in the 1980s is similar to the wholesale adoption of 360° systems. In the cast of tests, it led all too often to poor practice... There is every chance that 360° feedback systems will follow the same route if they are not introduced more carefully and, examined more critically than is the case at present (p. 82).[4]

CASE STUDY: PERFORMANCE APPRAISAL IN PRACTICE

Summary: *This section is an extended case study describing efforts to improve the effectiveness of performance appraisal in an investment bank. In this sort of performance-oriented (or achievement culture) environment, human resource systems do not command ready acceptance. As well as a substantial training effort, quality control is needed to prevent systematic overrating for reward purposes and substandard completion of forms.*

Having considered the theoretical background to performance appraisal, it is appropriate to turn to some practical issues involved in making performance appraisal an effective tool. This extended case study draws on the experiences gained in an investment bank: I describe the way in which the problems of systematic bias and poor quality returns were tackled. Some background on the appraisal process in the bank is necessary to set these experiences in context. It will be evident in the course of the discussion that an investment bank is an atypical environment, one where there is more than the usual resistance to personnel practices. However, it is suggested that if the measures used to improve the effectiveness of appraisal can produce results in this environment, they will be more effective in a more receptive milieu.

The culture in an investment bank is biased toward recognizing performance and rewarding contribution to the bottom line. This gives rise to an inherent problem in the delivery of personnel systems: on the one hand line managers recognize the necessity of clear guidelines to ensure equity of treatment throughout the organization; on the other, they demonstrate a readiness to bend the rules to their advantage if opportunity arises. Activities which are not seen to be directly aligned to bottom-line profitability are likely to be regarded as subordinate to the main objectives or even dismissed as irrelevant. The appraisal process provides the framework for managers to review staff and identify the extent of individual contributions. Even the most blinkered manager will accept the need to establish who has contributed significantly in his or her division and to evaluate that contribution against others. At the basic level, therefore, all managers accept the appraisal process as a review of past performance and acknowledge its role in the remuneration review process.

Another feature of the culture, however, is a hostility to what is perceived as bureaucracy, and an antipathy to form-filling.

One way in which line managers can reconcile these divergent attitudes is to accept performance appraisal as a principle but to dismiss the form and procedures as 'imposed by human resources'. This perception can be used to justify both a failure to adhere to the timetable imposed for the appraisal cycle and also poor quality completion of forms.

The human resource department has therefore developed mechanisms to improve the credibility of the system. First, training sessions have been introduced that are open to all staff who undertake the appraisal interview. The sessions take place in early autumn when the timetable for the appraisal round has been agreed, but before the forms have reached appraisers. Second, at the end of the appraisal round, a quality control exercise is conducted. The extent to which the appraiser has completed the form effectively is monitored against a number of criteria and the results collated by human resources and presented to the management committee.

THE TRAINING INITIATIVES

Different divisions within the bank respond in different ways to these initiatives. Participation in the training sessions, for example, varies greatly. Two stages of training are offered. First, all staff are invited, in groups, to attend a one-hour session in which the purpose of the appraisal form is underlined and any changes in procedures from previous years discussed. Second, all staff who have not already undergone such training are encouraged to attend a one-hour practice interview using closed circuit TV. A case study of a 'difficult' performance appraisal interview has been written for this purpose, and a member of the training team undertakes the practice interview and plays the role of the appraisee. As an alternative, managers may bring their own problem appraisal interview to this one-to-one session. The standard case study is reproduced in Figure 6.3.

Both training sessions have been endorsed by the management committee and hence add weight to their importance as part of the appraisal process. The human resource department in an investment bank does not, however, have the power to compel attendance – such power rests with line management in the divisions. Participation is encouraged by giving senior management feedback on attendance at sessions.

You will be undertaking an appraisal interview of a member of your staff.

He/she is one of the brightest people in the department, someone with considerable potential. However, relationships with other staff members are not good and he/she is regarded as difficult.

Having taken soundings from your colleagues, you feel that the following are the areas you wish to discuss:

- he/she is fully committed only when the work captures his/her imagination; otherwise he/she is casual and may not follow things through
- he/she can be secretive and doesn't always communicate – team work suffers as a result
- he/she can be impatient and impetuous.

Your view is that these are connected weaknesses.

The quality of the work produced is generally good, and you are anxious to secure improvement without deflating your staff member's morale.

Try, in the course of the interview, to secure a commitment to change.

Figure 6.3 Performance appraisal role-play case study

QUALITY CONTROL AND RATINGS DRIFT

The second activity designed to improve the effectiveness of the performance appraisal system is the quality control exercise. Some quality problems are generated as a result of a resistance to form-filling; others arise from multi-purpose usage.

As has been noted, a central problem arises because the performance appraisal process has more than one purpose. Differing emphasis can be placed on these purposes, although for many line managers the main interest is in the overall performance rating as this is known to be a significant determinant for salary purposes. This gives rise to a problem that can be characterized as 'ratings drift'.

The appraisal form used in the investment bank seeks to embrace three distinct areas: a review of past performance, measured against previously agreed objectives; the setting of future objectives; and agreement on training and development needs. To refer back to the analysis introduced earlier, it has elements of both judging and coaching and is both a reward and a performance review.

To line management the key feature of the form is the 'Summary of Performance' (see Figure 6.4). Despite its importance, in the words of one line manager: 'Performance Appraisal is a load of rubbish. You decide on the rating you want in the box and then make up a few words of narrative in the other sections to justify it'.

SUMMARY OF PERFORMANCE		(✔) your overall review
I ABSOLUTELY OUTSTANDING		An exceptional member of staff: performance consistently exceeds expected high standards
II ABOVE EXPECTED LEVEL		Performance frequently exceeds expected high standards
III EXPECTED LEVEL OF PERFORMANCE		In some respects exceeds expected high standards
		Meets the expected high standards
		In some respects does not meet the expected high standards
IV ROOM FOR IMPROVEMENT		Performance frequently falls below expected high standards
V UNSATISFACTORY		Performance does not meet basic requirements of the job
VI UNDER TRAINING		Performance is not accessible as the employee has been in position for less than 4 months

Figure 6.4 Performance ratings used in the investment bank

The appraisal cycle is deliberately timed to provide input to the remuneration review process so the results can be taken into consideration. Why is this a firm part of the programme when most of the commentators on the relationship between appraisal and salary review advocate the opposite? The answer is simple. The bank's culture would not accept more than one exercise. The task of the human resources department has been to build on this basic premise by highlighting the other aspects of the performance appraisal process. This has been achieved in two ways.

First, the department has sought to illustrate that setting clear objectives is closely linked to improving performance over the following twelve months. Specifically, appraisal training sessions have focused on setting quality objectives. Second, a link is drawn between having the skills and knowledge to do a job and the performance in that job. In some instances remedial training can have a marked effect on performance. In addition, an effort is made to promote the longer-term benefits which can be derived from continuous personal development at all levels.

Multi-purpose use of the appraisal process may not meet the approval of the purists but it has to be the way it operates in highly achievement-oriented companies. While managers are putting effort into evaluating past performance, the opportunity must be taken to heighten their awareness of the importance of setting objectives.

Ratings drift – the overrating of performance to increase remuneration – is an inevitable problem of any multi-purpose system. Once reward and performance review systems are merged, this problem can be reduced but never eliminated. In the investment bank, the link between the 'Summary of Performance' in Section V of the performance appraisal form and the salary increase applied in the following April is explicitly acknowledged. It is scarcely surprising, therefore, that the systematic overrating of staff is an ongoing problem, even though the requirement for equitable treatment is reinforced in performance appraisal training sessions and monitored through quality control.

In the group training sessions the fact that the performance appraisal interview is not solely, or even primarily, about salary is emphasized. It is emphasized that performance appraisal is only one of a number of factors that determine the eventual salary and bonus payments: company budgets, market data and broader compensation policy are the other major determinants. Staff who undertake appraisal interviews are advised not to discuss salary in the interview and are given guidance on how to handle the inevitable questions.

It must, however, be said that exhortations to avoid an emphasis on the salary implications of the appraisal process meet with more cynicism than any other aspect of appraisal training. Many line managers, aware of the link between the appraisal rating and salary increase, seek to use it to their advantage. For this reason, a measure of the spread of ratings – whether or not there is evidence of a systematic upward drift – is a key feature of the quality control exercise.

Each year divisions are given guidance on the expected distribution of their staff across the ratings. As part of the quality control exercise the analysis of the spread of overall ratings for each division is compared with the guidance on the recommended spread. Predictably, a higher percentage of staff appraised are placed in the top three categories than recommended in the guidance notes. Ratings drift is recognized as a major problem by the management committee and monitored by them. In the words of one member 'it is remarkable that two-thirds of the staff in ... division are recorded as above average when the division is performing less well than its peer groups in other companies'.

An encouraging result of such exhortations has been the growing practice of senior managers within a division meeting to reach an agreed view on ratings which correspond to guidelines. In one division, for example, team leaders and directors then meet to review team members. In this way there is an open forum to review staff, and all those who attend are able to give their views. Comparisons between staff of the same level or job family can therefore be made. This approach makes it difficult, though not impossible, for favoured employees to be over-rated.

MAINTAINING QUALITY

The need to enforce acceptable standards of form completion across different divisions has already been identified. Different line managers demonstrate very different degrees of commitment to the process and this extends across all aspects of form completion. Inspection and analysis of the returned performance appraisal forms has been a feature of the system since its inception. However, a more thorough and systematic exercise has been undertaken, culminating in the full report to the Bank's management committee with comparative data from each division.

Three broad categories are considered: timing – whether deadlines have been met; the spread of ratings; indications of a less than satisfactorily completed form. Timing is straightforward: the key figure is the percentage of forms outstanding after the due date. Publication of such percentage figures inevitably speeds up the completion of late forms. The second category permits the capture of data necessary to analyse ratings drift.

The third set of measures are all concerned with identifying the form which has received less than satisfactory attention from the appraiser. Four separate criteria are covered:

- *Insufficient comments in the sections of the form which deal with past performance* These sections record main tasks and objectives and also ask for an indication on how an employee approaches his or her work. Full comments on both positive and negative features are required.
- *Insufficient objectives set for the forthcoming year* The measure is to record the percentage of forms which identified three or less objectives for the forthcoming year. It is argued that this threshold must be passed if the broader requirements of any management job are to be fulfilled.
- *No development steps identified* The section of the form covering the ensuing

year also calls for training and development steps. Many returned forms merely list training courses without any comments. Any forms registering no steps at all are identified.

- *Inadequate comments by the employee* The percentage of forms where the employee recorded no comment is identified. Although it could be argued that this is a matter for the appraisee not the appraiser, in practice the attitude of the latter is likely to be influenced by the former. Part of the skill of the good appraiser is securing a thoughtful input from his or her subordinate.

The purpose of the quality control analysis is to identify the thoroughness with which appraisers have approached their task, and to provide comparative information on the even-handedness of approach between divisions.

IMPROVING THE PROCESS

As well as the requirement to monitor the quality of the forms to ensure that they have been adequately completed, there is a need to upgrade the whole process. Training the managers in understanding the purpose, their responsibility and the timetable of events is therefore an important way of improving the credibility of the process. Training them in the requirements of conducting a difficult appraisal interview effectively is equipping them with useful management skills. The former is the focus of the group training sessions: the latter the focus of one-to-one role-play sessions.

The agenda for attention at the group sessions has varied from year to year. Most recently it has concentrated on two elements; the need to improve the setting of objectives and the completion of the training and development details.

In the training sessions the characteristics of effective performance objectives are identified: these are reproduced in Figure 6.5.

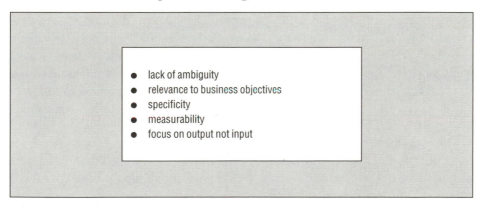

- lack of ambiguity
- relevance to business objectives
- specificity
- measurability
- focus on output not input

Figure 6.5 Characteristics of effective performance objectives

141

The extent to which practice departs from this model is well illustrated by the following objectives, all of which appeared in 1990 completed appraisal forms:

> As part of the newly formed (Group) within (Division) I would expect (Name) to make a full contribution to the development of business opportunities for the Group. This will involve continuing the existing programme of calling on professional intermediaries, as well as helping define and market to our chosen market sectors. I would expect (Name) to play a significant part in the initiative in conjunction with other members of the team.

This objective is imprecise and insufficiently focused but at least represents a genuine attempt by a manager to set an objective.

By contrast, the following objectives simply demonstrate loose thinking:

> Help cover my backside.

> Develop managerial skills.

> Improve organizational skills.

> To get motivated.

These last four examples were used in the performance appraisal training sessions as examples of poor objectives. Participants in the sessions were invited to consider why they are imprecise and how they could be improved.

This discussion may give the impression that performance appraisal is regarded by the human resources department as a defective and unsatisfactory process. This is far from the case. Despite shortcomings the annual performance appraisal at the investment bank provides all the essential information required for the pay review. Because the connection with the pay review is made explicit, the completion rate is close to 100 per cent; albeit not to the agreed timetable.

In addition, despite the varying degrees of enthusiasm displayed towards the other sections of the form, valuable information is generated for human resource management and planning. For example, members of the human resource management team are provided with essential information on day-to-day personnel issues. Potential internal transfers, ongoing performance/disciplinary issues and personality clashes are examples of early warning signals which are taken from a well-completed appraisal form. Information from the section on training needs on the performance appraisal form is transferred to the training database. Course provision is planned on the basis of the returns and individuals are booked or waiting-listed for course places.

These positive results, however, are achieved at a price. First, as is clear from the earlier discussion of performance appraisal in practice, a considerable amount of human resource time and energy is expended on gaining credibility for the process. Both the specialist training staff and human resource managers are involved in delivering training sessions and in encouraging staff to attend them.

The second price to be paid for this success is the abandonment of purity. As has been noted, separate reward and performance reviews have been dismissed as impractical and maintaining the theoretical distinctions as impossible. First, because line managers will only fill in one form. Second, because if they do not perceive a clear link with salary they will not do it. At the investment bank a 'one form for everything' approach works. So the definition of appraisal purpose used is deliberately imprecise. Theoretical models are of limited use in this situation. Separating reward review and potential review would mean that sufficient information would never be obtained on the latter. Information known to be collected for reward review is bound to be subject to bias and distortion, but is an essential starting point for the process. The other information collected provides input to staff management which would not otherwise be available.

Inevitably, therefore, it is necessary to work with a sub-optimal procedure. Bluntly, there is a need to live with sub-optimization and through a variety of activities and mechanisms to try to manage the difficulty and influence change. In this sort of achievement- or task-oriented environment human resource management is the art of the possible.

REFERENCES

1. Carlton, I. and Sloman, M. (1992), 'Performance Appraisal in Practice', *Human Resource Journal*, **2** (3), Spring.
2. (1992), *Performance Management in the UK: An Analysis of the Issues*, London: Institute of Personnel Management.
3. Armstrong, M. and Baron, A. (1998), *Performance Management: The New Realities*, London: Institute of Personnel and Development.
4. Fletcher, C. (1997), *Appraisal: Routes to Improved Performance*, Second Edition, London: Institute of Personnel and Development.
5. Ward, P. (1997), *360 Degree Feedback*, London: IPD.
6. Bracken, D.W. (1996), 'Multisource (360 Degree Feedback): Surveys for Individual and Organizational Development', in Allen I. Kraut (ed.), *Organizational Surveys: Tools for Assessment and Change*, San Francisco: Jossey-Bass/Society for Industrial and Organizational Professional Practice Series, Chapter 5, p. 118.
7. Borman, W.C, (1997), '360° Ratings: An Analysis of Assumptions and a Research Agenda for Evaluating the Validity', *Human Resource Management Review*, **7** (3), pp. 299–315.

7 Design and delivery

Progressing through the categories of the systematic training model, it is now appropriate to consider the design and delivery of training. Much of what is involved here is well documented. There is considerable material on the choice of training methods, the scheduling and balance of training events and ways of improving the effectiveness of the trainer. I do not attempt to duplicate this information in this chapter: readers who would appreciate further guidance are referred to the *Gower Handbook of Training and Development*.[1]

Instead my concern here is to offer an overview on some areas where attention is required to achieve best training practice. First, the following topics are considered in turn: improving the quality of on-the-job training; executive coaching and mentoring; training and equal opportunities; and the use of external consultants. On-the-job training is chosen because its importance is consistently understated. The other topics have all assumed greater importance in recent years. A clear understanding of the impact that they have on the training manager's job is essential.

The overview of these four topics is then followed by a more extended discussion of, first, technology based training, and second, training and knowledge management. These two related topics are of vital importance to the role of training in the new human resources. They are becoming more and more important and may offer new opportunities for the training manager.

If there is a single theme that underlies this chapter it is that the boundaries of training are becoming increasingly less distinct. Training shades into learning; learning shades into performance. A one-off training intervention with a clear start and finish is a rarity. This all demands a greater flexibility of approach from the trainer.

IMPROVED ON-THE-JOB TRAINING

Summary: *Half of training provision is delivered on the job, yet the whole topic is under-researched. Some practical ways of improving on-the-job training are suggested and a training module outlined.*

The most significant survey of training by UK employers (see Appendix I, pp. 255–7) showed that half of the training took place on the job; more costs were incurred in training on than off the job. On-the-job training is a fundamental way of moving forward new recruits, developing apprentices or other long-term trainees, teaching employees new skills when new equipment, technology and methods are introduced, and of updating and upgrading skills. Initiatives designed to improve the capacity of line managers in the delivery of training was seen to be a key feature of the best practice organizations surveyed for this book (see Appendix IV, p. 267).

This failure to pay attention to the quality of on-the-job training is hard to prove, but is evident in practice. It is probably most obvious in the service sector. The following extract from an Annual Report indicates a particularly casual attitude to skills enhancement on promotion.

> A Member enquired as to what training the staff received especially when they were promoted and cited the case of the Cellarman being promoted to Bars Manager. The Chairman replied that the Management Committee was satisfied with the Bars Manager otherwise he would not have been appointed. With regard to training, he had been understudy to the previous Steward for some time and had worked in bars for several years.

This extract is taken from the Annual Report of a well-known Welsh Rugby team (for the curious, they play in blue and black hooped shirts). Not only do its supporters suffer regular hidings on the field, they experience difficulty in drowning their sorrows afterwards.

A sustained effort to improve the quality of on-the-job training could yield considerable benefits. It also offers a particularly useful opportunity for making line managers aware of the importance of training, since so many of them will be involved in delivering on-the-job training. Defining this training is difficult, but a recent article by the IPD's policy adviser defined it as

> training that is planned and structural, takes place mainly at the normal work station of the trainee – although some instructions may also be provided in a special training area on site and where a manager, supervisor, trainer or peer colleague spends a significant time with the trainee to teach a set of skills that have been specified in advance. It also includes periods of instruction where there may be little or no useful output in terms of productivity (p. 28).[2]

Much on-the-job training is delivered on a one-to-one basis, and the same trainers will often instruct perhaps three or four people simultaneously. It seems likely that between one and two million people in the UK act as on-the-job trainers.

Surprisingly, the whole topic of on-the-job training is under-researched. Some principles based on case studies cited in a previous work[3] are listed here, together with an outline of activities for line managers designed to improve their effectiveness as on-the-job trainers. Readers are also referred to the 1997 article by the Institute of Personnel and Development's policy adviser, Mike Cannell, and an IPD guide[2].

These principles are basic rules of good practice which can be implemented in any organization:

- *Give on-the-job training the importance it deserves*   Evidence suggests that in almost every sector nearly as much training is delivered on the job as off the job and that it costs more. Many firms simply fail to recognize the extent of this activity.

  However, line managers do know which people receive on-the-job training and why, even though this information is often forthcoming only after extensive prompting.

  Recognizing who delivers on-the-job training within an organization is a first step towards more effective delivery. These generally unacknowledged trainers have a great deal of experience to contribute to the effective design of the overall training package in an organization. Identify them and seek their views, particularly when any major changes are planned.

- *Don't treat on-the-job training differently*   On-the-job training should be seen for what it is: a major element of an organization's total training provision. It should be subjected to exactly the same discipline, examination and scrutiny as the more visible methods of training that show up in invoices.

  On-the-job training should be viewed in the context of business objectives, particularly when significant cultural changes are contemplated. It is important to ensure that bad habits are not being reinforced by cynical, inadequate or simply unaware trainers at the workplace.

  Although on-the-job training is less visible and less tangible, the same basic disciplines should be applied as are used in systematic off-the-job training. It is important to identify what training is needed, plan appropriate training to meet this need, implement the training and then evaluate it. Imagination and ingenuity will be required to achieve this discipline, but the challenge should be welcomed and not used to excuse indifference.

- *Integrate on-the-job training with other methods*   On-the-job training works most effectively when supported by other training methods: it should not be employed in isolation. The efficiency of those responsible for delivering on-the-job training can be much enhanced if they are adequately supported. Technology-based training can be used to reinforce and supplement training objectives. Successful trainers treat on-the-job and off-the-job training as complementary activities.

Significantly, some successful examples of training initiatives have started from a recognition that existing on-the-job training is an inadequate mechanism for achieving change, and that an improvement in its delivery, and enhanced status for the trainers, is a key component of change.

● *Train the trainers*   The final suggestion offered is the most obvious one, but also the most difficult to implement. Given that half an organization's training effort is delivered through its under-recognized trainers acting on a part-time basis, an improvement in their effectiveness must pay considerable dividends.

Coaching – a Two-day Company Workshop

Prework

Before attending the workshop, participants are asked to send a questionnaire to 4–6 people. The questionnaire (similar to a 360° tool) asks respondents to rate the participant against a list of known coaching behaviours. The questionnaires are collated and the participant's strengths in coaching capacity and development areas in a coaching capacity are highlighted. The tutors use these to focus the content of the workshop. Participants are also asked to bring a live case to the workshop.

Day One

● Introductions and objectives
● What is coaching?
● The difference between coaching, counselling and directing
● The manager's role as a coach
● Recognizing the need for coaching

The coaching contract – the roles and responsibilities of the individual being coached, the manager as coach and the employing organisation, discussion of conflicts and constraints.

● Skills and qualities of a coach
● Benefits of coaching, coaching versus other learning interventions
● When to use coaching, using the Situational Leadership Model
● The GROW model of coaching

Discussion of the stages of the coaching cycle and the skills required.

G	GOAL	Set the goal or objective for the coaching programme
R	REALITY	Explore the reality of their current situation
O	OPTIONS	Look at options for improvement and development
W	WILL	Focus on actions which the learner is prepared to undertake, check competence and confidence levels

---

Figure 7.1   **A module for improving in-company coaching**

Skills practice – Coaching for performance development

Participants practise coaching an individual who has been identified as having potential to take on a different role. Using the GROW model they help identify specific activities which will build confidence and commitment. Observers identify what works well and what could be improved. Discussion and feedback. Video can also be used.

Day Two

Recap day one

- Informal/formal coaching
- Opportunities For Coaching
- Poor performance
- Delegation
- Career development
- New tasks
- Skill/will model

Discussion of the model and the need for the manager as coach to adapt their style in order to be most effective. Participants discuss what affects performance and learning. Using their live cases, they discuss what style and approach they will take to help the individual to develop.

- Advanced coaching and feedback skills
- Giving feedback

Discussion of the skills required for learning and development to take place. Introduction to the seven-step model of giving feedback. Confronting performance problems and using coaching to lead to performance improvement.

- Skills practice

Each participant practises their coaching skills, in triads, using their live cases. After the practice, the observer acts as a peer coach using the GROW model, helping the participant to identify what worked well and what could be improved. Discussion and feedback. Video can also be used.

- Action planning

Based on the pre-workshop feedback questionnaire and their experiences on the workshop, participants prepare a self-development plan, which will help them to develop their coaching skills further.

NB A follow-up workshop can also be arranged 6–12 months later, preceded by another 360° questionnaire to measure any performance change.

(Reproduced by kind permission of Cedar International.)

Figure 7.1   Concluded

EXECUTIVE COACHING AND MENTORING

Summary: *Individual coaching of senior managers has become a significant growth area in training in the late1990s – cynics could dismiss it as a fad. There are important issues of clarity of purpose and control to be considered if the value of coaching is to be determined.*

At its simplest, coaching is an intervention where one person assists another to achieve their potential over an extended period. In this sense it is a form of on-the-job development – analogous to the on-the-job training described in the previous section, but broader in scope and ambition. Figure 7.1 outlines a module designed to improve in-company coaching. Suitably adjusted, it can be used to improve the quality of the on-the-job training delivered in the workplace. Coaching has been a feature of training provision for decades. However, there are indications that the provision of tailored coaching for senior executives has become a significant growth area in the late 1990s. Such evidence is mainly anecdotal, but a plethora of articles in the quality newspapers is at least an indication of what appears to have become a trend.

One issue to be resolved at the outset is the purpose of coaching intervention. A clear definition may help and the following is taken from an internal Ernst & Young paper.[4]

Coaching, counselling and mentoring are all regarded as 'helping processes'; all can assist in accelerating the learning and performance of staff. They are defined as follows:

- **Coaching** is a process in which a manager, through direct discussion and guided activity, helps a colleague to solve a problem, or a task, more effectively than would otherwise have been the case. It also includes the process of producing personal development and action plans. Coaching is task-centred, in that it focuses upon the work processes, appropriate behaviours, and the actions the individual needs to take to improve performance.
- **Counselling** is a process that helps the individual resolve those personnel issues which impede performance or the development of new skills and attitudes. The style of delivery is usually non-directive/neutral. Counselling is person-centred, in that it focuses upon whatever the issues may be for an individual.
- **Mentoring** is a process which helps a person handle significant transitions in responsibility and/or status. It provides advice on such issues as the suitability of career goals, personal strategies and tactics. There will normally be a significant difference in seniority between mentors and those assisted.

Other organizations would use the terms in quite different ways. In part the above definitions were introduced to clarify the roles that should be fulfilled by internal staff in helping develop the less experienced. A number of underlying issues are of interest, however, irrespective of the organization. First, coaching, counselling and mentoring are interventions and require management and control. Second, those who are assisting others in this way need appropriate skills and sensitivity. If the intention is to deliver such support internally, using existing managers, a significant requirement for training will arise. An important distinction is made between task-centred helping (defined as coaching) and person-centred helping (defined as counselling).

As I have noted, a significant growth has taken place in externally delivered support for senior managers. The argument for this approach has been succinctly presented in an article by John Coleman of the Change Partnership – an organization specializing in the provision of this service.[5]

The Change Partnership draw a different distinction from that considered above. They view executive coaching as support delivered by someone external to the organization, and mentoring as support delivered by someone internal to the organization. Development of high fliers should be bespoke and the emphasis should shift from teaching to learning, and:

> coaching fills a gap in management development disciplines, by providing 'self-help' for individuals. While it may be used at any level, it is particularly important for those aspiring to the top jobs in an organization. It may be used to prepare for promotion, or a flying start afterwards, or to 'bed in' a newcomer to the organization; or where those attempting major change need an objective sounding board, mentor and Devil's Advocate – anywhere in fact where change processes demand new thinking, solutions or behaviour from top teams. Coaching offers an extra way forward. It is a 'live' system responding to changing individual and corporate needs as they occur (p. 38).

Given this statement of scope of coaching, it is not surprising that many significant executive coaching programmes are introduced as a constituent feature of a change management initiative. Such programmes could involve hundreds of top managers, each of whom would be involved in 35 to 40 hours of meetings over the year. These are obviously expensive, high-profile and high-risk initiatives.

Other questions on coaching concern the subject areas, which can range from hard business issues (support on finance or marketing) through to softer issues (concerned with life balance or stress management). Ethical problems arise when coaching moves into therapy, and when there is a danger of creating a dependency between coach and recipient. If external coaching of senior management continues to grow at its present rate, it is likely that these ethical issues will be the subject of much attention.

TRAINING AND EQUAL OPPORTUNITIES

Summary: *Equal Opportunities training is concerned with respect, sensitivity and* *good management practice. To be effective, it must therefore be embedded in all organizational policies and leadership and management practices. Therefore it cannot be an isolated intervention and should be seen as integral to cultural and organizational development.*

Equality of opportunity has been the subject of extensive legislation, policy formulation and training initiatives throughout the last 20 years. Its position on the business and management agenda has risen and fallen in direct correlation to the state of the economy and demographic projections. Issues such as Opportunity 2000 brought it back nearer to the top of some management agendas. Despite this, however, and the existence of many good policies and oft-stated intentions, statistics still show that equality of opportunity, in its truest sense, is far from being achieved. The question as to whether it is a dream or myth could rightly be posed since it is only now, with the combination of the changing structure of the workforce, the prospect of 'limitless' pay-outs and heightened publicity, that the matter is once again coming to the fore.

The term 'equal opportunities' training can cover a range of activities and approaches – intended to achieve a variety of objectives. In the introduction, I noted that, if this chapter had a common theme, that theme was that training interventions were blurred with other activities designed to promote organizational objectives. That observation is particularly apposite in the case of training to promote equal opportunities. Training interventions, if seen as stand-alone initiatives taken out of context, are unlikely to be effective.

The issue with equal opportunities training and making it a tangible reality in organizations includes putting a business case, raising awareness, challenging assumptions and, ultimately, changing behaviour. Making any policy and training intervention work in an organization is always a challenge; making an equal opportunities policy work is an even greater challenge. One of the issues is that, while most people agree, in theory, that equality of opportunity is a good thing, in practice they often still recruit, develop and promote in their own images, with seemingly rational arguments relating to 'team fit', customer profile, etc. When challenged many of these 'rational' arguments cannot be substantiated. Therefore, the aspiration to achieve equality of opportunity in organizations is all too frequently not matched by the observed reality. Success in this area requires a willingness to look at organizational practices and procedures and to ensure behaviour supports the intent. Training interventions are therefore but one part of the jigsaw. This ultimately means that managers have to be prepared to look at their own role in either furthering or blocking the achievement of equal opportunities. Since, arguably, organizations are asking their employees and indeed themselves to move faster than society (a glance at any advertising billboard will show a frequently stereotypical view of the world), this issue is a somewhat complex one.

Successful training initiatives in this area involve designing a process, which starts with where the organization is and where it needs to get to. Guidance is available for any trainer planning such interventions via the relevant advisory bodies – Equal Opportunities Commission (EOC), Commission for Racial Equality (CRE), Institute of Personnel and Development (IPD) and various other organizations listed in the Diversity register. Indeed the publication *Impact* focuses specifically on these issues and funds the British Diversity Awards.

A significant survey on equal opportunity training in the UK[6] revealed that such training could be interpreted narrowly to mean guidance on anti-discrimination legislation or on an organization's recruitment and selection procedures. Alternatively it could be wide-ranging, covering a variety of issues in equal opportunities policy. The aim might be to transmit information in one specific area or to be part of a wider strategy of promoting equal opportunities and practice. Gender, race and disability can be said to form the main focus of equal opportunity training. However, the treatment of other groups – gays, lesbians, older workers and ex-offenders – is specifically covered in some organizations' training initiatives. A number of these are including training on issues affecting people who are HIV positive or have AIDS. 'Awareness' courses in practice often not only focus on attitudes but can include information on legislation, how to implement good practice in recruitment and selection, and how to tackle racism in the organization.

The design of many events is undertaken in practice in the UK by in-house specialists. Helen Garrett and Judith Taylor have written a book offering useful guidance for trainers planning their own initiatives.[7] Training courses in recruitment and selection, for example, usually cover the following areas: equal opportunities legislation and its relevance to recruitment and selection; drawing up objectives criteria; job descriptions, advertising, shortlisting and interviewing procedures. The aim is to identify ways in which discrimination can occur at any stage of the procedures and examine ways to avoid it.

Equal opportunities training must be well planned. While this is true of all training interventions there is a real danger of cynicism and scepticism from those reluctant to recognize the need for such initiatives. The Commission for Racial Equality (CRE) in its guidance[8] emphasizes that training should be developed with 'particular attention to the needs of decision makers, including boards of management, selection, first line supervisors and managers and all key employees in positions of influence, including reception staff'.

As well as the need for planning, the CRE emphasizes that training will only be effective if: 'it gives trainees the knowledge and information that are essential to understand and recognize the scope for discrimination and couples this with the development of skills necessary to take effective steps in dealing with unlawful discrimination'.

Conditions for a successful programme are: senior management support;

continuing support after the event; back-up for changes in practice and policy; consideration of the resources needed. The CRE guide helpfully sets out specific minimum objectives for categories of employees.

All this indicates that the standard disciplines that should apply to all aspects of training management should be carried across into equal opportunities training. While this is scarcely a surprising conclusion, the importance for clarity of objectives cannot be over-emphasized.

USING EXTERNAL CONSULTANTS

Summary: *An area of importance to the training professional is the growing use of external suppliers for design and delivery. This topic is not well represented in the literature and much of what appears is written from the consultant's point of view. The value of using consultants is considered, distinguishing between their role as suppliers (or providers) and their role as change agents. The importance of involving line management is stressed and mechanisms for achieving this are outlined.*

In the discussion about alternative models for training management presented in Chapter 3 I considered training as consultancy. A distinction was made between the trainer acting as an in-house consultant and the need to manage the input of training consultants external to the organization. The former was explicitly rejected as a model for best training practice, though it was recognized that the training manager and trainer would be well advised to develop consultancy skills.

It is now appropriate, in this section on the new processes required in training management, to look at the issues involved in managing the contribution of external consultants. The proportion of training that will be delivered in this way will vary considerably from organization to organization (see, for example, the considerable differences observed in best practice organizations considered in Appendix IV, p. 267). Some will use no external consultants: typically these will be small organizations in the fragmented phase of training sophistication or large ones with extensive in-house training departments. Others, for the reasons outlined later in this chapter, will rely heavily on the contribution of external suppliers.

Some commentators suggest that the use of in-house consultants is likely to increase and indeed *should* increase. In their standard human resource text Torrington and Hall argue that, 'The best combination is for the organization to maintain a strong but lean training operation in-house, while using a substantial proportion of its training budget to deploy external expertise for specific assignments, but this is only possible in a large undertaking that can afford both' (pp. 403–4).[9]

To appreciate why they have reached this conclusion it is necessary to consider the value that external consultants can bring to the organization.

WHY USE CONSULTANTS?

Generally, consultants should be used if the value that they bring to the organization exceeds their fees. Within the context of this umbrella statement, however, it is possible to distinguish between a number of different types of contribution that they can make, and hence a number of justifications for their use. Before considering these, it should be noted that a growing use of consultants could be consistent with a general organizational trend.

Consultants can bring value to the organization for the following reasons.

First, they can assist the training manager in coping with the peaks and troughs of the demand for training activity. As anyone with practical experience will testify, no amount of planning can achieve a smooth workload for the training department over the year. An upsurge in workload can be caused by:

- a seasonal activity. A good example is the need for performance appraisal training that was identified in Chapter 6. The delivery of one-to-one role-play training sessions outlined there, for example, makes a heavy demand on the trainer's time
- a desire, often emanating from senior management, that all staff should undergo a particular type of training. A good example is a programme designed to have a significant effect on an organization's culture. Once this is requested, the emphasis is likely to be on speed of delivery and rapid throughput
- the greater than anticipated success of a particular programme leading to demands for repeats or extensions.

If the staffing of the training department is set at a level high enough to resource these demands internally, there will be periods of underemployment. It is precisely when these occur, and are disguised by spurious activity, that the training function's reputation suffers – not least in the perception of other human resource professionals.

The second reason why consultants are of potential value to the organization is the specialist expertise that they can bring. So far the terms 'consultants' and 'suppliers' have been used without distinction to describe external providers of training. Where this amounts to more than simply an extra pair of hands, the word 'consultant' is to be preferred to supplier; this term suggests some additional added value. The type of expertise must obviously depend on the type of organization, but it may well lie in the technical/functional area rather than in the area of management and interpersonal skills. The technical/functional requirements of the organization are likely to demand a very specific expertise and to change far more rapidly; the management and interpersonal skills requirements are more stable and are the stock-in-trade of most trainers. Many organizations have attempted to deal with the need for technical training by identifying line managers with a knowledge of the area and transferring them, or seconding them, to the training department. Sometimes this can be most successful; sometimes it can cause difficulties of acceptance and credibility. A serious problem arises if an in-house technical trainer is perceived by line management to be lacking in expertise or knowledge.

The third reason why consultants can add value is the sharpness of focus they can bring to the training process. This can arise in a number of ways. A decision to introduce an external consultant causes the organization to work at a number of issues on the type of training required. The training programme delivered by an external consultant can be sold internally as far more of an event – and more commitment can thus be secured from participants and their line managers. The ideas and thoughts that external consultants bring into the organization can provide a refreshing stimulus to the rest of the work of the training department.

The relationship between the training manager and the consultant is not without its problems. Before they are considered, however, I think it is helpful to identify two different ways in which consultants can be used and enlarge on the distinction already indicated.

SUPPLIERS AND CHANGE AGENTS

The above heading indicates polar opposites of the role that outside organizations or individuals can play in assisting with the provision of training.

On the one hand, a supplier can be employed by the organization as a provider with a tight remit and limited scope. An extreme case is the external supplier brought in for role-play training – for example, the one-to-one performance appraisal training described in Chapter 6. The significant feature here is that the individual is working firmly to the training manager's specification and is responsible for delivery but not design.

On the other hand, a consultant can be brought in to deliver a programme which addresses issues of cultural change. Many of these have been concerned with increasing customer awareness, or issues raised by the changed status of the organization (for example, privatization) or, more recently, total quality management. British Airways (on customer care) and British Telecom (on quality management) have undertaken such programmes, as has Anglia Railways, whose case study I presented in Chapter 4 (pp. 85–7). Often such projects are not regarded as training activities; they are the special concern of a chief executive and are managed by his or her office. Invariably, however, they contain a substantial training element and have implications for the training department. Here the consultancy is involved in both design and delivery.

These polar opposites raise some important issues in the management of the consultancy process. In the latter case, where consultants are used as change agents, they offer far more added value for the organization – a fact that is understandably reflected in their fees. A need here is to ensure that such added value is retained within the organization rather than being an ephemeral injection with limited long-run impact – the 'sheep-dip' of cultural change. It is therefore necessary that the training department arranges with the consultancy whereby there is an in-house capacity at a later date to deliver aspects of the programme or to reinforce it.

When an external supplier is simply working as a provider under the direction of the training manager, the management issues are more straightforward. However, there are few external bodies – whatever service they offer – who would not claim that they could give far more value to the organization if they were more closely involved in training management.

CHOOSING CONSULTANTS

It is essential that the training manager feels comfortable with his or her suppliers or consultants. In general terms external consultants should be good enough to cope with tough organizational cultures – quickly, cheaply and without too much hand-holding. Too many consultants are poor at fitting in culturally and also may wish to bring their own pet theories or solutions. The process of initial change is of vital importance and can be divided into the following stages:

- agreement of specification
- identification and choice of supplier
- formulation of programme
- selection and agreement.

Useful information, and a series of practical checklists, on managing all stages of process are set out in Bailey and Sproston's *Choosing and Using Training Consultants.*[10]

In determining the choice of consultants, it is important to consider which of these reasons discussed have led to the decision to outsource the training activity. Certainly, for some tasks, there are large numbers of consultants available; for others, where special expertise is required, the choice is more limited. Because low investment is required to become a consultant, the barriers to entry into these markets are easy to overcome. A training manager, in serving the needs of his or her organization, must ask what is involved in securing value from external consultants.

Figure 7.2 should make it easier to determine value for money. It is presented as a two-by-two matrix (sometimes called a Boston Box after the Boston Consulting Group who used a two variable classification in strategy analysis).

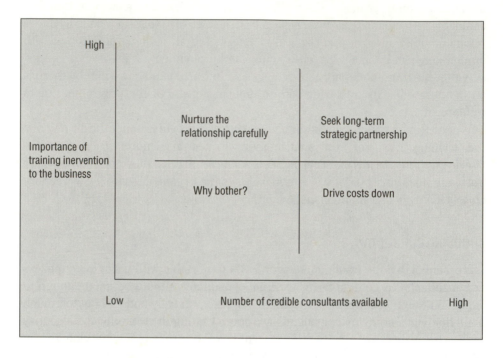

Figure 7.2   Using external consultants: determining value for money

The first point to note is that the more difficult area for the training manager to select and direct consultants is the left-hand side (the south-west and north-west corners). The fewer the potential consultants the more difficult the choice, and the training manager's power to demand customization of programmes is reduced. The most difficult area is where the activity or product delivered to the consultant is of high strategic importance to the business. A good example, drawn from my own experience in investment banking, is the provision of training for security traders in complex financial option and derivative products. In the early 1990s this was of paramount importance to the future diversification of the business – yet only a handful of external suppliers had the credibility to deliver such training. All were in demand from competition and were well aware of their relative power and market value. Respectful, almost kid-glove treatment, was required. However, if there are few suppliers and the activity and product is not important to the business, the value of the training intervention is questionable – the south-west box quadrant is therefore labelled 'Why bother?'

As the number of credible consultants increases so the training manager's task becomes easier. The power balance has tilted in his or her direction. This provides an opportunity in two respects. For interventions that are important to the business there is scope for careful selection and for developing long-term collaborative or strategic partnership. In this arrangement the external supplier will be expected to have a good awareness of, and sensitivity to, client needs. There may be an opportunity to enter into an exclusive contract.

The best scope for driving down rates lies in the bottom right-hand or south-east corner. Here there are plenty of suppliers and the intervention is not of strategic importance. This could apply to a range of low-level inter-personal or soft skills training: interviewing skills, assertiveness skills, or time management. There is an opportunity for negotiating good rates and volume discounts here. Beware the external consultant who seeks a premium for special expertise or charges development costs so they may gain a unique understanding of the organization's requirements – the latter is the training manager's job.

Once the decision to use a consultant has been made, the next stage is the specification. This involves the determination and outline of the consultancy intervention. Beyond this general statement the varying circumstances make it hard to be detailed. Some specifications derive from a need identified by line managers (for example, training in a specific computer system or other technical training); others from the training manager (for example, a recognition that more creative thinking would be of benefit). The general principle that line management should be involved at an early stage applies in both cases; even when a training need is identified exclusively within the training department, the active participation of line management in the specification will be of benefit, a topic developed in the next section.

It is at the specification stage that the choice between the use of external consultants and resourcing in-house must be made. Complex formulas are rarely necessary. Essentially the first question is whether the in-house trainers have the ability to deliver; if so, it is then a question whether they have the capacity. Only subsequently do economic calculations become relevant. Few in-house training establishments can deliver a course on the interpretation of European accounts; but most are capable of delivering a course on interview skills training. The second stage is to consider the managerial cost of the in-house trainer's time against the day rate charged by the consultant. An illustrative calculation is set out as Figure 7.3.

Once a decision has been made to resource the training event externally, the next stage is to identify suitable suppliers. Larger organizations will have an existing pool of preferred individuals or companies, who will be able to deliver within their appropriate range at a standard day rate. If it is necessary to find new external

At the time of writing, consultancy rates for standard interpersonal skills training (such as presentational skills) typically vary between £700 + VAT and £1 500 + VAT per day. Open courses run by external agencies lie in the range of £500–£600 + VAT per person. Assuming the in-house trainer is paid £30 000 per annum, after adding 40 per cent for on-costs, and assuming an availability of 200 working days a year, this implies a daily opportunity cost of £175. The choice on the delivery of the two-day training event for six participants, therefore, lies between:

- an external supplier at, say, £1 600 + VAT (£800 per day × 2) and the cost of hiring premises and equipment if not already available
- sending the six participants on an external course at £3 000 + VAT (£500 per participant, though bulk discounts may apply)
- delivering in-house at an opportunity cost of £350 (£175 per day× 2) and the cost of premises and equipment if not available.

A first glance suggests that it would always be easier to resource in-house; the simple calculation above is the justification for maintaining a training department. However, the training department may not always be able to deliver at the appropriate time and the external supplier could well have superior expertise. Such a calculation should always be made, but the most important question wil be without fail the effectiveness of the training.

Figure 7.3 Alternative costs of training delivery: an illustrative calculation

suppliers or consultants there are two ways of proceeding: published sources (for example, the National Training Index) and personal recommendations. The second source is as effective as the training manager's network of contacts. If he or she is active in the very accessible professional networks, assembling a list of potential suppliers should be straightforward.

Once suitable suppliers have been identified, the training manager can issue a programme outline or invitation to tender. Undoubtedly the supplier would wish to develop such a specification and offer alternative perspectives and recommended approaches – he or she should be encouraged in this activity as a way of adding value. However, the training manager must not abdicate responsibility for training events for which he or she carries accountability within the organization.

Selection and agreement, the final stage of the process, is the most straightforward and follows as a consequence of the previous three. Where possible line managers should be involved, and I consider this in the next section.

INVOLVING LINE MANAGEMENT

By this stage the need to increase the involvement of line managers in training activity will have been accepted. A brief summary of the advantages of greater involvement of line managers at the design and delivery stage, however, embraces the following factors:

- involving line managers in the design and delivery of training improves their awareness of the potential benefits of training and its inherent limitations. The organization's appreciation of training is thus enhanced

- more immediately, the quality of any training event is improved if an appropriate line manager owns the event. He or she will ensure committed attendance from participants, and effective post-course reinforcement will occur
- the potential participation of line managers as trainers adds weight to any training event; it emphasizes its relevance to ongoing activity in the workplace; it adds variety to the event and may identify hidden talents among the managers and increase their confidence.

Assuming that the organization is making use of consultants to contribute to the training effort on anything other than an occasional *ad-hoc* basis, the management of the consultancy process offers the training manager a valuable opportunity to define his or her relationship with line management. In particular, the consultancy relationship can actively encourage the responsibility and responsiveness of line management; in this way it can help the organization to develop a more sophisticated approach to training.

This can be achieved by formalizing the relationship of the consultant within the organization and explicitly involving relevant line management in the choice of the supplier. There are considerable benefits to all parties if the line manager whose staff are to be trained is involved in preparing a specification that is used as the basis for a competitive tendering process usually known by consultancy firms as a 'beauty parade'. The procedure is quite simple. First, a specification is prepared giving broad indications of what is required: Figure 7.4 reproduces a specification for a short event designed for developing creative thinking.

Three or four suitable consultants/suppliers would then be shortlisted, invited to submit costed proposals and to present details of their approach, background and experience to the relevant line manager and training manager.

As anyone with experience of such a process will confirm, it is remarkable how such presentations clarify the purpose and potential for this type of training event – thus enabling the line manager, who is acting as product champion, to express more fully what he or she had in mind. This serves to emphasize the place of supply-side as well as demand-led activity in training design.

One of the problems with implementing such a transparent process is a degree of coyness that is present in some trainers about the use of the consultants. This must be dealt with by controlling the consultants rather than letting them have control. Few sensible consultants object to the use of competitive tender procedures (and most of those that do should be avoided); most consultants or external suppliers welcome the opportunity to match needs against specifications – and would use the opportunity to develop the specification. Most consultants are prepared to be transparent about their pricing policy and it is in the broader interest of the training community that such transparency is encouraged.

DEVELOPING NEW PRODUCTS THROUGH CREATIVE TECHNIQUES

(Description of the organization's size and scope.)

There are indication that the potential synergy between the different activities has not yet been fully realized. There are opportunities for increased cross-selling and, more importantly, for developing new and innovative products drawing on the widest expertise within the Division.

Accordingly, you are invited to indicate your interest in facilitating a series of new product workshops.

The design and extent of the workshops is a matter for the consultant but as an indication we would expect the workshops:

a) to involve 8/10 senior professionals at a time
b) to last about 24 hours and to be held at a residential centre.

At this stage our approach is still in its early stages but we would be pleased to learn if you feel equipped to deliver on this basis. If so, could you indicate:

a) your preferred design for the activity – please feel free to depart from the outline suggested above
b) an indication of your favoured approach
c) an estimate of the costs involved
d) some outline details of the staff who would act as facilitators.

Please feel free to contact (Name and Telephone Number).

Figure 7.4   Illustrative course specification for external suppliers

The training manager should be wary of consultancy firms that refuse to participate in competitive tender procedures or to disclose their day rates. It is astonishing how shy some training managers can be in requesting the latter. Most experienced training managers will have heard consultants justify excessive day rates on the ground that they alone can offer a real understanding of the client organization's needs; some accompany this with a request for paid exploratory work to improve this understanding.

If a note of cynicism appears in the above paragraph, I hope that the reader will excuse it as a reaction to overselling by consultants. Undoubtedly, training consultants and suppliers have a great deal to offer the organization, and better services are usually reflected in higher prices – in general, the market rules. However, it is in the interest of the wider training community and training managers in particular to improve the efficiency of the market by ensuring that better information (and open pricing) brings about better 'market clearance' – a closer match between supply and demand.

OPPORTUNITIES AND THREATS

Joint design of the specification for an external provider can be regarded as an opportunity offered by the use of consultants. It can assist in building the relationship with line management. If this presents an opportunity, threats may occur if the consultant does not respect and appreciate the training manager's position in the process and his or her responsibilities for overall training strategy. There are two connected problems here: what can be called the boundary issue, and issues surrounding selling on within the organization.

The boundary issue relates to the training manager's accountability. Because he or she carries managerial responsibility for obtaining the maximum leverage for training spend, it must be his or her judgement on where there is potential for adding value through training. The training manager should be as forthright in discouraging and preventing some training activities as in encouraging others. A real danger to this role arises if, as is particularly possible in heavily decentralized organizations, consultants or suppliers attempt to engage in direct selling to line managers without the training manager's knowledge and acquiescence. The need to prevent such activity is discussed in the later section on the Code of Behaviour. This is not simply a matter of petulance or pique on the part of the training manager – though few problems can cause quite so much avoidable irritation. It arises because *ad hoc* training activities can severely inhibit the development of a coordinated training strategy for the organization as a whole. One of the main tenets of consultancy practice is that the client owns the problem while the consultant offers independent advice or delivers a defined service. By choosing to work as consultants the suppliers are outside the organizational boundary, however valued their services and close their relationship with the training department.

The corresponding danger of the abuse of the consultancy relationship by the training manager must also be avoided. It takes a different form. In particular, training managers must avoid exploiting the consultant's enthusiasm and, as has happened in recent times, a regrettable anxiety to go to considerable unpaid efforts to obtain work.

There are, for example, obvious attractions for the training manager to get consultants to do his or her thinking. For example, if four or five consultants were invited to submit proposals for an interviewing training programme for members of staff involved in graduate recruitment, the combined product that arrived on the training manager's desk would be comprehensive and stimulating. It would also, if the training manager had the resources, provide a sufficient course outline for internal delivery. To act in this way would be unethical.

A subtler manifestation of this practice is to invite too many organizations to submit complex proposals or attend a 'beauty parade'. Parts of the public sector, particularly local authorities, have been considered to engage in such practices

To some extent this can be seen as the training manager playing safe and being over-anxious to ensure that tender procedures are satisfied. For major consultancy contracts the production of pre-qualification documents (a short statement indicating previous relevant experience and other facts indicating suitability for the assignment in question), followed by an initial exploratory meeting (the survey meeting) with selected consultants, some of whom will then submit detailed tenders, is acceptable practice. To invite consultants to put time and energy into fruitless activity is wrong.

What is at issue is that the training manager must not invite consultants to engage in activity where there are no reasonable prospects of paid work resulting. At all stages of the relationship, therefore, it is incumbent on the manager to be open and forthcoming on these prospects. In the later 1980s and early 1990s there has been an increase in the number of consultants, reflecting the fragmentation of some of the larger consultancy firms, the growing attractiveness of the activity to independent-minded professionals, and (often regrettably) involuntary consultancy engaged in by former in-house trainers following redundancy. Anecdotal evidence only is available, but there has been a consequent upsurge in cold canvass calling and expensive brochures arriving in many training departments. The temptation to agree to initial meetings and, more importantly, to accept corporate hospitality, must be resisted if there is no serious prospect of the relationship developing profitably for the consultant. Given the capability of the good consultants to generate suggestions and offer insights in ways that can add considerable value to the organization, the above may appear to be unduly harsh. However, if Torrington and Hall[9] are right in their view of the best way forward for the training function, effective management of the consultancy relationship is essential. This will require discipline on the part of the training professional.

All the above is summarized in Figure 7.5, which is presented as a code of behaviour for an effective relationship between training manager and consultant.

TECHNOLOGY-BASED TRAINING AND DISTANCE LEARNING

Summary: *Traditional wisdom suggests that changes in the design and delivery of training events should be demand-led – deriving solely from identified business needs. However, some supply-led activity may be beneficial, and technology-based products offer opportunities for the trainer. It is important to keep abreast of developments and recognize that technology is a tool rather than a panacea.*

It could be argued that the opportunities presented by technological advances could bring about major changes in training: new technologies offer more than simply better training aids; potentially they could lead to a totally new approach to

Building an effective relationship with external consultants who deliver training events or otherwise support the training effort requires

the TRAINING MANAGER to

- produce a clear specification of what is required from a consultancy input
- avoid exploiting the consultant by requesting effort where there is no prospect of paid work
- be open and forthcoming on the prospects for paid work
- ensure that all bills are paid promptly

and the CONSULTANT to

- respect the boundaries of the relationship, and to recognize that the training manager is ultimately accountable for the quality of the training event
- keep the training manager aware of contacts with the organization and to desist from trying to sell directly to line managers without approval
- provide reasonable information on price structures.

Figure 7.5   **A code of behaviour for working with external consultants**

delivery. A reappraisal of the role of training could be driven by the changing techniques available to trainers.

Supply-led changes run contrary to the way in which training delivery has traditionally been viewed. Changes in approach should be demand-led, the changing needs of the business determining the appropriate reaction from the trainer. However, as soon as it is accepted that the training function has a role in articulating, as well as responding to, training needs, some supply-led activity is not only inevitable but potentially beneficial. New techniques, by raising line management awareness of training possibilities, may make a wider contribution through gaining acceptance for increased training activity.

Few developments in training have attracted as much attention in recent years as technology-based training and the opportunity that these new approaches create for distance learning. Some initiatives have received high profile media attention; some have been the subject of aggressive marketing campaigns. Among the initiatives are:

- the growing release of training products delivered on computer disks/videos and CD ROMs
- the potential attractions of delivering training through the internet or intranet (where networks are on an organization's computers with access restricted to authorized users)
- the establishment of internal learning resource centres which provide a comprehensive range of technology-based products available for employees on demand.

- the growing publicity on corporate universities which may or not have a distance learning aspect.

In addition, at the time of writing, the Government is making the University for Industry a significant component of its employment and training strategy (see Appendix II, p. 263).

Such initiatives have dramatically increased the potential leverage of the trainer in the organization and open up a number of new and more sophisticated options for learning. These developments, and the opportunities they afford, are considered in a plethora of books and articles on the new technology and its application. A most valuable guide was published in 1998 by the Institute of Personnel and Development (IPD),[11] and contains a glossary of terms, guidance and advice and case studies giving four different examples of successful use. This book will not duplicate such discussions and analysis but instead will attempt to place the technological developments in some overall context.

A starting point for this analysis is the proposition that new technology offers an opportunity in tailoring and designing training interventions for the individual learner. This statement might seem, at first, to conflict with accepted wisdom on technology-based training. Surely its main advantage is the cheap mass reproduction of user-friendly learning material – for example, the easy availability of computer-based training disks and videos at multiple outlets within the company? This is true but only part of the picture. Sending disks and videos to the high street shop or building society branch is no different in character from sending a large workbook.

The reasons why technology-based training offers a new opportunity for the trainer, and deserves a section in this chapter, stem from its flexibility and ease of access to the user. In addition, the new sophisticated products allow an element of choice. Computer-managed learning environments have gone far beyond the 'linear video' (a workbook on the screen).

Technology-based training (TBT) (which, as the IPD Guide[11] notes is sometimes used as an alternative phrase for CBT (computer-based training)) includes audio, video, telephone or video conferencing as well as CBT. Figure 7.6 summarizes the advantages and disadvantages of TBT as a training method.

A cursory inspection of Figure 7.6 suggests, to quote from a useful article, that:

> the most effective application of CBT is in a situation where there are a limited number of correct variables and where the right response is clear cut, such as imparting factual information, be it product knowledge or corporate systems. In situations where you might say that the 'correctness' is more relative, such as in developing interpersonal or complicated business decision-making skills, it is of significantly less value.[12]

In short, technology-based training is a valuable vehicle for learning technical skills, particularly where a large population is involved, or a changing population

---

ADVANTAGES OF TBT

- it enables learners to study at a time of their own choosing
- it enables learners to study at their own pace
- it can offer a high level of interaction with immediate feedback
- it provides opportunities for learners to check their understanding
- it can be made readily available at different locations and offers privacy
- it is versatile when it comes to on-screen display of information
- it can keep student records automatically
- it can be cost-effective, depending on the circumstances.

DISADVANTAGES OF TBT

- it is relatively inflexible, depending on a pre-produced program
- it requires a greater self-discipline and commitment by the manager or individual, since there is no trainer or peer group present to ensure participation
- it may induce a sense of isolation as individuals work on their own
- it does not permit direct personal reinforcement and hence the motivational effects of training are forgone
- it can prove costly as expensive hardware is required and if tailored, as opposed to generic, programs are required.

(Adapted from Lawar (see Ref. 12) and Wynn (see Ref. 13).)

Figure 7.6   Advantages and disadvantages of technology-based training

with people entering the organization at different times. Simple TBT is of limited value, however, in teaching soft skills such as communication, teamwork or decision-making.

More sophisticated opportunities are emerging from the development of new techniques. The training and learning opportunities, however, arise as a consequence of the technological developments; the primary driving force behind such developments is always the broader business use. The training manager's task is, therefore, to ensure that where new technology has potential value in the training arena this is given full consideration at the design stage.

It is understandable that such developments have created interest among training managers and trainers. However, some caution is necessary in reviewing the opportunities made available. First, because for many trainers, technology is fascinating for its own sake; there can be a tendency to use the new equipment just to show what it can do, when alternative, more everyday, methods would be equally effective and much cheaper. Second, the impetus for change comes from new technologies developed elsewhere, which are then adapted to training situations; it does not come from trainers defining requirements and then seeking new solutions by designing appropriate technology.

If properly managed and introduced, however, technology-based training offers a new opportunity for the trainer because of its flexibility and ease of access. It can permit training which is more accessible, quicker, more effective and better related to user needs. It must, however, be integrated with other forms of training delivery and should never be viewed in isolation.

To some readers the above discussion may appear timid and cautious. Nevertheless,the survey of best practice organizations undertaken for this book (see Appendix IV, p. 269) showed that very few organizations had wholeheartedly embraced technology as a means of delivery. The use of technology was an area of concern and interest – but few respondents displayed confidence in their current provision.

Undoubtedly some training managers believe that technology-based training delivered through distance learning contains the seeds to rewrite the rules of training. At an extreme, the new opportunity may bring about the demise of course-based training. This is most unlikely, but two initiatives which have received high-profile attention deserve close attention.

The first is the potential offered by the intranet: this has already been defined as the use of internet technology to network an organization's computers, with restricted access to authorized users. The Ford Motor Company, an organization with a record for innovation in training, has invested heavily in learning resource centres. It is now investigating the potential to deliver training to its dispersed workforce and suppliers using an intranet. This is described in an issue of *Employee Development Bulletin*,[14] which discusses the history and potential of intranets delivered training more fully.

The second high profile initiative is the publicity surrounding the concept of the Corporate University. Companies in very different sections of the economy have received attention: Motorola, Unipart, McDonalds and British Aerospace are examples of organizations using the term.

The concept of the Corporate University is, at the time of writing, somewhat elusive and ill-defined. The term can be used to describe an association between a company and a business school to provide ready access to training for employees and a collaborative approach to development. The term can also be used to describe in-house facilities that produce comprehensive training for employees: these can be based on delivery through technology (for example using the intranet); it can involve open, or unrestricted, access to all facilities for a wide range of employees. At the least ambitious the term can be used to describe a rebadging and relaundering of existing training, a partnership with a business school, and the purchase of some CBT material.

Time alone will demonstrate the significance of such initiatives. However, the link between training and technology is of critical importance to the development of the training profession and the following section, on knowledge management, will consider another aspect of this link.

TRAINING AND KNOWLEDGE MANAGEMENT

Summary: *Knowledge management, which can be defined as the art of creating value from an organization's intangible assets, is a new and exciting topic. It has a great deal to contribute to the new competitive model. While the links with training practice are still emerging, it is possible to identify a number of potential contributions from training.*

A key element of the new competitive model is that competitive advantage can be achieved through the skills and knowledge of a sophisticated workforce (see Figure 1.1, page 6). What is required is to ensure that the capability of the workforce is not only developed (an evident role for the training function) but that it is harnessed across the organization. This underlying theme, expressed in different forms, appeared in a number of guises in the review of the output from management thinkers considered in Chapter 1. It was, for example, integral to Hamel and Prahalad's concept of core competencies. As was also noted, (in Chapter 1, p. 16), Charles Handy talked of the 'Triple I' organization in which competitive advantage is based in knowledge and the ability to use that knowledge.

This broad concept has given rise to an emerging activity in which the 'knowledge initiatives' are multiplying to gain maximum advantage in 'knowledge creation'. 'Knowledge management' is now seen as a vital organizational task and 'knowledge officers' are appointed to oversee the process. What does all this mean for the training professional? In this section the underlying concept will be considered further and some practical guidance suggested. However, a word of warning is necessary. This area is developing rapidly and, more so than any other topic considered in this book, new ideas will emerge and new practical approaches to knowledge management will be formulated and articulated.

The concept of most practical value to the trainer is that of knowledge management. This will be defined more fully later in this section, but at this stage it can be regarded as a systematic attempt to chart, cultivate and promote an organization's intellectual assets. The fashion for knowledge management has reflected a desire to ensure that someone is looking after the intellectual capital. Such assets are intangible, but they are important. Andrew Mayo, a leading UK author and consultant and former Director of Personnel at ICL Europe, has argued that:

> The most commonly understood components of [the value of a business] are tangible: fixed assets and other money-related items that appear on the balance sheet. But in almost all organisations, these tangible assets represent less than half, and sometimes as little as 5 per cent, of the true valuation. Even heavily capital-intensive companies find that two-thirds of their value lies in intangible assets – intangible in that they are hard to measure and sometimes difficult to hang on to (p. 34).[15]

Part of these intangible assets that make up the market value of an organization can be described as intellectual capital. This has been defined by Tom Stewart as 'the sum of everything everybody in a company knows that gives it a competitive edge'. In his seminal book,[16] Stewart identifies three sorts of capital: human capital (broadly the individual competence of the organization's employees), structural capital (the internal structures that make the organization work) and customer capital (the organization's relationships with its customers). It is beyond dispute that training and development must have a role to play in developing an organization's intellectual capital by adding to the capability of the individual employees. Intellectual capital, while a useful concept, is only of value to the organization when it is applied. This leads to the concept of knowledge management.

A powerful case for knowledge management was offered by Ikujiro Nonaka in an influential *Harvard Business Review* article and a subsequent book.[17,18] Nonaka, who has become the first Professor of Knowledge (at Berkeley, California), based his approach on an examination of companies who are 'Famous for their ability to respond quickly to customers, create new markets, rapidly develop new products, and dominate emergent technologies. The secret of their success is their unique approach to managing the creation of new knowledge' (pp. 96–7).[17]

The second sentence from the above quotation indicates one of the possible sources of confusion. There is a difference between managing the creation of new knowledge and managing the organizational effectiveness of the existing knowledge. This distinction has important implications for the contribution that could be expected from the training function.

According to Nonaka, new knowledge always starts with the individual and the task is to make that personal knowledge available to others. Some knowledge is explicit: this is formal and systematic and can easily be communicated and shared ('in product specifications or a scientific formula or a computer program'). Another sort of knowledge is highly personal: tacit knowledge is hard to formalize and, therefore, difficult to communicate to others. Tacit knowledge consists 'partly of technical skills – the kind of hard-to-pin-down skills captured in the term "know-how"'. It also consists of 'mental models, beliefs and perspectives so ingrained that we take them for granted, and therefore cannot easily articulate them' (p. 98).

In any organization knowledge can be created in a number of different ways (tacit to tacit, explicit to explicit, tacit to explicit, explicit to tacit). However, it is the knowledge creation process involved in making tacit knowledge explicit that has direct implications for organizational design and managerial roles and responsibilities. If the structures and practices are appropriate, managers can synthesize the company's tacit knowledge, make it explicit and incorporate in into new technologies and products.

Nonaka's approach is based on creating an appropriate organizational culture, so that knowledge creation can be seen as key and is embedded in processes and systems. Some Japanese companies, from which he draws many of his examples, put 'knowledge creation exactly where it belongs: at the very centre of a company's human resources strategy' (p. 97).[17] His approach does, however, set him apart from many other writers on knowledge in two respects. First, he shows far less interest in information technology. Knowledge creation is not equated with the establishment of computer databases storing and sharing facts. Second, he argues that Japanese companies succeed because there is a conscious overlapping of information, business activities and managerial responsibility. A tight organization with no slack is inimical to knowledge creation.

From this brief exposition of Nonaka's work, it is evident that knowledge creation and knowledge management are two subtly different concepts. Karl Sveiby, a prominent writer on the topic,[19] defines knowledge management as 'the art of creating value from an organization's intangible assets'. In his useful web site (http://www.sveiby.com.au) he has collected information on a series of knowledge management initiatives undertaken by companies and practitioners. The headings that he uses to classify them reflect his own approach to measuring and presenting intangible assets: the Intangible Asset Monitor. This approach, which gives a good indication of the range of interventions which can be included under the heading of knowledge management initiatives, is set out in Figure 7.7.

As Sveiby's taxonomy demonstrates, the boundaries of knowledge management are potentially very broad indeed – ranging from approaches to mass marketing through to the innovative use of mentors. Most of the initiatives that are currently being described in the training literature, however, fall under the

---

EXTERNAL STRUCTURE INITIATIVES

- gain knowledge from customers
- offer customers additional knowledge

INTERNAL STRUCTURE INITIATIVES

- build knowledge sharing culture
- create new revenues from existing knowledge
- capture individual's tacit knowledge, store it, spread it and reuse it
- measure knowledge creating processes and intangible assets

COMPETENCE INITIATIVES

- create careers based on knowledge management
- create micro environment for tacit knowledge transfer
- learn from simulators and pilot installations

(Reproduced with permission from Karl Sveiby.)

Figure 7.7 Knowledge management initiatives: Sveiby's classification

categories of building a knowledge-sharing culture and capturing, storing and spreading individuals' tacit knowledge. The latter is often seen in terms of creating databases to capture existing knowledge and best practice. The former involves creating an attitude within the organization that encourages the development of the latter. A good and accessible example was contained in an article by Elizabeth Lank, Programme Director, Knowledge Management, at ICL.[20] In this article she describes how, as a business imperative, a new project including a café-style information service was set up to develop a knowledge-sharing culture. The new technologies could make knowledge accessible throughout the organization.

A project undertaken by the Open University Business School team, who were developing a course in Managing Knowledge, also provided a broad overview[21] of initiatives following a search of web sites. They then offered the following comprehensive definition:

> Knowledge management is the process of continually managing knowledge of all kinds to meet existing and emerging needs, to identify and exploit existing and acquired knowledge assets and to develop new opportunities (p. 387).

A whole series of activities can take place designed to support this process, including the following people aspects:

> training, development, recruitment, motivation, retention, organization, job design, cultural change and the encouragement of thinking, participation and creativity, and the management of all types of employment contract (p. 388).

The above appears to embrace almost the whole of human resource activity!

Knowledge management must help make a reality of the new competitive model (see Figure 1.1, p. 6). This model, it should be recalled, positioned training as fundamental to competitive strategy. Can we offer more guidance to the training professional than simply find out what is going on in knowledge management and try to get involved? More guidance is possible and this is set out in Figure 7.8, which sets out a list of initiatives that the training professional should consider. All are legitimate (and indeed essential) areas for training involvement; which of them are appropriate must depend on the circumstances of the organization.

The list is straightforward and the only item which may need elaboration is the last. The suggestion here is that course-based training can be enhanced by the use of databases at both the pre- and post-course stages. Course material (for example case studies) can be generated from the standard company knowledge management exchanges and made available through an intranet. After the course learning reinforcement can be increased through database discussion using the same medium.

Knowledge management is a hot current topic. Reports and conferences abound. Although partial surveys suggest that more organizations are introducing knowledge management initiatives, the survey of best practice organizations

Depending on the circumstances of the organization and the sophistication of the existing knowledge management infrastructure, the training professional should:

- ensure that adequate familiarization training is given in the knowledge management philosophy and processes – especially at induction
- introduce a specific training initiative in creativity to enhance knowledge generation
- support culture change initiatives which are designed to enhance cross-department transfer of information
- ensure that adequate IT training is in place to support knowledge databases
- introduce pre- and post-course reinforcement of course-based training using database discussion sites linked to existing knowledge systems.

Figure 7.8   Potential contribution from training to knowledge management

undertaken for this book (see Appendix IV, p. 269) produced little evidence of significant current initiatives. As is depressingly often the case, the ownership of publicized projects seems to be outside training or human resources. The Institute of Personnel and Development is, at the time of writing, making knowledge management a priority and significant guidance is likely to emerge. Ultimately, however, it is down to the individual practitioner to grasp the opportunity afforded by this new discipline. Resource-based strategy has crept up on the training profession and caught us unawares. It would be a tragedy if the same were true for knowledge management.

REFERENCES

1. Prior J. (ed.) (1994), *Gower Handbook of Training and Development*, Second Edition, Aldershot: Gower.
2. Cannell, M. (1997), 'Practice Makes Perfect', *Personnel Management*, **3** (5), March, and (1997), *On-the-Job Training*, London: Institute of Personnel and Development.
3. Sloman M. (1989), 'On-the-Job Training: A Costly Poor Relation', *Personnel Management*, **21** (2), February.
4. Internal Ernst & Young Paper, *The Helping Process: Coaching Counselling & Mentoring*. I am grateful to my colleague Mike Laws for permission to reproduce his work.
5. Coleman, J. (1997), 'Coaching and its Role in Senior Management Development, Organization & People', 4.3, pp.37–9. I am also grateful to Peter Hogarth his colleague at The Change Partnership, for his ideas.
6. *Equality Training: an EOR survey of employer provision* (1991) EOR No. 37, May/June, and *Case Studies in Equality Training* (1991), EOR No. 39, September/October.
7. Garrett, H. and Taylor, J. (1993), *How to Design and Deliver Equal Opportunities Training*, London: Kogan Page.
8. 'Training: Implementating racial equality at work, a curriculum guide', London: CRE, summarized in EOR No. 39, September/October, 1991.
9. Torrington, D. and Hall, L. (1991), *Personnel Management: A new approach*, London: Prentice Hall.
10. Bailey, D. and Sproston, C. (1993), *Choosing and Using Training Consultants*, Aldershot: Gower.

11. (1998), *The IPD Guide on Training Technology*, London: Institute for Personnel and Development.
12. Lawar, D. (1991), 'CBT – a cost effective option?', *Training Personnel*, **3**, March.
13. Wynn, P. (1991), 'Computer-based training' in Prior, J. (ed.), *Handbook of Training and Development*, Second Edition, Aldershot: Gower.
14. 'Intranets: Delivering Just-in-Time Learning', *Employee Development Bulletin* (1998), **103**, July, pp. 7–12.
15. Mayo, A. (1998), 'Memory Bankers', *Personnel Management*, **4** (2), 22 January, p. 34.
16. Stewart, T. (1997), *Intellectual Capital*, London: Nicholas Brealey.
17. Nonaka, I. (1991), 'The Knowledge Creating Company', *Harvard Business Review*, **69** (6), pp. 96–104.
18. Nonaka, I. and Taakkeuchi, H. (1993), *The Knowledge Creating Company: How Japanese Companies Create the Dynamics of Innovation*, Oxford: Oxford University Press.
19. Sveiby, K.E. (1997), *The New Organizational Wealth*, San Francisco: Berrett-Koehler.
20. Lank, E. (1998), 'Café Society', *People Management*, **4** (4), 19 February.
21. Quintas, P. Lefrere, P. and Jones, G. (1997), 'Knowledge Management: A Strategic Agenda', *Long Range Planning*, **30** (3), pp. 385–91.

8 New approaches to measurement

The need for the training function to demonstrate that spending money on training is justifiable follows as an inevitable consequence of the new human resources.

Measuring the effectiveness of training interventions and the provision of appropriate management is therefore the most important challenge in implementing best training practice. It is also one of the most neglected, both in theory and in practice.

Seeking competitive advantage through people means a higher commitment of resources, of both time and money. In the course of the public debate on the desirability of a compulsory training levy, expenditure figures of 1.5–2 per cent of payroll were suggested as a minimum (see Appendix II, p. 261). In 1994 the Department of Trade and Industry and the Confederation of British Industry suggested that in best practice 'winning' companies as much as 10 per cent of employees' time is spent on training (see Chapter 1, p. 8). The Industrial Society conducts a regular survey of training spend. For the calendar year 1997, they reported that organizations spent an average of 1.12 per cent of their annual turnover on training. Training spend now represents approximately 2.9 per cent of the average organization's wage bill.[1]

If organizations devote substantial resources to training, they need to ensure that value for money is obtained. First, that there is strategy in place to ensure that resources are deployed effectively. Second, that each individual intervention is properly managed and controlled. Both these requirements are discussed in this chapter. The first is wide in scope and concerns measurements and information systems; the second is mainly concerned with training evaluation.

While there is a comprehensive literature on evaluation, comparatively little guidance is available on the place of measurement information systems in training. Textbooks do discuss the importance of training records; budgets and internal pricing receive an occasional mention. However, there is little comprehensive analysis of information systems and their role in effective training management.

OLD ISSUES IN A NEW CONTEXT

Summary: *The need to manage and control training spend has been recognized as important for decades. What is new, however, is that, in the modern organization, responsibility for this process has become diffuse and the process more difficult.*

The following is a simple and unexceptionable statement of the requirement to measure corporate training:

> *Firm-wide training activities should be seen to reflect business needs and strategic priorities. Course-based training activities, must be seen to have a clear relevance to the business. All activities must be undertaken in the most cost-effective way and be monitored and controlled.*

This statement, which is taken from an internal Ernst & Young document, could have been written at any time over the last thirty years. It indicates a need to introduce discipline to ensure that training spend is deployed effectively. What has changed over the last thirty years is that the construction of the appropriate disciplinary framework has become a more complex activity. This has created a major new challenge for the training manager. Indeed, if the traditional expression of responsibility is, 'the training manager's role is to ensure that training courses are appropriately structured using the systematic training model and that rigorous evaluation is undertaken', the modern statement would be 'all those responsible for training must ensure that training interventions meet business requirements in a cost-effective way'. This is a much broader responsibility and one that is more widely shared within the organization.

This different emphasis reflects changing perceptions of the role that training should play, and consequently of the management of the training process. The most significant forces (leading to this revised perception) are:

- greater devolution of responsibility for training decisions to line managers
- the blurring of the boundaries between training and more general business activity
- the wider, sometimes less explicit, objectives of course-based training activity.

The impact of each of these forces will be governed by the circumstances of the particular organization. Less sophisticated companies, where training interventions are fewer, will find that traditional evaluation methods grounded in the systematic training model may suffice. Sophisticated companies, where training is seen as a competitive weapon, will have encountered all the above forces and all three are outlined briefly below.

The devolution of responsibility for training decisions to line managers is now a well-observed trend (see, for example, the Price Waterhouse/Cranfield study discussed in Chapter 2, p. 28) and one that progressive training managers would wish to encourage. The case for such devolution is two-fold: only the business (and the line managers in particular) can be aware of an individual's skills/knowledge deficiencies, and recommend training; if the business and line managers are involved in training decisions they will pay more attention to the training initiative and its effectiveness will consequently increase. There is an important implication here, one which is illustrated in Figure 5.5, p. 108. There the systematic training model is shown as a sequential hierarchy rather than a continuous loop. At the top level, the entry level where training needs are identified, it is reasonable to expect the business and line managers to carry a heavy responsibility – here they may require the advice and support from the training professional, reflecting the latter's particular expertise. However, the business and line managers' acceptance of responsibility will diminish as the training progresses. Certainly the design and implementation of the appropriate evaluation framework will be seen as the job of the training specialist. Line managers will play their role as good corporate citizens (by undertaking post-course briefing, for example), but that is likely to be the extent of their involvement.

The second force which has led to changing perceptions of the role of training concerns blurring of the boundaries between training and more general business activity. This is an inevitable product of the new human resources. The individual must accept greater personal responsibility for self-development and this involves continuously seeking learning opportunities in the workplace. Such learning opportunities may involve no more than the exchange of information with internal specialists. If course-based training is involved, much of the benefit may result through the planned post-course application of what has been learned. It therefore becomes more difficult to try to evaluate the effects of a training event in isolation.

The third force is related and concerns the way in which the objectives of the course-based training have widened. Course-based training events are often seen as opportunities for consolidating organizational objectives – including building a culture and breaking down barriers.

Consider two courses which are part of the Executive Series at Ernst & Young. These are aimed at partners and senior managers (the two most senior levels in the organization), and are three-day events; the training is delivered by a mixture of external business school faculty and internal specialists from Ernst & Young. The aim of the courses is 'to expand participants' commercial skills in support of the business advisory role'; one concentrates on skills, the other on commercial awareness. The learning objectives of the courses can be specified (improved appreciation of the knowledge management system, acquisition of negotiation skills, etc.). However, there are significant cultural objectives that are implicit to the courses and are central to their design. These include: the opportunity for participants who are under consideration for entry into partnership to gain an appreciation of the business challenges facing the firm and how they should be

PLANNING

- training events not linked to business needs
- training delivered at the wrong time in individual's development
- insufficient numbers of participants at training event
- duplication of activity across the business denying opportunity for economies of scale
- lack of awareness in the business leading to non-participation of suitable candidates
- course too long to benefit participants
- poor mix of participants preventing cross-fertilization of ideas.

USE OF EXTERNAL TRAINING CONSULTANTS

- sub standard/inadequate consultants used
- consultants paid too much
- consultants unaware of organization's business needs

PARTICIPANTS

- participants sent on inappropriate courses
- participants cancelling from courses
- no opportunity given to practise knowledge/skills acquired
- inadequate pre-course briefing
- inappropriate prior expectations
- participant does not fully participate in course when present at venue
- participants have received similar training before joining organization.

Figure 8.1 Sources of wasteage and leakage from training

met; the opportunity for networking, building up contacts, leading to the elimination of 'silo' mentality; and the provision of a wider range of products and services to clients. Narrowly-based traditional evaluation methods may fail to recognize these less tangible outcomes often identified by participants as a major benefit of the event. Another benefit, also often missed, is the chance to reflect on the job away from the day-to-day pressures.

Significant spending must always be subject to scrutiny. Training spending is always vulnerable because courses are often highly visible – particularly the more adventurous or ambitious. Moreover, as the process becomes more complex, the potential for leakage or wastage becomes greater. Figure 8.1 gives a list of potential sources of wastage and leakage identified for training courses in Ernst & Young. The challenge for the training manager, therefore, extends beyond ensuring that effective post-course evaluation is in place. It involves the construction of an appropriate framework to ensure the overall effectiveness of the training effort.

A HOLISTIC APPROACH: THE DISCIPLINARY FRAMEWORK

Summary: *The growing complexity of training interventions, and the more diffuse responsibility, is not an excuse for neglect. What is required is a holistic approach based on the concept of a disciplinary framework.*

The management of training in an organization that has adopted the new human resources has become far more complex. This is not an excuse for neglecting a rigorous approach to measurement and evaluation. Because responsibility for this activity has become more diffuse, it has not become any less important. On the contrary, since training spend will be higher and the expectations of the impact from the training activity has become commensurately greater, measurement and evaluation are more important. Best practice organizations (see the survey outlined in Appendix IV, p. 269) are concerned to demonstrate value for money from training. If appropriate controls are not in place, training can become an easy target in any cost-cutting exercise.

Training, however costed, is a significant expense of running the business. Moreover, it is one that, whether presented in a budget or not, is visible to line managers. Training can be perceived as an avoidable expense; one that is easy to cut in hard times. At the very least, attendance at a training event can be postponed and money 'saved'. Nothing causes more embarrassment to the training manager than being unable to answer questions on training spend because the information is not available. This serves to reinforce any underlying prejudice that the hard-bitten manager has that training is a soggy discipline managed unprofessionally.

Any experienced training manager will know that such prejudices abound. It is all too easy to question the relevance and cost of interpersonal skills courses; it is easy for the outsider to regard the training manager's presence on a residential course as a holiday. The zenith of such sentiments may have been achieved in an article in the *Sun* newspaper reproduced in *Personnel Management Plus* (August, 1991):

> A British Rail training manager has given his full support to a culture-building course which was branded 'a huge free booze-up' by a national tabloid newspaper. In a front-page story obtained by reporters working under cover, the *Sun* claimed last month that workers on the course at the Portland Heights Hotel in Dorset had taken part in late-night drinking sessions paid for by British Rail.
>
> Among those quoted was a trainee who dismissed the Myers-Briggs psychometric test he had undergone as 'crap'. Charles Nicholls, total quality manager for BR's South East Region ... said that there were strict guidelines covering the amount of drink provided to trainees. Nicholls said the courses would continue: 'They will not stop us that way. We are going to win.' He claimed that the suggestion in the newspaper that British Rail was spending £4 000 a week on the courses was inaccurate, but he was unable to give the real figure because of commercial confidentiality. He added that the improvement in attitude and culture resulting from the course was reflected in improved staff performance.

Any training professional reading that article would send an enormous wave of fellowfeeling to Mr Nicholls. The course sounds no different from run-of-the-mill training events which take place in thousands of organizations throughout the country. Myers-Briggs, for example, is recognized as one of the most valuable personality instruments available to the training manager. Residential courses facilitate the cross-fertilization of ideas (sometimes over a drink). Against this background the stated costs involved (which were denied by BR as inaccurate) do not appear excessive.

The purpose in reproducing the passage from the *Sun* is that such articles would command a resonance with the less progressive line managers who regard all training as a 'waste of time'. An indication of a clear and responsible attitude to cost-control is therefore indispensable. So, too, is the provision of relevant and valid data on training activity and results for the line manager.

What is required, therefore, is the development and implementation of a framework to ensure the effectiveness of the training effort. Such a disciplinary framework for corporate training spend is more than just evaluation. It involves a considered approach to measuring and monitoring the effectiveness of training, wherever and whenever it occurs within the organization – irrespective of the responsibility for the day-to-day management of implementation. This requires a holistic approach: the creation of a framework or system which is more than the sum of its parts. If the training manager can develop such a disciplinary framework, he or she will have demonstrated a capability and understanding that will enhance the credibility of the role of the function. The disciplinary framework is described in Figure 8.2.

The disciplinary framework is a considered approach to measuring and monitoring the effectiveness of training, whenever and wherever it occurs. Elements of the framework are:

- evaluation
- monitoring/measurement
- reporting.

Figure 8.2   New approaches to measurement: the disciplinary framework

The evaluation of individual training events will continue to be a key element in the disciplinary framework. Changing practice in evaluation will be discussed later. However, two other elements have assumed greater importance: these are the wider monitoring/measurement of training activity and the reporting on training activity. The second of these two elements, reporting, will be considered in Chapter 10, pp. 241–2.

As is to be expected, given the importance of the disciplinary framework, a number of commentators have developed models or approaches. These models have been formulated in the wider business context, or for the human resources function as a whole. One approach which is worthy of consideration is that developed by Jac Fitz-enz of the Saratoga Institute – a performance measurement research and consulting company. Fitz-enz has made a significant contribution to the benchmarking of human resource activity (the comparison of data with similar/best practice inside and outside the company). His thesis was developed in his book *How to Measure Human Resources Management*.[2] His approach is wide in scope and ambition and offers valuable insights on the creation of a disciplinary framework.

Fitz-enz's work is accessible and persuasive. He argues that HR professionals should not only make their function more responsive to organizational changes, they must prove their contribution to the bottom line. This demands the accurate measurement of the efficiency and productivity of all human resource activity.

According to Fitz-enz, organizational success requires the production of performance data in a form that is meaningful to audiences. The plural 'audiences' rather than audience is deliberate. Fitz-enz identifies a number of audiences: the human resources department, other departments and their managers, and senior managers. Given this diverse constituency for the human resource profession, he offers the following advice:

> if you want to be successful over the long-term, you have to do three things well: you have to excel at your job; you have to perform in areas that positively impact the mission and purpose of the larger organisation; and, last, but also very important, you have to be able to use information about your performance to prove to the organisation that you are doing an excellent job and that you should be given whatever it is you are seeking (p. 14).

These words have a resonance for today's training manager. Not only must the job of designing and delivering training be carried out well, but this job must not be undertaken in a silo. Training must have an organizational impact and this impact must be demonstrated. This requires the production and promulgation of the right numbers to the right audiences at the right time.

Fitz-enz's work contains an expression of his view on the positioning of human resources as a partner in the organization. To achieve this the contribution must be measured. A measurement system 'provides a frame of reference that helps management carry out several important responsibilities ... Measurement focuses the staff on important issues; clarifies expectations, involves, motivates and fosters creativity and brings human resources closer to line departments' (pp. 129–30).

Fitz-enz develops a strategic planning system and discusses how the components of the human resources system (pay, benefits, employee relations, career development, etc.) can be measured in the context of this system. Fitz-enz is an advocate of benchmarking but his main contribution to the debate is his development of a holistic approach. His argument is illustrated through a series of 'gems' (he describes these as simple and significant points to remember). A selection of the more important gems that illustrates his approach are set out in Figure 8.3.

- direction and control are impossible without data
- you must understand the business if you expect to add value
- measurement of operating results cannot and need not be as precise as laboratory research
- reports are an opportunity to sell your point of view
- a little information is more valuable than a mountain of data
- we do not need more data, we need to understand how to use the data we have.

Reproduced with permission from J Fitz-enz *How to Measure Human Resources Management*

Figure 8.3   Measuring HRM: some Fitz-enz 'gems'

THE BALANCED SCORECARD

Summary: *Two US academics and consultants have developed a new approach to managing corporate performance though effective information: the Balanced Scorecard. Although its scope extends beyond human resources, it is of considerable interest to the training function.*

The Balanced Scorecard is an approach to using management information as a strategic driver for the organization. It has been formulated by the US academics and consultants Robert Kaplan and David Norton, and was introduced in 1992 in an article in the *Harvard Business Review* (HBR) and subsequently developed in two later HBR articles and in a book published in 1996.[3,4,5,6]

Training managers should be aware of the Balanced Scorecard for the following reasons. First, because it is a concept which has attracted considerable attention in the current management debate: a significant number of leading organizations have adopted it as part of their strategic implementation system. An awareness of the Balanced Scorecard is therefore necessary if the training manager is to be seen as an aware participant in any debate in management tools. Second, and most important, if the training manager's own organization is using the Balanced Scorecard, the provision of training information should be seen as part of the Scorecard. Indeed, if this is not the case, the training manager should be concerned about the importance given to training as a business driver.

There is a third reason for understanding the Balanced Scorecard approach – even if it has not been adopted by the organization and has no advocates among the Board or Senior Managers. A consideration of the Balanced Scorecard offers insights on the importance of management information and its relevance to the strategic process. It helps shed light on what the training managers should seek to provide and why.

In their book, Kaplan and Norton introduce the Balanced Scorecard in the following terms:

> The collision between the irresistible force to build long-range competitive capabilities and the immovable object of the historical-cost financial accounting model has created a new synthesis: the Balanced Scorecard. The Balanced Scorecard retains traditional financial measures. But financial measures tell the story of past events, an adequate story for industrial age companies for which investments in long-term capabilities and customer relationships were not critical for success. These financial measures are inadequate, however, for guiding and evaluating the journey that information age companies must make to create future value through investment in suppliers, employees, processes, technology and innovation (p. 7).[6]

The starting point then, is a recognition that companies competing in the information age need to measure much more than traditional financial/accounting indicators. Organizations need to build and deliver value added to customers and their information systems must focus on the performance indicators that are critical to this process. Financial/accounting indicators should not be discarded, but they are insufficiently comprehensive, therefore:

> The Balanced Scorecard complements financial measures of past performance with measures of the drivers of future performance. The objectives and measures of the Scorecard are derived from an organization's vision and strategy. The objectives and measures view organizational performance from four perspectives: financial, customer, internal business process and learning and growth (p. 8).

It is the Balanced Scorecard's use of the four perspectives (including, significantly, learning and growth) that has captured much attention and helped to make the concept popular. Before discussing this aspect, however, it is important to consider some other implications of the quotations presented immediately above.

The Balanced Scorecard is indeed balanced in the sense that it includes financial and non-financial measures. It is, none the less, primarily a tool aimed at assisting the organization in implementing its strategic objectives. Board-level commitment and Executive Sponsorship are essential if the Scorecard is to be used as its authors advocate. It is not simply a matter of formulating some attractive non-financial measures and monitoring them alongside the financial ones. Kaplan and Norton see the Balanced Scorecard as more than a measurement system. It has evolved into a management system and can become a management philosophy.

The starting point is therefore the key strategic objectives of the business. Aligning and focusing activity is needed to achieve this overall strategy. This demands the identification of the two or three key activities that should occupy the attention of managers and staff in all parts of the organization. The measures must be kept simple if they are to be actionable. The Scorecard is therefore cascaded down and appropriate measures identified at the different levels. Its advocates would therefore claim that it is an important tool for promoting teamworking and for communicating the goals of the organization.

As has been noted, vision and strategy are translated into operational terms using four perspectives (reproduced in Figure 8.4.) This was well expressed in the first (1992) *Harvard Business Review* article, which stated that the Balance Scorecard

> provides answers to four basic questions:
>
> - How do customers see us? (customer perspective)
> - What must we excel at? (internal perspective)
> - Can we continue to improve and create value? (innovation and learning perspective)
> - How do we look to shareholders? (financial perspective) (p. 72).[3]

Kaplan and Norton would argue that this is not a stakeholder perspective – identifying those parties who have an interest or stake in organizational performance from whatever viewpoint. The Scorecard identifies what matters for the strategy and vision and then devises and uses appropriate measures.

Full information and discussions on each of the four perspectives is contained in Kaplan and Norton's 1996 book.[6] It should be observed that 'innovation and learning' in the initial exposition of 1992 had become 'learning and growth' in 1996. This reflects partly a gradual evolution through use, and it is fair to say that individual development has been recognized as of greater importance.

> Ultimately, the ability to meet ambitious targets for financial, customer and internal business process objectives depends upon the organizational capabilities for learning and growth. The enablers for learning and growth come primarily from three sources: employees, systems and organizational alignment. Strategies for superior performance will generally require significant investments in people, systems and processes that build organizational capabilities. Consequently, objectives and measures for these enablers of superior performance in the future should be an integral part of any organization's Balanced Scorecard.
>
> A core group of three employee-based measures – satisfaction, productivity and retention – provide outcome measures from investments in employees, systems, and organizational alignment (p. 146).

SOURCES OF INFORMATION

Summary: *Volumes of training activity and the costs of training will provide the main sources of information for the training manager. For all its deficiencies the number of days' off-the-job training is a most useful measure. Ways of improving data-capture repay investigation and wider yardsticks should be sought. Computerized training information systems can, if introduced and managed effectively, add considerable value.*

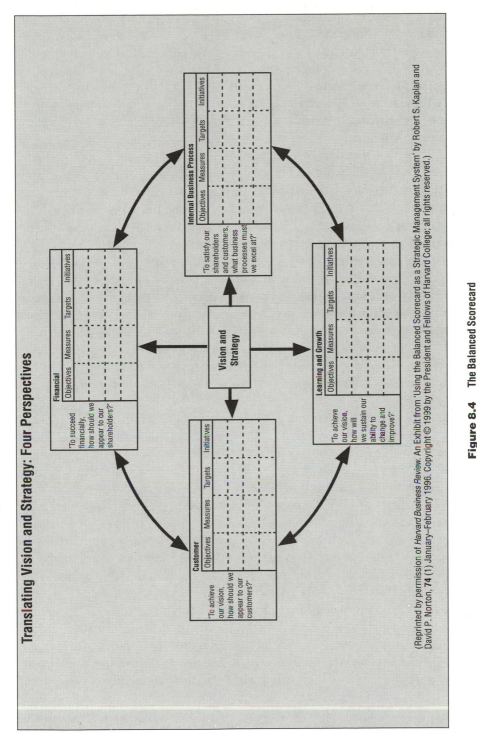

Figure 8.4   The Balanced Scorecard

(Reprinted by permission of *Harvard Business Review*. An Exhibit from 'Using the Balanced Scorecard as a Strategic Management System' by Robert S. Kaplan and David P. Norton, **74** (1) January–February 1996. Copyright © 1999 by the President and Fellows of Harvard College; all rights reserved.)

The training manager must make appropriate information available throughout the organization. This is the third element (reporting) of the disciplinary framework described in Figure 8.2. He or she must provide the data to monitor and control costs and volumes of training activity, and provide feedback for the training function and for line managers.

An inevitable danger in providing information is to concentrate on those aspects of training that are readily capable of measurement. These divide broadly into two categories: volumes and costs.

Most line managers and employees tend to regard training as a series of events. Advocates of the learning organization may regard this as unfortunate, since training should become so integrated into day-to-day activity that the boundary is no longer apparent. This may be true when an organization has achieved a high level of sophistication. Today's reality in the UK is that, for most managers, training events are what can be recognized and hence recorded.

The events that are most easily recognized mainly relate to off-the-job training activities – from residential and non-residential training courses to shorter in-house training modules. Nowadays one might add participation in distance-learning activities that take place with the employer's support. It should be emphasized that this latter category of activity is still properly regarded as off-the-job training – training which takes place away from the employee's normal place of work. Such computer-based training as takes place at the employee's workplace is a marginal category in terms of definition, but is probably best regarded as on-the-job training.

Participation in off-the-job training events, expressed in terms of number of days or hours of training received, is the most accessible training measure. With all its deficiencies as a measure of training sophistication, it is well worth systematic recording. It permits the comparison of training within the organization over time as data is captured on a monthly or quarterly basis, comparison between different business activities or formations and, if treated with caution, comparison with sectoral or national training activity.

There are two main problems with excessive reliance on such a measure. First, in any practical situation there will be an incomplete capture of training events. A well-observed organizational situation is for a central training function to be responsible for the provision of a proportion (often very high) of training activities, and for the data on these activities to be recorded comprehensively. The remaining training activities which are delivered at a decentralized level are not always recorded. Since a training objective is to encourage the ownership of training activities by line managers, paradoxically the more sophisticated the organization the more difficult it is to achieve comprehensive data capture. Partial capture of data is well known to training managers who use training databases for course information; increasingly these are linked to personnel information systems. The information held on such databases often relates to company-wide courses but not one-off events or special courses.

Data obtained on training events initiated by line managers can be captured; if necessary this can be achieved by translating training costs into estimated volumes of training activities.

The second main problem in capturing data on training volumes has already been recognized. What participants recollect, and hence are recordable, are off-the-job training events. Data relating to on-the-job training events and other less clear-cut forms of training activity is far more elusive. As a result, the volume of training activity is likely to be understated. This may not be as much a problem as might appear, because the understatement is likely to be consistent throughout the organization. In general, the higher the level of off-the-job training, the more likely it is that other forms of training will be taking place. Conversely, an absence of off-the-job training is likely to be associated with minimal on-the-job training. Additionally, it is possible to capture data on wider training activity by periodic sampling inside the organization, either through the mechanism of focus groups (described in Chapter 5) or by a full-scale audit of training activities.

The second principal source of accessible data is the cost of training. In almost all organizations (except of course the non-trainers) at least some information is available about the costs of training. It does, however, need to be treated with caution. The extent of the capture of cost information varies according to the approach to training management in the organization concerned.

Two aspects of training management are of particular importance here: the extent to which training budgets are maintained; and whether a system of charging for internal courses is implemented (with the costs of attendance at training courses delivered by in-house trainers being charged back proportionately to the participant's division). If both budgets and internal charging operate, the opportunities for constructing effective information systems from cost-data are considerable; if neither, there is nevertheless likely to be some cost information available. All organizations (if they do nothing else) record, monitor and maintain invoices, and those relating to participation at training courses (often including accommodation and travel) and the services of training consultants will be available. If they are not already monitored by the training function (and the question should then be asked 'why not?'), they will repay detailed examination.

Moreover, it is by no means difficult, through examination of past training records, to convert training spend as recorded by invoices into an approximate measure of the volume of training activity. A rough rule of thumb is that £300 on an invoice equals one-day's off-the-job training. This correspondence can be of particular value in bringing together data from training events which are delivered in-house – generally recorded in volume terms – and the training activity managed at a local level in a decentralized organization – generally recorded as spend on invoices.

The most important measure of training activity that will be recognized by line managers is, of course, evaluation information. This centres largely on the benefits as opposed to the costs of training and will be the subject of the next section of this chapter. Here, however, it is worth re-emphasizing a point made earlier: the importance and value of multiple data sources in giving a reliable and rounded picture. The innovative training manager, as well as monitoring costs and volumes, should therefore consider whether any useful information could be derived from other, less obvious, indicators of training activity. Statistics on the use of training facilities, for example, could repay systematic investigation, as could the number and source of inquiries to the training department. Computerized training information, which will be considered next, can dramatically alter the provision of information.

Once an organization decides to manage a portfolio of in-house training courses, it will inevitably consider the way in which information technology systems can facilitate training administration. In simple terms, the choice lies between home-grown systems or specific training packages. Within these two options, home-grown systems can range from simple spreadsheets through to a sophisticated tailored database developed in-house; purchased packages can extend from the simple course-booking system to a sophisticated module that is part of an overall approach to human resource management.

Extensive literature is available in the choice of systems and the potential benefits and drawbacks. The IPD organizes an annual exhibition/conference on Computers in Personnel. As technology advances so the scope of such systems increases. A 1998 survey reported in *People Management* suggested that half the organizations polled were either seeking a new human resources information system or expecting to buy one within the next two years.

At one time a human resource information system was little more than an electronic filing cabinet for sharing data and generating reports. Information systems are now seen as a potential source of competitive advantage. HR information systems can help solve the complex problems of providing appropriate management information on training. However, there are dangers and pitfalls which should be taken into account.

Computerized training systems can automate training administration. This automation can cover: identifying/selecting participants, scheduling course sessions, assigning equipment, sending joining instructions, maintaining evaluation records. As a consequence individual training records can be maintained and made available. In Ernst & Young, for example, the training administration system is used to generate information for reports for an individual's annual continuing professional education record.

Obviously all information must be up to date and the trend is towards the integration of human resources and payroll data. Beyond this there is an emerging trend to what are styled 'enterprise systems'. These are integrated business systems which contain financial, customer, manufacturing and supply chain information as well as human resources. The German software house SAP is the best-known supplier of enterprise systems with PeopleSoft, Oracle and Baan among their competitors. In an enterprise system, a control database is used to maintain information that supports a series of diverse applications – including human resource planning and training.

On the positive side, the generation of reports on training activity has become far easier. There are, nevertheless, dangers in generating reports because they are a feature of the system – rather than because they supply useful management information. It is helpful here to return to Fitz-enz's concept of the audiences rather than audience for information on training. The information architecture must be planned so that unnecessary data is not generated.

Additionally, most training administration systems will, albeit for a cost, provide dispersed access. This means that local human resource managers can use local terminals to check on course availability, individual participation and to book individuals on courses. They can also produce reports on training incidence for their relevant population. Individuals can call up information about training courses and initiate appropriate action. Access to information can be restricted if required.

Computerized training information systems are potentially of enormous benefit. Regular updating is essential and full integration with other systems is much to be preferred. However, the most important implication for the argument developed in this chapter is that the reporting should not be driven by the system. Reporting should be driven by customers' (Fitz-enz's audiences) need for management information.

APPROACHES TO EVALUATION

Summary: *Evaluation may be defined in a number of ways and a hierarchical categorization of activities is helpful. Three broad approaches – evaluation as measurement, intervention, and the systems approach – are outlined, and some underlying problems discussed. One reason for the deficiency in evaluation practice could be a lack of self-discipline on the part of the trainer.*

The evaluation of training courses is a vitally important weapon in a training manager's armoury. Evaluation is a key component of any systematic approach to training; indeed, heightened feedback from evaluation is a feature of the more sophisticated models. A greater concern to measure the effectiveness of training and development is regarded by the Ashridge Management Research Group as a defining characteristic of the most advanced 'focused' approach to training and development (see Ref. 7, Chapter 3). Those who require recognition for their training effort under the UK Government Schemes must prove that they undertake effective evaluation. Entrants for the National Training Award are encouraged to focus on organizational benefit and give tangible results where possible. Any organization wishing to be recognized as an 'Investor in People' must demonstrate that it evaluates investment in training and development in order to assess achievement and improve effectiveness. However, repeated surveys suggest that evaluation is frequently neglected. This cannot be for lack of practical guidance. Much useful information and advice is contained in the Institute of Personnel and Development/Investors in People UK Publication on making training pay.[7] This publication is very practical and contains a series of models and templates.

The following ten-stage process is used as the basis for introducing practical techniques:

- link training explicitly to the organizational needs
- decide measures of success at the start
- design and implement the training programme
- select the evaluation methods/toolkits
- evaluate participants' reaction
- evaluate training: participants and managers
- assess impact on individual performance
- analyse impact on organizational performance
- identify return on investment
- publicize results.

One possible reason for such an apparent contradiction between the textbook emphasis on evaluation and deficiencies in practice could be a confusion about what is meant by evaluation. The term can be understood at a number of different levels, and definitions vary accordingly. A standard glossary of training terms distinguishes between evaluation and validation and offers the following definition of the former:

> The assessment of the total value of a training system, training course or training programme in social as well as financial terms. Evaluation differs from *validation* in that it attempts to assess the overall cost benefit of the course or programme, and not just the achievement of its laid-down objectives. The term is also used in the general judgmental sense of the continuous monitoring of a programme or of the *training function* as a whole (see Ref. 1, Chapter 3).

The glossary also distinguishes between internal validation (whether the training programme has achieved the objectives specified) and external validation (whether the objectives were appropriate).

Categorization into a hierarchy of evaluation activity is a recurrent theme in the work of commentators. For example, a UK commentator, Tony Hamblin, offers a broad definition of evaluation as:

> any attempt to obtain information (feedback) on the effects of a training programme and to assess the value of the training in the light of that information (p. 8).[8]

Hamblin then suggests that there are five levels at which evaluation can take place: reactions, learning, job behaviour, organization and ultimate value.

The most common evaluation framework adopted by training practitioners in the USA, the Kirkpatrick model, offers four levels of evaluation:

- reaction – how well did training participants like the programme?
- learning – what knowledge (principles, facts and techniques) did participants gain from the programme?
- behaviour – what positive changes in participants' job behaviour stemmed from the training programme?
- results – what were the training programme's organizational effects in terms of reduced costs, improved quality of work, increased quantity of work and so forth?[9]

It is apparent that evaluation can be implemented at a series of different levels. At the lowest level (Kirkpatrick's 'reaction') participant responses are easy to collect but provide little information about the value of training to the organization. At the highest level (Kirkpatrick's 'results') the information is most difficult to capture but the results are most valuable to the organization. It is important that the training manager is aware of the purpose of the evaluation exercise before embarking on it.

Jack J. Phillips, a US commentator, has focused his attention on the return on investment (ROI) on training. He has correctly argued that measuring the ROI in training and development has consistently been one of the most critical issues facing training managers. In an important and accessible book (p. 9),[10] he has presented a practical process model for determining ROI. Significantly, he regards ROI as building on Kirkpatrick's four levels, adding a fifth level which compares the monetary value of the results with the costs of the programme, usually expressed as a percentage.

Textbooks on training evaluation offer a number of different categorizations and classifications of evaluation. For practical purposes, three approaches to evaluation may usefully be distinguished: evaluation as measurement, evaluation as intervention, a systems approach to evaluation. Most commentators incorporate aspects of all three in their analysis and the approaches represent broad bands rather than absolute distinctions. However, such a discussion highlights the practical issues involved in implementing effective evaluation.

MEASUREMENT

The following is a useful summary statement of the measurement method:

> To be useful and effective, evaluation must involve rigorous procedures based upon relevant research, properly integrated with all other aspects of programme development. Although some outcomes of training are difficult to anticipate, predict or measure, problems often occur due to ambiguous or unstated goals. Hence the emphasis ... on clear and explicit specification of objectives. Also ... suitable criteria should be established at an early stage, with pre-testing of trainees to enable progress to be monitored and subsequent assessment of how well these objectives have been achieved (p. 133).[11]

Key features of this approach are integration, clear and unambiguous goals, and testing before and after the event. The measurement approach represents an ideal situation. Many textbooks on training outline the approach, offer guidance on practical methods of data-capture (observation, questionnaires, etc.) and look at the various practical difficulties involved in implementation. The IPD's publication *Making Training Pay*[7] is recommended, as is Kearns and Miller's *Measuring the Impact of Training on the Bottom Line.*[12] Kearns and Miller's valuable work extends the ROI/numerical approach to measuring training effectiveness to its practical limits.

INTERVENTION

It is the practical difficulties of implementation that have, in part, led to the development of more sophisticated approaches to evaluation. There is an evident problem of demonstrating clear links between training objectives and organizational goals – particularly in management training. One answer is to integrate evaluation into the training process and regard evaluation as a component of effective training.

Research undertaken at the Centre for the Study of Management Learning at Lancaster University has identified the post-course questionnaire (or reactionnaire) as the most commonly used method of evaluation, though it is recognized to be of limited value. An alternative is to integrate evaluation more fully into the learning process: participants should be asked to complete questionnaires before and after the course, focusing on the learning experienced and its application; afterwards, participants and their bosses should be asked to complete questionnaires which review the effects of the course.

This perspective regards evaluation as an important form of organizational intervention that can produce a variety of effects beyond the immediate training goal.

This has been best developed by a member of the Lancaster University faculty, Mark Easterby-Smith, who identified four general purposes of evaluation:

- *Proving* – demonstrating conclusively that something has happened as a result of training and development activity
- *Improving* – trying to ensure that either current or future training activities become better than they are at present
- *Controlling* – ensuring that trainers and courses operate as intended by a central designer
- *Learning* – which treats evaluation as an integral part of the learning process itself.

Easterby-Smith suggests that recent developments in evaluation, while not denying the value of measurement, have tended to place greater emphasis on how the information will actually be used. Since evaluation cannot easily be divorced from the training event, Easterby-Smith argues that, with planning, it can contribute to the learning process itself by reinforcing the training objectives. Hence it becomes an intervention in, and component of, the training process.[13,14]

A SYSTEMS APPROACH

The third approach to evaluation can be labelled a systems approach – though it should not be confused with the systematic training model which treats evaluation as measurement. It is best expressed in the study undertaken by Carnevale and Schulz for the American Society for Training and Development (ASTD). The study found that most American companies evaluate their training programmes in some fashion and build evaluation design into programme design when objectives are established. In addition, they found that evaluators are increasingly using multiple data sources, combining quantitative and qualitative data. This suggests that, in this respect, American practice is well in advance of that in the UK.

Where the ASTD study is of particular value is that its recommendations are firmly embedded in realism.

> It's difficult to isolate the beneficial organizational results of training. Nonetheless, training specialists need to work from an understanding of organization-level goals and objectives. In many cases, it is possible and feasible to link training contributions to organizational improvements. Doing so doesn't require absolute isolation of training's contributions. Rather it requires indicators that demonstrate training's valuable role within the organization's systems (p. S-16).[15]

> Training is one operating system within an organization, and training should be evaluated as a system in support of other systems. In other words, training must contribute to achievement of the goals of the departments it serves and, through these, contribute to organizational objectives. This view of training necessitates the use of systematic means for performing training and linking its role to the goals of higher systems. Evaluation of training is the main method used to assess whether training is accomplishing desired effects of sufficient value (p. S-16).

The ASTD report recognizes that, since evaluation is an activity which will take place within an organization, it will be constrained by the organization's willingness to cooperate. Some sub-optimization is unavoidable, but one way of tackling the problem is to seek multiple sources of data because such sources give a rounded view and build stronger support for evaluation findings. More rigorous evaluation designs therefore have the following characteristics:

- they collect data from many, perhaps all, participants
- they collect data more than once, possibly many times
- they evaluate more at the organizational results level
- they employ quantitative data-collection methods
- they are more expensive
- they are more time-consuming
- they yield formal reports
- they are used for making decisions about program continuation or cutback (that is, they are summative)
- they are used when training's success is critical for safety or strategic business purposes (p. S-21).

EVALUATION: A PRACTICAL APPROACH

Summary: *The evaluation approach used in an investment bank is outlined. The model and two questionnaires are reproduced. The detailed interview questionnaire is structured to assess the effect of a course across four ascending categories.*

This chapter concludes with an outline of a recommended evaluation system – based on the approach used in an investment bank. The system is illustrated in three figures:

- the overall design (8.5)
- the end-of-course reactionnaire (8.6)
- the questionnaire used in one-to-one interviews (8.7)

It can be seen that the general design (Figure 8.5) is firmly rooted in the alternative recommended by Carnevale and Schulz for the ASTD – the systems approach. It follows the Kirkpatrick model and seeks to capture information at the four levels. It also seeks to collect data from multiple sources: from course reactionnaires, interviews with participants after the training event; interviews with business heads; other relevant results. In addition, there is an expressed commitment to devise comprehensive measures of evaluation and to consider and deal with the systems issues – a recognition that training is only one of the operating systems in the organization and should not be viewed in isolation.

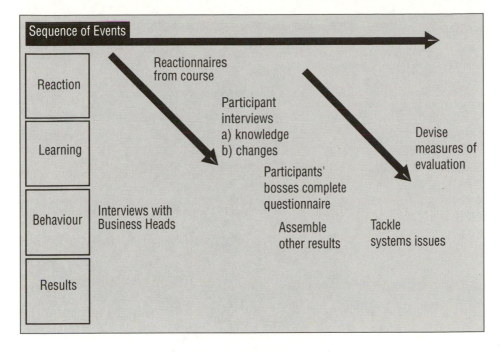

Figure 8.5   Evaluation design

This design is intended as an objective rather than a reflection of standard operating practice. It indicates how things should be done rather than how they are usually done. For example, participants' bosses are not always aware of the purposes of the training event and these interviews can produce limited results. However, an appropriate overall design helps put evaluation activity in its context.

The end-of-course reactionnaire (Figure 8.6) is unexceptional. It is designed to ensure that basic information is collected and maintained. Although to a limited extent it could be regarded as an intervention in the training process, that is not its primary intention. The reinforcement of the learning points should take place within the training event itself, not as part of the ritual closure. Information from such reactionnaires is of limited value, but it is important that it is collected. Certainly if the event is delivered by an in-house trainer, familiar in the organization and known to be collecting such information, it is a bold participant who will circle the rating marked 'poor' and offer entirely negative comments. The reality is that the dissatisfied internal client will be gentle to avoid controversy and will save the negative feedback until he or she returns to colleagues at the workplace – where it will gain currency as damaging anecdotal evidence. By introducing the ten-point scale, it is at least possible to record and codify information over a period – and thus to identify any sustained decline in the value of the course.

TRAINING EVALUATION REACTIONNAIRE

It is important that we review the extent to which courses meet the needs of participants so that we can continually improve the training being offered.

Please complete this questionnaire and hand it to your course tutor at the end of the course.

NAME:..
DIVISION/DEPARTMENT:..
COURSE NAME: ....
DATE: ....

1. Please circle your rating for the course on the following 10 point scale:

  1 ----- 2 ----- 3 ----- 4 ----- 5 ----- 6 ----- 7 ----- 8 ----- 9 ----- 10
  Poor   Moderate   Good   Excellent

2. What were your objectives for attending the course?

3. To what extent were they met?

4. Please summarize what you judge to be any additional benefits to you from having attended the course.

5. How will you be able to apply what you have learned to your job?

6. Do you have any suggestions for improvement of the course?

7. Would you recommend the course to colleagues having a similar need to yourself?

Figure 8.6   End-of-course reactionnaire

The interview questionnaire (Figure 8.7) is of much greater value. The example reproduced is intended for use some three to six months after the participant has completed the training. It is designed for a one-hour discussion between the training manager and the course participant. The aim is to collect information which allows the value of the course for the participants to be classified in four categories:

I   no benefit
II   general benefit, but unable to be specific
III benefit which has been applied in the work situation, but unable to quantify bottom line impact
IV   precise and quantifiable effects for the organization.

It can be seen that the classification is accomplished by a series of trigger questions (numbers 6, 7, and 8); it is here that the training manager must probe. In addition, the questionnaire follows the 'evaluation as intervention' model by obtaining information designed to improve course design and reinforce learning.

Clearly, the further down the list the more justifiable the training event. Some caution is necessary, however, because of the underlying problems in evaluation that were identified in the earlier section. The interviews are much more likely to produce Category IV results in the technical training area than in the interpersonal skills area.

Results from each event must be interpreted in their context and can be compared with results from similar events. The questionnaire is a comparative, not an absolute, instrument.

This approach is resource-intensive; one-to-one interviews do take time. However, the effective training manager will be constantly seeking feedback from training events: when others are responsible for delivering, he or she will visit the event or activity and seek out the nuances that indicate whether things are going well or whether there is scope for improvement. The evaluation design presented above is offered as a way of enhancing and codifying this process. Given the value of evaluation, emphasized throughout this chapter in the wider context of information systems, resources and efforts are well spent on this activity.

EXTENDING THE EVALUATION MODEL

Summary: *A fundamental academic criticism of the Kirkpatrick model, that advanced by Holton, is considered. This criticism comes from a research perspective, and suggests that a new approach based on training outcomes and linkages could assist in designing an extended framework for post-course evaluation.*

TRAINING EVALUATION INTERVIEW QUESTIONNAIRE

Name of course: FINANCIAL RISK ANALYSIS

Objectives of (Learning/Behaviour) Evaluation are:

Identify, from participants, what knowledge has resulted from the training events and what positive changes have resulted. Thus leading to measurement of bottom line effects.

Objectives of Course are:

To expand and enhance ability to interpret financial information and to form conclusions regarding financial risk.

To provide an introduction to corporate finance through investment appraisal.

Course Content:

Flexibility in accounting
Review of ration analysis/Dupont Pyramid
Working capital dynamics
Cost structure: fixed and variable costs
Contribution/breakeven analysis
Cash flow analysis
Fixed capital, depreciation and capital expenditure
DCF
Investment appraisal

Name: Date:

Business Area/Formation:

Date Attended Course:

1.   Why did you attend the course?

    – you requested to attend
    – your boss told you to attend
    – Personnel told you to attend
    – mutual agreement with your boss

2.   What did you hope to achieve as a result of attending the course? Refer to pre-course questionnaire.

Figure 8.7   One-to-one interview evaluation questionnaire

3. What are your overall comments on the course?

4. Which topics/aspects of the course have you been able to put into practice and how often?

5. Which topics/aspects of the course have you been unable to use? Why?

6. What positive knowledge/skills have resulted?
   (I/II trigger question: something must be here for it to be in category II – otherwise category I)

7. Can you think of a situation where these new skills or knowledge have been applied (probe for critical incidents)? (II/III trigger question: something must be here for it to be in category III – otherwise category II)

8. As a result of attending the course and putting your new skills into practice, do you think that you have had an impact on the 'bottom line'? If yes, please quantify. (If the candidate can quantify his/her impact on the bottom line put them in category IV, otherwise category III.)

9. Have your manager's expectation of the training you received been fulfilled?

10. What further help can your manager or the company offer you?

Figure 8.7   Concluded

A more vigorous challenge to evaluation based on the Kirkpatrick model was developed by Elwood Holton III of Louisiana State University. In a neglected article published in the US *Human Resource Development Quarterly,* Holton offers some powerful arguments which led to a spirited debate with Kirkpatrick himself.

Though this was not his primary intention, Holton's article suggests ways of improving evaluation practice. It has immediate implication for the design of evaluation questionnaires.

Holton argues that there is a need for new theory and research to develop a fully specified researchable evaluation model. The four-level Kirkpatrick model is really 'a taxonomy of outcomes and is flawed as an evaluation model' (p. 5).[16]

Much of the debate between Holton and Kirkpatrick considers whether the latter's model is truly a model and, indeed, whether Kirkpatrick intended it to be one. Holton regards it as a taxonomy – simply defined as a classification system. Some of the debate is semantic, centring on the distinction between model and taxonomies – though the protagonists generate some heat. One aspect of the debate is of particular interest to the training manager: this is Holton's proposition that a new model needs not only to specify outcomes, but also to account for the intervening variables that affect outcomes, and indicate causal relationships.

A very important point is at issue here. Although Holton's interests are directed towards academic research, the focus on intervening variables and causal relationships can help in improving evaluation practice. To take account of these variables and relationships, Holton proposes a conceptual model: this model also offers practical guidance.

To understand the argument it is helpful to consider one of his key criticisms of the Kirkpatrick model: this concerns the link between reactions and learning. Holton argues that in the Kirkpatrick model, as it stands, this link is uncertain (because it is a taxonomy or classification rather than a model). Drawing on research, Holton argues that trainees' reactions act as a moderator or mediator of learning. There is not a simple causal link between the Kirkpatrick levels: in practical terms the reaction does not have to be favourable for learning to take place; changes in behaviour do not have to be preceded by learning.

Recognizing this uncertainty, Holton argues that there is a complex system of influences on training outcomes that must be measured if training is to be accurately evaluated. Moreover, such a conceptual model, 'would enable practitioners to diagnose correctly barriers to training effectiveness'.

The model Holton proposes identifies three primary outcomes:

- learning, achievement of the learning outcomes desired in an HRD intervention

- individual performance, the change in the individual as a result of the learning being applied on the job
- organizational results, which occur as a result of the change in individual performance.

The first two primary outcomes are changes in individual behaviours that are intended results. Learning is primarily an internal behaviour: performance is a visible external behaviour. However these outcomes are also a function of ability, motivation and broader environmental influences. Holton's model is reproduced in figure 8.8. It identifies and represents a sequence of influences which all affect the three desired outcomes. As well as the primary influences of ability, motivation and environmental influences there are secondary influences identified at the top of the figure. Trainers will recognize the legitimacy of all of these influences (which will vary accordingly to circumstances). A brief summary of some of the relationships may assist.

Motivation to learn (self-explanatory) is directly related to learning (hence the bold arrow). Primary influences on the motivation to learn (narrow arrows) are intervention readiness (the participants' desire to enter and participate in the programme), job attitude (the trainees' attitude to the organization and the job), and the trainees' personality characteristics.

Motivation to transfer is the trainees' desire to utilize their learning on the job. The degree to which trainees' expectations about training are met has a significant impact on their attitude after receiving training. This can be described as intervention fulfilment and hence is shown as a primary influence on motivation to transfer.

Expected utility/return on investment (ROI) concerns the pay-off from training. Obviously this is a primary influence on organizational results but also affects motivation to transfer. Transfer climate and transfer design are both primary influences on individual performance. The former concerns the situational constraints in the workplace (manager support for training and the use of rewards, for example). The latter concerns the extent to which the design of the training itself facilitates the participants' transfer of learning. The other variables are described as they are defined in common parlance. The model as presented is complex. The underlying ideas are simple and the result productive.

Training interventions are designed to produce desirable outcomes: these outcomes are affected by a series of influences. Holton's model illustrates these main influences and postulates linkages between them. His is a research model: the training manager's requirements are practical. How can this conceptual mapping improve evaluation practice?

This question is a powerful one and can only be answered in the context of the particular organization. At the heart of the answer, however, is a requirement that

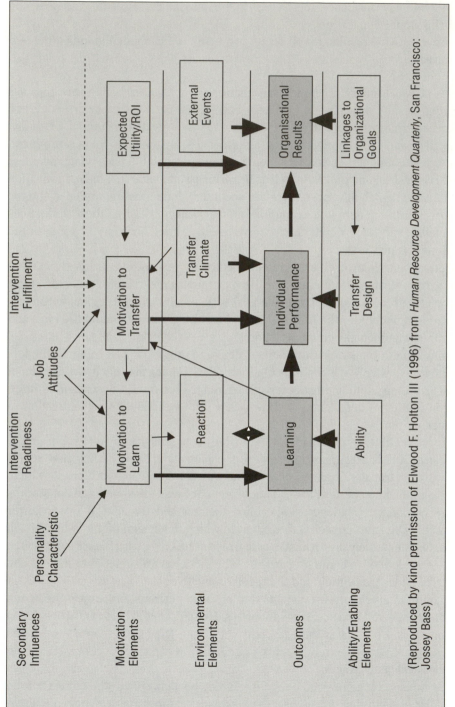

Figure 8.8 HRD evaluation research and measurement model (The Holton model)

(Reproduced by kind permission of Elwood F. Holton III (1996) from *Human Resource Development Quarterly*, San Francisco: Jossey Bass)

all those involved in the management of the training process understand and undertake their responsibilities. This brings the discussion back to the disciplinary framework first, introduced as Figure 8.2. One of the key roles for the training manager is designing and maintaining the training framework. This concept is extended in Figure 8.9.

In a corporate, modern, complex organization training spend should be reviewed using a wide disciplinary framework.

● all parties involved in decisions on training interventions (commissioning, designing or delivering) will have responsibilities for their part in the framework.
● the training manager must accept a particular responsibility for the construction and maintenance of the framework.
● key elements of the framework are:
  – evaluation
  – overall monitoring and measurement
  – reporting.
● evaluation should extend beyond the post-course reactionnaire. However, this is still a useful document, particularly if it is extended to take account of primary and secondary effects.

Figure 8.9   Key features of the new approach to measurement

The training manager must determine where the wastage/leakages from training arise (see Figure 8.1 for some illustrations). Then he or she must take systematic action to improve the effectiveness of training spend. The Holton model provides conceptual insights on how this practical process can be undertaken.

REFERENCES

1. The Industrial Society (1997), *Training Trends 27, Training Budgets & Spending*, London: Industrial Society.
2. Fitz-enz, J. (1995), *How to Measure Human Resources Management*, New York: McGraw Hill.
3. Kaplan, R.S. and Norton, D.P. (1992), 'The Balanced Scorecard – Measures that Drive Performance', *Harvard Business Review*, **70** (1), January–February, p. 71.
4. Kaplan, R.S. and Norton, D.P. (1993), 'Putting the Balanced Scorecard to Work', *Harvard Business Review*, **71** (5), September–October, pp. 134–47.
5. Kaplan, R.S. and Norton D.P. (1996), 'Using the Balanced Scorecard as a Strategic Management System', *Harvard Business Review*, **74** (1), January–February, pp.75–85.
6. Kaplan, R.S. and Norton D.P. (1996), *The Balanced Scorecard*, Boston: Harvard Business School Press.
7. Beaton, L. and Richards, S. (1997), *Making Training Pay*, London: Institute of Personnel and Development and Investors in People.
8. Hamblin, A.C. (1974), *Evaluation and Control of Training*, Maidenhead: McGraw Hill.
9. Kirkpatrick D.L. (1975), *Evaluating Training Programs,* American Society for Training and Development, Alexandria Va: ASTD.
10. Phillips, J.J. (1997), *Return on Investment in Training and Performance Improvement Programs*, Houston: Gulf Publishing.
11. Torrington, D. and Chapman, J. (1975), *Personnel Management*, London: Prentice-Hall.

12. Kearns, P. and Miller, T. (1996), *Measuring the Impact of Training and Development on the Bottom Line – An Evaluation Tool Kit to make Training Pay*, Hitchin: Technical Communications.
13. Easterby-Smith, M. and Tanton, M. (1985), 'Turning Course and Evaluation From an End to a Means', *Personnel Management*, **17** (4), April.
14. Easterby-Smith, M. (1994), *Evaluation of Management Education, Training and Development*, Second Edition, Aldershot: Gower.
15. Carnevale, A.P. and Schulz, E.R. (1990), *Return on Investment: Accounting for Training*, American Society for Training and Development, Alexandria Va: ASTD.
16. Holton, E.F. III (1996), 'The Flawed Four-Level Evaluation Model', *Human Resource Development Quarterly*, **7** (1), Spring, pp. 5–21.

Part III
Managing the Training Function

Introduction to Part III

In this final part of the book I consider a model of the place that the training function should occupy in the modern organization. It is argued that there can be no definitive, unique answer to the question 'what is best?' Any answer must be contingent. It must reflect the strategic business objectives of the organization and also the extent of the appreciation and recognition of the value of training; this latter is an aspect of what will be called the organization's training culture.

At the beginning of Chapter 1 I maintained that a new confidence was evident throughout the training profession. I argued that changes in the corporate and business environment have created opportunities for a significantly enhanced organizational contribution from training. Subsequent exploration and discussion has found solid grounds for this optimism: competition through people has given rise to what has been called the new human resources. Training and development have a key role to play.

Two words of caution are necessary, however. First, that as yet there is no sustained evidence in the UK this is being borne out by what is happening. A discussion on (the paucity of) statistical information on UK training is presented in Appendix I, p. 255. However, the main conclusion is that, although some progress is taking place, there is a wide difference in levels of training activity in organizations. The climate may be favourable for improvement, but commitment is needed to produce action, achievement and demonstrable results.

The second word of caution must be addressed to the training profession itself. There is still a need to adopt a harder edge with clear models that will command immediate respect from managers in the wider organization. It is they who will determine the support that will be given to the training effort. One depressing feature follows from reflection on Parts I and II of this book. The decisive thinking that influences the approach to best practice has taken place outside human resources in general and training in particular. It is the strategic planners, economists and confident management gurus who are shaping the training manager's agenda.

Positively, we have a golden opportunity. Negatively, if we don't get it right now we have only ourselves to blame. The current climate offers a chance to shape the role of training and gain respect for the profession, as a central contributor to business growth rather than a peripheral adjunct. Paradoxically it is easier to see how this can be done at the level of the individual organization that at the national level. Although different circumstances require different approaches, in general it is possible to give a series of statements on modern training practice which, taken together, have general validity and are capable of application in most organizations. An elaboration of this approach forms the subject matter for Chapter 9; the consequent demands on the training professional are considered in Chapter 10. It is a fundamental premise of the book that the new approach should be firmly embedded in operating reality. Hence the previous two parts of the book have concentrated on aspects of the changing environment facing the training professional.

In the course of Parts I and II key issues in modern training emerged. Gradually, a new approach has taken shape. I present this in detail, and discuss its implications, in this final part of the book.

9 The role of the training function

In Chapter 3 I undertook a review of models of training management. I argued that, although the models available all had their limitations, developing an appropriate training model is a worthwhile activity. Figure 3.9 (p. 65) suggested that an effective model offers the trainer a structural and disciplined framework in which to work.

However, one approach does not fit all. General principles can be advanced of how an effective model can be developed. Planning and the management of the organization's training culture are the two key elements whatever the circumstances. Beyond this a contingent approach is required which will depend on the individual situation: a different focus is required in smaller developing organizations from that needed in leading-edge sophisticated companies that compete though knowledge workers.

The systematic training model provides a useful starting point for such a discussion. First, however, a brief excursion is necessary to underline the need for greater precision of terminology.

THE BIG IDEA

Summary: *Over the last decade the human resource profession has been easily influenced by big ideas generated elsewhere. While this may have helped keep the function involved in the most important organizational changes, there is now a need for greater precision.*

This brief interlude is about sloppy thinking. The argument is that, by too eagerly adopting the latest management fad, the training profession has damaged itself. The new favourable climate demands greater rigour.

Such a charge is hard to prove, but should have some resonance with practitioners who have been active in training over the last decade. The implication is that the age of downsizing, delayering, tough lean organizations and (in some places) 'macho' management, was not an easy one for the training professional. Training was an easy target in any cost-cutting exercise. To achieve organizational credibility, human resources professionals in general, and trainers in particular, seized on prevalent grand conceptual themes – or Big Ideas.

In the early 1990s, at the height of this period, this sentiment was perceptively captured in an article in *Personnel Management*. The author, Stephen Connock, argued that few human resource managers can remain immune from Big Ideas, which he defined as satisfying at least three criteria:

- the idea must be universally applicable in all sectors and to all sizes of organization
- it must have a memorable label
- it must be self-evidently valid; 'no one for example would challenge the importance of improving customer service'.

Although it is easy to be cynical about big ideas, they are, as Connock suggested, 'important' in their ability to focus or re-focus attention on simple, universal and self-evidently valid subjects'[1].

Quality management and business process re-engineering are big ideas whose time appears to have passed. A glance at the bookshelves of the Library at the Institute of Personnel and Development will bear testimony to the number of attempts, many of them commendable in their own way, to 'fit' training into one or other of the prevalent conceptual frameworks – and thus give it managerial credibility in the context of the time. The learning organization (see Chapter 3, p. 58), has been a particularly woolly big idea. Marvellously compelling for the training manager, but often meaning comparatively little in practice. It was even argued by two leading commentators at the time that 'when companies establish total quality management as a way of life, they are in fact establishing a learning organization'. Two big ideas for the price of one!

One can sympathize with the former US Labor Secretary Robert Reich when he argued, 'Rarely has a term moved so rapidly from obscurity to meaninglessness without passing through an intervening period of coherence.'

Imprecision is not however the exclusive property of the trainer and Reich used this phrase twice in a four month period, first at the OECD Conference in Paris (June 1994) to describe flexibility, then at the National Alliance of Business in Dallas (September 1994) to describe competitiveness.[2]

Oscar Wilde is alleged to have said, 'America is the only nation to pass from barbarism to decadence without the intervening stage of civilisation.'

The above interlude serves only to introduce a plea: training now has the opportunity to become far more hard-edged. It will be argued that a structured and disciplined approach and simple consistent vocabulary leading to clear communication will follow from effective planning and management of the training culture. A further consideration of training models provides a useful introduction.

TRAINING MODELS RECONSIDERED

Summary: *Changes in the business context mean that the systematic training model can no longer supply a sufficient framework for the trainer. The consultancy model and the learning organization also have limitations. A new model is introduced.*

Training, however defined, is an intervention in the organization. The first part of the book identified a number of changes in the context in which the training intervention takes place. Globalization and the communication revolution have redefined the market. This has led to competition through people and to the concept of resource-based strategy. Knowledge workers have created, through changing perceptions of careers, new demands and pressures on the training manager. This has given rise to the new human resources which aims to both develop competitive advantage though people and reinforce it through appropriate policies on encouragement, involvement and commitment.

In this new context, the definitions of training and development can usefully be revisited and the following descriptions offered:

- Human resource development deals with the establishment of the internal structures and processes needed to create the organization wide competencies that allow the business to compete.
- Training is the process of acquiring the individual competencies and knowledge related to work requirements by formal structured or guided means, but excluding general supervision and job-specific innovations. Training is now necessary for competitive purposes and for individual growth and survival.

It can be seen that the description of training has been extended beyond the definition offered in the Introduction (p. xix). The second sentence emphasizes the dual forces that drive the demand for training. Human resource development is described in its broader organizational context as a wide process. The word 'competencies', a term which seems to have staying power, is used in its different senses in both descriptions – and the adjectives (organization wide and individual) should clarify the difference.

Training interventions will be determined by the nature of the business (how does the firm compete?) and the organization's culture (particularly the acceptance by line managers of the importance of training). Market competition and organizational change have merged in practice as the two most powerful forces influencing training strategy (see Appendix IV, p. 269). However, the impact of these forces will vary and the approach must be contingent and must depend on the circumstances. Will models help and, specifically, what is the value of the systematic training model?

The inadequacies of the systematic training model of training management were identified in Chapter 3. Taken on its own, this model can no longer supply a sufficient framework in which the training professional can operate. Although the systematic training model remains of value as a disciplined way of structuring activities it has a number of limitations. In particular:

● it demands a precision of approach which fits uneasily into training objectives which arise from looser organizational structures
● it ignores the need for supply-side activity where the trainer attempts to generate options for line management, rather than simply responding to stated needs
● it does not consider issues that arise because of changing organizational relationships, particularly the devolution of responsibility to line management
● it defines training objectives narrowly, ignoring the link with development and the other human resource benefits that can be captured by a proactive training function.

The limitations of the systematic training model have given rise, albeit implicitly rather than explicitly, to two new approaches to training management: the consultancy model and the learning organization.

The consultancy model of training management has attracted considerable interest. It cannot, however, be regarded as giving more than a partial perspective of the place and role of training. If it is viewed as a way of determining the approach in its entirety serious drawbacks become apparent. In the main, though not all consultants would agree, consultancy is an input purchased from outside the organization. The underlying problem is owned by the client; the consultant gives specialist independent advice or offers a defined service. Repeat business is secured by achieving client satisfaction.

Modern training practice, though, requires the person responsible for the delivery of the training resource to become fully integrated in the management process. This is not to deny the reality or attractiveness of a model, prevalent in larger organizations, of part of the training resource being designated purely as training providers; for many companies a separate management training centre fills this role admirably.

What is disputed is whether it is desirable for the training function *as a whole* to seek to place itself in an internal consultancy role. A training professional must strive to become far more than an internal consultant. Proactive training involves taking management responsibility as well as giving internal clients satisfaction.

The prevention of waste of resources through unnecessary training activity, for example, requires deliberate management intervention rather than the reaction of a consultant.

The drawbacks with the second new approach, the learning organization, are less apparent – mainly because the commentaries that can be grouped under this heading are disparate and frequently aspirational rather than practical. In the discussion of the learning organization as a model in Chapter 3 (p. 58), it was argued that the term 'learning organization' lacks precision. The lowest common denominator list of characteristics set out in Figure 3.7 (p. 61) were worthy in intention, but could not be said to constitute a sea change in thinking about the place of training. Indeed, Professor David Guest and Kate Mackenzie Davey (in an article considered earlier in the context of career management (see Ref. 16, Chapter 2)) argued that 'concepts such as the learning organisation and self-development tend to dissolve on closer inspection' and 'the learning organisation literature perpetuated a naïve view of both the individual and the organisation, and how cultural change could be achieved. Indeed the learning organisation is unlikely to be an effective vehicle for organisational change, working best instead in a culture which supports many of its ideals' (p. 25).

Is the learning organization simply a big idea whose time has passed? Time alone will tell, but it is possible to identify a number of strands which, if an effort is made to articulate them with precision, could add up to a coherent model.

Some of these strands were identified in the discussion of the learning organization as a possible model in Chapter 3. First, learning could be regarded as a continuous process rather than a set of discrete training activities. Then deliberate efforts are made to inculcate learning into all business activities. Precision would demand hard evidence that this occurs: that reward systems are linked to contributions to learning; that learning reviews take place after significant projects, for example.

Second, and as consequence, there is an acceptance that the organization should encourage its employees to participate in learning over and above what is required for narrow business requirements.

There is a third strand which has not been greatly in evidence in the literature to date and was therefore not identified in the discussion in Chapter 3. This is a deliberate policy to increase the skills capabilities and application of knowledge workers through interventions designed to encourage them to learn. This is a subtle point, but to appreciate its significance it is helpful to return to the definition of learning contained in the Introduction to this book. Here learning was defined as the 'physical and mental processes involved in changing one's normal behavioural patterns and habits from the norm'. An important shorthand distinction between training and learning was then put forward:

> Learning lies within the domain of the individual, can result from a whole range of experiences, and can be positive, negative or neutral from the organization's point of view. Training lies within the domain of the organization: it is an intervention designed to produce behaviours from individuals which have positive organizational results.

In a learning organization, then, the training intervention would be deliberately designed to foster learning – which lies within the domain of the individual. The implications of such a policy raise some hard questions: does responsibility lie entirely with the individual who can choose what he or she wishes to learn (is no training imposed?); is the organization sure that individuals are equipped, or are willing to accept such responsibility?

The true learning organization then would be one where efforts are made to inculcate learning in all activities; where it is accepted that learning should take place beyond what is narrowly required as essential; and where training interventions are designed to encourage individual learning (at its extreme, whatever the consequences). The precise mix of training interventions would vary: but, typically, the organization would encourage open access to distance learning, would try to create learning groups, would introduce learning contracts and would put considerable efforts into creating a culture where all managers saw staff development as part of their responsibilities – and were held accountable for their efforts. Almost certainly, in addition, the current unsolved riddle of corporate training, the link with knowledge management, would have been satisfactorily resolved and the edges of learning, knowledge and performance blurred into one continuous activity.

For some organizations this may be a legitimate aspiration; for others it may even resemble current activity. For most, however, this approach would be inappropriate. The resources (in both time and money) needed to create such an environment are considerable – and are, in addition, difficult to predict or control. At its extreme, the rigorously defined learning organization may demand an open-ended commitment to individual learning.

For this reason, arguments that the training manager should focus his or her attention on 'learning' rather than 'training' should be viewed critically. Part of the training interventions should, in most organizations, consist of initiatives which create effective individual learning. Nevertheless, whatever the sophistication and ambitions of the organization, these are unlikely to comprise the entire focus of the appropriate training interventions.

In summary, then, 'the learning organization' can become a credible model for a small elite of corporations. For much of the recent debate, though, the term has been used loosely and without thought, and in situations where these sophisticated conditions cannot apply. As an aim this may be laudable. Sometimes in the recent past, however, a declared intention to create a learning organization has been seen as a test of a training manager's professional virility. The most important question, 'what does the concept of the learning organization mean for *me* and in *my firm*?' has been ignored. In many cases there is a huge disparity between the reality of the situation and the nirvana of the learning organization. For many trainers the concept of the learning organization may prove to be damaging and counter-productive as a model for progress. It asks too great a leap of faith from most managers and does not describe situations that they can recognize. Indeed, the very phrase 'learning organization' could be regarded as unhelpful; it is firmly 'trainer-speak' and does not carry a high likelihood of achieving resonance with a hard-bitten manager who is struggling to achieve short-term financial targets.

Something different in terms of a model is required. While one approach does not fit all, it is possible to give general guidelines. These are set out in Figures 9.1 and 9.2. The two key features of the approach – articulating the training strategy and plan and managing the training culture – will then be considered in turn.

MODERN TRAINING PRACTICE REQUIRES

- the articulation of a training strategy and plan with clear targets and clear control, and hence clear accountability.

THE TRAINING RESOURCE THUS

- makes a significant and distinctive contribution to the development of both the organization-wide and individual competencies and to the process of skills enhancement that must necessarily take place in the modern organization
- assists in the capture of wider human resource benefits through the more effective development of people in the organization.

THIS IS ACHIEVED IN PART BY

- developing an appropriate training *culture* for the organization in which managers at all levels embrace the role for training in achieving business plans.

The training function must operate at strategic, tactical and operational levels.

Figure 9.1   **Requirements of modern training practice**

TRAINING STRATEGY AND PLANS

Summary: *The preparation and promotion of a training strategy and its expression as a plan is a key task for the training manager. Both strategy and plans should be made explicit and tangible; written formats and diagrams can assist in communication. If the organization does not have an accessible business strategy, the training manager can nevertheless proceed by offering a model based on Investors in People or on performance management.*

THE ROLE OF THE TRAINING PROFESSIONAL IS TO

● develop and articulate the training strategy and plan
● promote the training culture.

THIS IS ACHIEVED BY

● defining and developing the appropriate relationship with all managers, giving special consideration to the place of the other human resource professionals and achieving the maximum leverage for the training resource within the organization
● adopting a proactive role and presenting supply-side alternatives to management
● developing an appropriate management information and a disciplinary framework to ensure that resources are managed and controlled effectively.

Figure 9.2   The role of the training professional

Both strategy and planning are components of a strategic planning process. Strategy is the high-level activity that generates insights and matches what a company can do with what it might do. Plans exist to cope with the immediate needs of an organization: they operate under a pre-set timetable and demand structured documentation. In practice, the distinction is less important than it might appear: what matters is the effectiveness of the process.

One of the clearest findings to emerge from the survey of best practice organizations undertaken for this book was the importance of the training plan. This plan was given in written form, generally produced by a human resource or training specialist, expressed in budgetary terms and linked to the commercial needs of the business (see Appendix IV, p. 269).

As has been emphasized throughout, the human resource strategy and planning processes must be consistent (aligned) with those in place elsewhere in the organization. Outside best practice organizations, strategic planning processes will vary considerably, and may not exist at all. At this minimum level, however, it is still possible to express a training strategy as a statement of intent and to formulate a training plan which can be defined as 'a statement drawn up in the context of an organization's corporate objectives, which indicates training objectives and approaches, selection procedures for training, timetables and methods of training'.

A primary responsibility of the training manager within the organization is to formulate appropriate training strategy. He or she then must secure agreement for this strategy from senior management, prepare a plan and promulgate and promote it throughout the organization, thus ensuring its implementation.

To some training professionals the above statement may seem so obvious as to require no elaboration; to others the process involved in developing a strategy and plans will appear to be incidental to their main tasks in the organization; to a third group, the statement, while germane, demands development and elaboration before it is accepted.

In fact there are both theoretical and practical reasons why such a statement attracts challenges; here there is a need to return to the discussion on alternative training models in Chapter 3. There I outlined both the systematic training model and the National Training Award model. It was noted that the systematic training model suggests an approach which is partial – it is a discipline structured to tackle training requirements as they arise. The National Training Award Model treats training as an independent sub-system of the organization, with training requirements driven entirely by needs articulated elsewhere. Both models implicitly place training in a reactive role – though the advocates of the models could argue with some justification that that was not their intention. Neither model implies that there is necessarily a need for an overall training strategy. Investors in People, by contrast, implicitly recognizes the importance of a training strategy.

The practical challenge to the statement arises from the observation that explicit training strategies are far from universal. There is an absence of comprehensive sustained statistics on employees' training in the UK. However, the evidence suggests that formal training strategies may be the exception rather than the rule. If training managers are not in practice formulating strategies and planning, it is questionable whether such an activity should be given a key position in the new model.

These are all reasonable objections, and the reader may conclude that formulating a training strategy is an unnecessary indulgence – but this would be mistaken. Running themes throughout this book have been the need to persuade people at all levels of the importance of training activity, the need to recognize the importance of devolving responsibility to line managers, the need to ensure that the devolved function is adequately controlled and monitored, and the need to gain the maximum leverage for training activity so that it is deployed to best effect. Meeting those needs demands ongoing discussion within the organization on the deployment of training resources – in short, the training manager must ensure that the function does not become marginalized. A successful way of avoiding this is for the place of training to be expressed in terms that are understood and accepted within the organization. This is what is implied by the training manager's responsibility for formulating an appropriate strategy and for developing plans.

It could also be argued that a training strategy should be expressed implicitly rather than explicitly. In this case there would be no need for a written document because the strategy was widely understood. At the highest level of sophistication, it may be that training philosophy is so thoroughly ingrained in organizational behaviour that an explicit statement is unnecessary. However, such situations in the UK today are likely to be rare. In most cases there is a need to heighten awareness of the importance of training, and an articulated strategy and plan offer a valuable mechanism in achieving that aim for two reasons.

First, because an explicit statement of the role of training can be communicated within the organization. It indicates to progressive line managers what is involved in discharging their responsibility for the effective development of their staff. It also provides a yardstick against which the less progressive can be measured. For this reason it is important that strategy and plans are expressed at an operational level in terms that the line manager can readily embrace – the tendency of trainers to develop their own vocabulary has been an evident handicap to effective communication. Managers face multiple demands on their time, and questions that to the trainer may seem unduly prosaic ('how many days training should my staff receive?') require straight answers rather than an improving lecture.

The second reason for putting forward a strategy and plan is because an explicit statement of the role of training focuses attention on the resources spent on training and the opportunity cost involved in using those resources. For some organizations the key cost will be the expenditure on training events (course fees, accommodation and other items that show up on invoices). For others the key cost will be the time spent away from the job, and underlying dissatisfaction with the results from training will be expressed through future unwillingness to release staff to participate in training activity. Whatever the situation, an explicit statement does ensure that there will be a recognition of the choices involved in expending the training effort. At its simplest, they force the organization to consider whether time at off-the-job training events is best used in developing management skills and extending and updating technical knowledge, or on more specialized activities like language or computer training.

Given an acceptance of the need for a formal training strategy and plan, how is it to be produced? This will depend on the planning process adopted in the training manager's own organization, the structure and position of the human resources, and the nature of competition and the organization's culture. Some fundamental questions are set out in Figure 9.3. Figures 9.4 and 9.5 are presented as guides for the training manager in providing input to the strategic planning process in their own organization. They are not prescriptive. They are no more than frameworks that may tackle the programme in different contexts.

In this spirit, Figure 9.3 is a list of key questions for the training manager to consider at the outset when seeking to formulate his or her contribution to the strategic planning process; Figure 9.4 is drawn from the analysis undertaken by Professor Shaun Tyson of Cranfield,[3] and this identifies the elements of a human resource plan; Figure 9.5 presents the elements that should influence and find expression in a training plan. None should come as a surprise; with the exception of marketing, selling and communication, all have been considered earlier in this book.

POLICY QUESTIONS

What is the basis of the organization's competitive advantage?
- how does the firm compete?
- what is the nature of the environment, i.e. the market?

What are the human resource issues that underpin effective competition?
- what people skills does the organization need to succeed?
- how can these skills be developed?

PROCESS QUESTIONS

What is the business planning process that takes place within the organization?
- who is responsible for the planning?
- at what stage, and how, are the human resource policies considered?

How should the appropriate human resource policies be determined and implemented?
- what is achievable best practice under the circumstances?
- who owns these policies?
- how should they be communicated and monitored?

Figure 9.3   Key questions on strategic planning

Where an organization has neither an articulated strategy nor has accepted the contribution of training, the training manager will need to be proactive. The promotion within the organization of a framework which allows the training strategy to be developed is then recommended. This is an illustration, at the highest level, of the trainer taking a supply-side initiative. How to proceed must depend, again, on the circumstances of the organization, but two general frameworks are suggested: Investors in People and performance management. Both are described more fully elsewhere in this book – the former in Chapter 3 (p. 52), the latter in Chapter 6 (p. 128).

Although Investors in People explicitly rejects a uniform approach to training and development (recognizing differences caused by size, structure, markets and culture), its standards and indicators for assessment purposes offer a clear guidance on what is required to link training with business objectives. Among the relevant suggestions is that training needs should be regularly reviewed against business objectives – which are expressed in a written but flexible business plan. This should be underpinned by a training or skills audit with a distinct business focus; the skills of existing employees should be developed in line with business objectives; the organization must evaluate how its development of people is contributing to business objectives. Promotion of Investors in People within the organization can address the issues involved in formulating and implementing training's contribution to the strategic planning process: it provides a valuable framework for such discussions.

THE BASIS OF COMPETITION	
How does the firm compete? What are the key skills that must be enhanced, developed or protected?	

THE INFLUENCES	
A reflection of the organization's philosophy of management (what are the organization's values and how should they be reflected in the management process?)	
Review of external influences – political/economic	
Technical/ social/specific legislative trends or changes anticipated	
Main business trends as they are likely to affect human resources (expansion, contraction, and any collaborative arrangements)	

THE ROLE OF THE DEVELOPMENT FUNCTION	
Description of the service from the human resource function (relationships with line management, the expertise required in the function, and the way it should operate in the future)	

(Adapted from: Tyson, S., *Strategic Prospects for HRM*, London: IPD (1995.)

Figure 9.4 Elements of a human resource plan

An alternative framework, though of a less structured kind, is offered by performance management. The key elements (communicating a vision, setting targets, evaluating and monitoring) are generally accepted as consistent with best human resource practice. Moreover the model is compatible with any broader organizational initiative.

In the absence of an existing high-profile change initiative, the proactive training manager can use Investors in People or performance management as a model. A training strategy can be voiced and a plan formulated, using a 'bottom-up' approach where the organization has no articulated business strategy.

Once the training strategy has been formulated, it must be expressed in a way

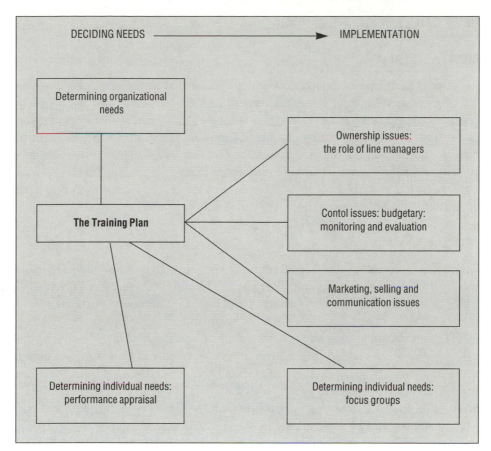

Figure 9.5   The training plan: significant influences

that is understood throughout the organization. Clear targets and control and accountability mechanisms are then required. If responsibility for the delivery of effective training is embedded through the organization and is no longer the exclusive responsibility of designated training staff, it is essential that such responsibilities are made transparent. How this is to be achieved is considered in the next chapter, where the implications for the trainer will be discussed.

The second key element of best modern training practice – the management of the training culture – is considered in the final section of this chapter. First, however, I present a short case study of Chartwell Land.[4] This illustrates how training can be part of the strategic planning process in a smaller organization. One approach may not fit all, but the need for appropriate discipline is universal.

CASE STUDY: A TRAINING PLAN

CHARTWELL LAND

Chartwell Land plc is a property company employing 54 staff. During the 1990s its training and development was transformed. In 1994 it became the first property company to secure Investors in People status. In 1995 it won both a Regional and National Training Award in recognition of 'continuous strategic commitment to effective training and development over the last four years'. It also received a special award for the exemplary use of Investors in People standards. It can serve as a model of what is feasible given a commitment from the top and the consistent application of appropriate methods.

Background

Chartwell Land is a specialist retail property company. It was created in 1987 as a wholly owned subsidiary of Kingfisher plc, the holding company for Woolworths, Comet, B&Q and Superdrug. Chartwell Land manages a property portfolio valued at over £750m. It has a development arm (acquiring and developing sites) and an investment arm (investing in properties with growth potential and managing a property portfolio). The main business units are supported by finance, company secretarial, marketing, personnel/training and research staff. In addition there are the normal administrative and secretarial staff.

The staff are a highly professional mix of Chartered Surveyors, Accountants and Project Managers (who are often themselves qualified surveyors (RICS)). The company has a flat management structure with an emphasis on project-based work. As well as internal teamworking, Chartwell Land's professional staff work as individuals or in teams coordinating external groups of agents, architects and contractors.

In its early days Chartwell Land was a more diversified business. It refocused its strategy between 1990 and 1993 concentrating on the retail business. It operates in a highly commercial market place, facing competition from other retail property companies for sites and from institutional investors in developing its portfolio.

Training strategy

In 1991, as the new business strategy was being introduced, a Personnel and Training Manager was appointed. The 1993 edition of the company's Strategic Plan stated that there had been 'no formal training to date but occasional participation in topic specific and other Group programmes'. Topic-specific training referred mainly to technical and specialist seminars. At the time, and subsequently, strategic planning was mainly driven by the Managing Director and other Directors. A single Strategic Document existed and focused on setting objectives and financial targets for the component business areas.

The new Personnel and Training Manager set about his task in two stages:

a) he identified and sought endorsement for a training strategy
b) once this endorsement had been obtained, he translated this strategy into a specific training plan.

Identification and endorsement

The process of needs assessment involved:

a) a detailed consideration of the 1991 Strategic Plan to identify major themes. Training and succession planning were mentioned in the Plan in broad terms but there was limited detail or specifics
b) one-to-one interviews with the Directors and Managers seeking their views on business development and the training and development implications
c) training needs analysis of other members of staff. The organization was sufficiently small to allow the Personnel and Training Manager to interview all the staff personally.

Once these activities had been completed a presentation was made to the Board. An extract of the Company Strategic Plan and an interpretation of key development needs was presented for each business unit.

Five important areas of training and development needs across the business were then highlighted. These are set out in Figure 9.6. The key areas were broad in scope and ambition. As can be seen they were categorized into short-term, medium-term and long-term objectives. They received endorsement from the Board.

Creating the plan

Once the training objectives had been agreed, the Personnel and Training Manager was given the task of establishing a specific plan. This comprised three elements:

a) training policy objectives, which followed directly from the strategy
b) budgetary and cost control considerations
c) monitoring and validation.

After a detailed presentation of cost estimates, the Board agreed to set the annual training spend at about £80 000 (approximately £1 600 per head). Once this had been agreed the plan could be restated for each of the five key areas. Although some information must remain confidential, the plan took the format set out in Figure 9.7.

1. Professional development

Short-term:
- Continuous professional development statement
- PCL seminars
- Internal resources
- Confidence building for finance

Medium-term:
- Specialist lecturers
- CPD research
- Continuous legislation update

Long-term:
- Central CPD / continuous professional education database
- Construction management course

2. Commercial development

Short-term:
- Computer literacy / internal assistance
- Financial skills training

Medium-term:
- Systems consolidation
- Internal negotiations training
- 1:1 coaching/finance

Long-term:
- Commercial development programme

3. Management development

Short-term:
- Management skills training
- Time management programme

Medium-term:
- Management modules
- 1:1 coaching
- Disciplinary skills

Long-term:
- Business schools
- MBAs

4. Corporate development

Short-term:
- Guest speakers
- Induction
- Selection training

Medium-term:
- Team-building events
- Recruitment screening

Long-term:
- Communication systems
- Competencies
- Personality profiling

5. Secretarial development

Short-term:
- Follow-up training
- Evaluate course providers
- Enhance property knowledge

Medium-term:
- Manager involvement
- Minute taking

Long-term:
- Commercial development

Figure 9.6   Chartwell case study: key training and development needs

---

PROFESSIONAL DEVELOPMENT

Training Objectives

'To assist staff in maintaining high standards of professional and technical competencies and to keep them updated on knowledge and information necessary for the successful execution of their jobs.'
Illustrative specific objectives were:

Short-term (3–4 months)	Timescale
Issue statement and policy guidelines to professional staff regarding Continuous Professional Development.	30.09.91

Medium-term (5–9 months)	Timescale
Use specialist lecturers from the property market to deliver 'tailor-made' programme in-house covering such areas as Investment Appraisal and general property market developments.	28.02.92

Long-term	Timescale
Establish a central database or resource centre for professional staff with access to videos, journals, books and other relevant publications.	30.09.92

Similar timed objectives were prepared for the other four areas: commercial development, management development, corporate development and secretarial development.

Specific brief statements on cost control and validation were included in the plan.

Figure 9.7   Chartwell case study: the plan format

Implementation and progress

Due to the size of the organization it was not thought appropriate to devolve budgetary control to business units – the training budget has been held centrally and managed by the Personnel and Training Manager. All training requests are forwarded through him – thus he is aware of all activity.

Every month a report is prepared for the Managing Director giving details of all training spend against budget. It is discussed in the course of a regular monthly two-way meeting on personnel issues. Board-level presentations on training are received on average about twice a year: immediately before and after the annual appraisal round. The Training Plan itself is reviewed, updated and rewritten about once every 18 months.

Considerable emphasis is put on the evaluation of training events and, where possible, a financial return is sought (for example, from negotiation skills); if not, some evidence of performance improvement is expected (for example from presentation skills). A specific post-course implementation form is in use, beyond the standard end-of-course form. Succession planning data, at the most senior level, is provided for a group-wide review.

Some observations

Training at Chartwell Land has undoubtedly been a success. The technical process used to formulate the training plan has been sound; and the method of presentation has offered a clear vehicle for communication throughout the organization. Over time, training and development has evolved into a broader statement of human resource strategy. Chartwell Land has moved away from *ad hoc* training initiatives into a sophisticated training culture with a greater emphasis on self-development.

Although the steps taken have been technically correct in the context of the organisation, success reflects in the main the determination of key individuals. Both the professional Personnel and Training Manager and the Managing Director were prepared to think long-term and plan accordingly. Sustained and consistent progress was therefore possible.

TRAINING CULTURE

Summary: *Training culture is a multi-faceted measure of the place that training holds in the life of the organization. It is related to the level and sophistication of training, and also to the extent to which it is pervasive. It is a relative concept. Part of the training manager's job is to identify, articulate, manage and monitor the training culture.*

Underpinning the other activities for the training function is the need to manage the training culture within the organization. It is the second key element of the new model. This can be divided into a number of subsidiary activities: the need to identify the most appropriate culture for the organization; the need to determine the current level of training culture; the need to ascertain ways in which any gap between existing and desired levels can be bridged (this is one of the main purposes of the training strategy); the need to monitor progress as the training culture is developed.

Training culture is a measure of the place that training holds in the life of the organization. It is related to:

● the sheer volume of training activity that is going on
● the extent to which such activity pervades the organization and is integrated into normal activities

- the sophistication of approaches used, the extent to which the organization has moved away from off-the-job training events that happen in isolation.

Training culture is, therefore, a relative rather than an absolute concept. As has been noted, the Ashridge model is one of the more valuable tools available to the training manager. The proposition that training and development can operate at three different levels of sophistication – fragmented, formalized and focused – is an implicit statement of the concept of a variable training culture. The table reproduced in Figure 3.6 (p. 57) offered a list of features or manifestations of training culture operating at a number of levels. In the absence of any other indicators, the list in Figure 3.6 would provide the training manager with a route map for positioning the prevailing level of culture and plotting subsequent progress. Arguably, some of the Ashridge features would have less relevance than others and the training professional would need to adapt the list to his or her circumstances.

An alternative list of features of training culture can be generated from the Investors in People (IiP) programme. This list is presented in Figure 9.8. The nine features have been adapted from a series of Investors in People assessment indicators, particularly those linked with the national standards on taking action to train and develop individuals and on reviewing training and development needs.

The list set out in Figure 9.8 can be subdivided into four groups concerning:

- the contribution to strategic planning (the first two features)
- needs identification (the third, fourth, fifth and sixth)
- gaining acceptance (the seventh feature and the qualifying statement at the foot of the proposition)
- monitoring and evaluating activity (the eighth and ninth features).

However the training culture is defined, it must be seen as a yardstick for gauging position and progress. There is no absolute situation in which training and development can be said to have achieved a state of grace, and training culture can be said to have arrived. To re-emphasize, the task of the training professional is to identify the organization's requirements and current position, and to manage progress. The task is not simply to drive the organization up an advancing training curve.

This last point needs stressing, not least because the commonly-held assumption among trainers is that training is a good thing and hence any increase in training activity is beneficial to the organization. Given a general recognition that the UK undertrains, this assumption is understandable. However, it will not always command acceptance with senior managers, as anyone who any practical experience of operating either in the private or the public sector will know. In this respect trainers can be their own worst enemies: they have a vested interest in an increased volume of activity and should understand that line managers will be

TRAINING CULTURE IS A MEASURE OF THE EXTENT TO WHICH THE ORGANIZATION

- has a plan which identifies the place of training and development in the fulfilment of business objectives
- identifies the resources available for training and development
- reviews training and development needs regularly against business objectives
- ensures that all employees are given the training necessary to do current and future jobs and are also given development opportunities
- encourages employees themselves to identify and meet job-related and development needs
- has a process for the regular review of the training and development needs of all employees by appropriate managers
- identifies the responsibility for developing people to be carried by each manager, and ensures that managers are competent to undertake such responsibility
- sets clear targets, clear control and clear accountability for training activities
- evaluates the outcomes of training and development activities and communicates the results

AND OF THE EXTENT TO WHICH THE ABOVE ARE APPRECIATED, ACCEPTED AND UNDERSTOOD WITHIN THE ORGANIZATION AND ARE ACTIVELY ENDORSED BY TOP MANAGEMENT.

Figure 9.8　Training culture

aware of this if they try to oversell. A useful first step in gaining greater credibility will be an explicit statement of recognition that the level and content of training activity should reflect the requirements of the organization. There is a resource cost involved, and not every organization will become a super-trainer or, using the Ashridge categorization, achieve a focused approach (see discussion in Chapter 3, p. 56).

There is a second, more subtle, point to be made here. Improving the training culture has to be a gradual process. To return to the Ashridge model, an organization cannot move from a fragmented approach straight to the training sophistication of the focused approach. One of the attractions of the Ashridge model has been identified as a clear ladder of progression, in which movement from fragmented to focused must include a passage through the formalized phase. Consider an example concerning the role of line management in identifying training needs. If training is generally perceived as a luxury or waste of time (fragmented approach), and the intention is to ensure that the main responsibility for training rests with line management (focused approach), there is a long, painful process to be undertaken in shifting attitudes. One way of achieving this is to encourage line managers to become more involved in training and development through their role as appraisers (characteristic of the formalized approach). This was the justification for the inclusion, in Part II, of a chapter on performance appraisal.

Most training managers in most organizations will face the task of developing the training culture. Because of the general state of training in the UK, the objective will be to achieve an improvement in the formulation of training strategy and its greater acceptance, better identification of needs and more appropriate monitoring and evaluation – in other words, a heightening of the training culture. The implications of this for the work of training manager, and of the other issues considered above, will be considered in the next chapter.

REFERENCES

1. Connock, S. (1992), 'The Importance of Big Ideas to HR Managers', *Personnel Management*, **24** (6), June.
2. I am grateful to Warren S. Sinsheimer for finding the source of the US delivery of this quotation and drawing my attention to the double use.
3. Tyson, S. (1995), *Strategic Prospects for HMR*, London: IPD, pp. 7–8.
4. I am grateful to Gary Miles and to Chartwell Land for permission to reproduce this case study, which first appeared in Croners' *Training and Development*.

10 The implications for the trainer

In the previous chapter I reviewed the role of the training function in the modern organization, and now consider the implications of this new role for the training manager. Three broad topics are covered: what are the consequences of the new role? What tasks will be undertaken by him or her? What skills will be required?

By this stage it should be evident that the training function in an organization should not be equated with the role and activities of those people who are designated trainers. If the latter are succeeding, training will have become a pervasive activity delivered by many people at all levels – a concept which finds its extreme expression in the learning organization. Indeed, one issue that this chapter considers is whether the training profession should survive in the future, or whether it should seek to manage its own extinction.

Although this pessimistic outcome is dismissed, it becomes obvious in the course of this discussion that the future place for the training professional in the organization remains to be determined. There are some powerful, and potentially contradictory, pressures at work. However, these provide more opportunities than threats and, if the training profession recognizes them and reacts accordingly, some exciting choices are available.

THE ROLE OF THE TRAINER

Summary: *The role that the trainer should play in the organization is a subject of continuing discussion. Current practices demonstrate wide differences with respect to delivery of training. The main choice for the trainer lies between acting as a strategic-facilitator or as a deliverer. The former role must be filled somewhere in the organization. Defining the relationship with the rest of the human resource function and contributing to their input to the strategic-planning process is of vital importance.*

In Chapter 9 I identified the role of the training professional as developing and articulating the training strategy and plans and promoting the training culture (see Figure 9.2, p. 216). The activities required to achieve these tasks include: strategy formulation; needs identification; gaining acceptance for the strategy and plans; monitoring and evaluation. The delivery of training as such does not appear in the above list – even though many training professionals would put this forward as the major justification of their presence in the organization. The extent to which the training function perceives itself as a supplier of training or as a manager of training activity is at the heart of the current debate on its role.

Even the most cursory inspection of the organizational place occupied by the training function in the UK will show that current practices vary. In the survey of best practice organizations considerable differences of approach to both the organization and delivery of training were recorded (see Appendix IV, pp. 274–5). Sometimes the most senior person responsible for training is within the headquarters' human resource function and carries other responsibilities. In other cases the most senior person is located at a training centre and is responsible for the delivery of what is clearly seen as a specialized function.

In 1990 an important study examined 'the ways in which the role of the trainer is changing and whether trainers themselves can be effectively managed and developed': *The Training and Development of Trainers,*[1] was based on an in-depth study of 23 companies, conducted by the Policy Studies Institute. After considering the economic and social forces that had revitalized and enhanced the training function, the report identified two issues central to the argument of this book.

First, it recognized that the training role within the organization was becoming far less compartmentalized:

> responsibility for 'delivering' training is passing from those who have 'training' in their job title to ALL managers. In this way, training is increasingly integrated within every function and every manager becomes a 'training' manager. A philosophy of HRD – human resource development – permeates the whole organisation.

As a consequence it was suggested that changes were inevitable in the role of the designated trainer. Trainers would be less involved in giving direct instruction and 'their role increasingly shifts to one of facilitating, advising and promoting good training' (p. 7).

The report went on to recognize the emergence of different types of trainers. This is the second issue. In particular, the report identified:

- strategic trainers, senior trainers who need to operate effectively with top-level managers in the organization
- practitioners, or specialist designated trainers, who need to facilitate training and support those who provide training as part of their everyday managerial responsibilities

● line managers, supervisors and others who need to be committed to training and development of their staff and acquire coaching skills.

At the heart of any discussion on the future of the training function is a choice between opposites. Both offer a legitimate and potentially valuable place for the training professional in the organization; they do, however, demand two very different orientations and require two very different skill bases in the trainer. A review of many articles on the role of the trainer leaves the reader with the impression that this dichotomy is not always appreciated. Bluntly, the training professional can rarely have it both ways. A choice must be made between what can be conveniently labelled the strategic-facilitator role and the deliverer role.

The 'strategic-facilitator' role is the one that has been a recurring theme throughout this book – the phrase is taken from the Institute of Personnel Management's analysis of performance management in the UK (see Ref. 2, Chapter 6). Acting as a strategic-facilitator involves taking a clear managerial responsibility for the overall provision of training in the organization and its effectiveness – in particular a responsibility for the development of the training culture.

In the alternative 'deliverer' role, the training professional does not assume primary management responsibility for the training effort; such responsibility lies elsewhere in the organization, with either the human resource function or line management, or a combination of both. Instead, the training professional is relatively detached and he or she offers a specialized service of advice, design and delivery, with the aim of meeting needs identified by those responsible for the management of the function.

This second role could easily be confused with the consultancy model discussed in Chapter 3 and accordingly dismissed as a pattern for future training provision. There is, however, a subtle distinction. What has been rejected is that the training function as a whole should operate as an internal consultancy. Within an organization of any appreciable size there is a requirement for both the strategic-facilitator role and the deliverer role to be fulfilled. The problem is how this should be done.

Any organization that takes training seriously must ensure that both roles are undertaken. In practice, however, there is a tendency to underestimate the important differences in the demands made of the training professional. Only anecdotal evidence is available here, but it seems that the dichotomy is often realized only when a new appointment is made. If an organization has to recruit someone to head the training function, those responsible for selection are obliged to clarify their thinking on what is required and could be faced with candidates who offer considerable expertise on training delivery, but questionable skills when it comes to the strategic-facilitator role that underpins the effectiveness of the function as a whole.

There is extensive literature on the orientation of the trainer as deliverer; less is available on the orientation of the trainer as strategic-facilitator. If the training professional wishes, or is required, to fulfil the strategic-facilitator role, it is essential that he or she is placed firmly in the mainstream of the organization. At the strategic level the important relationships will be with senior management and those responsible for strategic planning; at the tactical level the relationships with other human resource professionals are indispensable.

This underlines the importance of securing for training a prominent and influential position in the human resource department. Because of the organizational structures prevalent in the UK, it is difficult to see where else this role could be located – though in the longer term it is possible that it could be seen as a component of strategic planning and placed within that discipline.

However, the location of the role within human resources does not mean that it will be performed effectively. Much will depend on the structure of the human resources department and, in particular, the capability of the function to perform in a strategic manner. The training professional who wishes to fill a strategic-facilitator role must be prepared to devote some of his or her energy to assisting the broader human resource function in redirecting its own activities. He or she must be active in developing the function's contribution to the strategic-planning system and ensure that the strategic human resources drivers (see Figure 4.1, p. 74) are aligned with business requirements. The training professional cannot stand aloof from other human resource activities and expect to operate effectively in isolation.

This calls for a joint development of the capability of the human resource department involving training and the other members of the human resource department. How this can be accomplished must depend on the circumstances of the organization; the receptiveness of key members of the department is probably the most important factor. One successful method used is based on the concept of strategic milestones. Another is the use of the Balanced Scorecard (see Chapter 8, p. 182). An application of the former method has been described in a journal article[2] and is summarized below.

In a UK investment bank, the human resource department, together with the rest of the business, was asked to establish strategic milestones for a five-year period. The department's performance would be measured against the achievement of these milestones by agreed target dates. The milestones were designed to assist in the achievement of corporate strategy and reinforce accountability and responsibility. It was made clear that the submission of the milestones would be treated as an application for scarce resources.

In total 18 separate strategic milestones were produced as output from the exercise. All were intended to improve the effectiveness of the organization and hence follow through to the bottom line. Others were designed to improve professional skills, which underpin supply-led capability development. A number of them were designed to improve integration within the different business areas.

The format of the milestones was the same throughout: each carried a description, an implementation date, a measure of success and an indication of the behaviour from the business area. Wherever possible the measure of success was expressed in quantifiable terms.

An innovative feature of this format was the behaviour expected of business areas. Most of the milestones were contingent on positive support elsewhere in the organization: the request for their production as part of the management plan gave the personnel department the opportunity to make this contingent relationship explicit. The intention was not to threaten or attempt to batter the business area into submission – a 'fortress personnel' approach. Instead, the aim was to emphasize how much the achievement of personnel objectives is a joint approach between line management.

Those milestones that were most explicitly concerned with human resource development are set out in Figure 10.1, together with some comments on subsequent progress.

The production of milestones is only one approach to the joint development of the capability of the human resource department. What is important is that an approach is undertaken: the process involved can be as important as the product.

In summary, if the training professional has ambitions to fulfil the strategic-facilitator role, he or she must seek a high level of integration with the human resource department and help that department in securing an appropriate position in the organization – how this is done depends on the circumstances of the organization.

All this prompts the interesting question of whether the training function should survive in the long term? If training is fully integrated with human resources, and human resources integrated with the organization, is there a future for a specialism of training management? If human resource strategy (of which training is a key component) is built into business strategy, the decision as to who does what is surely subordinate.

One can sympathize with these sentiments without wholly endorsing their conclusion. It may be that, in the organization of the future, an effective training strategy will be accepted to such an extent that there is no longer a need for an individual to carry managerial responsibility for ensuring its implementation. The organization of today in the UK, however, has not yet accepted training, development or any thoughtful human resource policies as given. For some time to come there will clearly be a role for the training professional and it is important that he or she equips himself or herself with the necessary skills. Effective training management, through the strategic-facilitator role, is essential for the modern organization. The training professional may prefer the delivery role. He or she may have the luxury of choice; the organization does not.

Milestones	Date	Measures of success	Reaction/behaviour by Business Area
1 Analyse competences	1st Quarter 1991	Generic competences identified and accepted	Contribute to and understand potential value of such a tool
Competency analysis is an essential underpinning of other milestones. It is essential that business areas accept ownership of these competences and share agreement on their importance.			
2 Directors' development centre	2nd Quarter 1991	100 per cent of newly appointed directors to attend	Business Areas' acceptance of status of Director and recognition of the value of the centre
The first Directors' Development centre has now been held and proved to be a major integrative activity. Problems are likely to arise in terms of resistance from individual staff to participation. It is essential that there is full support for the activity and an acceptance by Business Areas of the importance of the Director in management as well as technical process.			
3 Career families	3rd Quarter 1991	Complete career families for accountants, technologists,	Business Areas' ownership and organizational support for career structure
A major problem for an investment bank is reducing the turnover of professional staff. The identification of career families, paths where people with technical expertise can move from a job in one business area to a job in another, is an important first step. In practice it is likely to prove easier to identify career families for accountants and technologists than for other jobs within the company. Business Areas must, however, be prepared to recognize the importance of a career structure and release valued staff to join another area.			
4 Improvement effectiveness of induction process	4th Quarter 1991	90 per cent of new staff attend a company Induction, 90 per cent of staff receive three months follow-up discussion, 90 per cent of staff receive six months formal reviews. Greater awareness and interest in other business areas.	Release of speakers and time to the process
This milestone, again is significant in terms of the tight targets for measurement of success. Often Business Areas are reluctant to release staff for external activities.			
5 Established structured training/development programme for technical and interpersonal skills for each Business Area	4th Quarter 1992	Each Business Area to have a published core curriculum	To assist in the identification of training needs
Different Business Areas will show different degrees of enthusiasm to the production of a core curriculum. Some of these Business Areas, which feel positive towards training, will regard it as an exciting challenge and contribute fully. Others will be reluctant and will need to be carefully nurtured. It is essential not to do the job for them since then they will not own the eventual product.			
6 Cross-career movements	4th Quarter 1995	One in 10 staff will have worked in more than one Business Area	Cultural acceptance. Acceptance of milestones on remuneration.
This is an important integrative milestone and one of the most difficult to achieve. There is a willingness on the part of the Business Areas to allow staff to move at junior level; there is also support for movement within the graduate training scheme. At senior level, there will be a reluctance to lose valued staff. Absence of cross-career movement is a major barrier to integration.			

Figure 10.1   Some strategic milestones

THE TASKS OF THE TRAINER

Summary: *Two perspectives on the trainer's task are considered. First, regardless of the role of the training manager, skills enhancement is perceived as the main justification for the existence of the training function in the organization. This activity must take place at the strategic, tactical and operational level. The second perspective comes from an analysis of modern systematic training, this can be viewed as a five-stage process and each stage presents its own problems.*

At the beginning of this chapter I argued that successful training is a pervasive activity, delivered by many people at all levels. Someone must take clear managerial responsibility for the overall provision of training in the organization and its effectiveness. If this responsibility is carried by the training manager, this is described as the strategic-facilitator role.

The job description and role of the training manager will vary between organizations, as will the commitment and responsiveness of line managers to the training effort. Whatever the situation, individual skills enhancement (alternatively expressed as developing individual competencies) will be seen as the main justification for training. It is this contribution that distinguishes training and development activity from other facets of human resource management. The training professional, to justify his or her existence, must have expertise appropriate to the organization and an ability to translate that expertise into visible results in terms of enhanced skills.

In some circumstances, particularly in smaller and less sophisticated organizations, the trainer will implement the skills programme directly by spending most of his or her time on in-house training activity. In the smallest organizations, where there is no training function as such, the programme of skills enhancement will be delivered by external bodies, whether consultants or public institutions. At the other extreme, where training activity has expanded to the level where the senior member of the designated training staff exercises purely management responsibilities, his or her activities will ultimately be directed towards enhancing the skills in the organization.

Again, the above statements would command general acceptance. What is perhaps less widely recognized is: first, that the process of skills enhancement must take place at different levels; second, that the training function should think beyond the narrowly-defined, short-term impact of training programmes and help capture the wider human resource benefits. Moreover, the demands made on the training professional at each of the strategic, tactical and operational levels are subtly different – a feature summarized in Figure 10.2.

The strategic level has been the subject of a full discussion in the previous chapter. The issues here relate to resource deployment – ensuring that the train-

AT THE STRATEGIC LEVEL

- assistance in the generation of the organization's competitive capabilities
- an expession of the training implications of the organization's plan/objectives, with particular attention to any issues of culture management
- a clear link between short-term training activities and longer-term development requirements.

AT THE TACTICAL LEVEL

- a significant contribution to the pivotal role that the human resource function must play in developing competitive advantage through people, in particular voicing the future skills required and how they should be met
- that training programmes are consistent and congruent with business objectives.

AT THE OPERATIONAL LEVEL

- implementation of a continuous programme of ongoing skills enhancement for the sophisticated workers required by the future organization; such a programme to have gained the full support of, and hopefully be driven by, line management.

Figure 10.2   Demands of modern training practice

ing effort is appropriately focused. In addition to the points already made on consolidating the link between training and the strategic planning process, it is worth re-emphasizing the importance of an explicit recognition of corporate culture. If the organization is undergoing deliberate and planned cultural change without at least supporting activity from the training function, an inevitable conclusion must be that the function has limited esteem in the eyes of senior management.

I have also examined the requirement that the training function should help capture wider human resource benefits. All training managers are aware that an effective training programme contributes to team-building, increased awareness of the organization's strengths (training events bring people together), and a general confidence in the employer. It is this aspect of training that spills over into development and forms the interface with other human resource activities. Much of this is implicitly, but not explicitly, accepted. Training professionals believe that a high-profile, well-managed training programme is an indicator of a progressive modern employer – but they are loath to say this. Part of the reason may be that such wider benefits are hard, if not impossible, to measure, and advocacy of such by-products of training activity may appear self-indulgent. This is unfortunate: the capture of wider benefits is a legitimate part of the training function's job. What is advocated here is a more hard-nosed approach to identifying, articulating and monitoring such benefits.

It is at the next level, the tactical level, that the training professional begins to exercise choices among the available methods of delivery. Here the expertise of the training manager should be used to determine, for example, the potential place for distance learning as opposed to training courses in skills training. Here also the choice must be made between generic training modules that can be made widely available within the organization at the expense of some specificity, or more narrowly-focused customized modules that have considerable relevance, though at the expense of cross-functional awareness generated within the training activity. This expertise, based on knowledge, experience and awareness, is another defining characteristic of the distinctive contribution that the organization has a right to expect from its training manager. At the tactical level, too, the need to capture wider human resource benefits should be taken into account.

A necessary feature of working at this level is the need to prevent, or at least discourage, training activity which is at odds with the overall strategy and inconsistent with the main thrust of skills enhancement. Even in the context of a comparatively low level of training activity, not all training is necessarily good for the organization. Some may duplicate activity which is already available elsewhere; some may simply be superfluous and represent a waste of resources. Programmes must be consistent and congruent with overall objectives.

It is perhaps easiest to see the process of skills enhancement taking place at the third level, the operating level. It is here that the day-to-day requirements are recognized and needs met. Within the UK population of trainers there is enormous expertise, painstakingly built up over a period of years, in delivering effective training. This expertise is vitally important, and is generally recognized as such by managers in an organization. It includes activities as diverse as training in interviewing skills, computer systems and basic accountancy. Also included are those activities well-known to training managers as 'remedial training', though never labelled as such.

The above insight on the task of the trainer follows from a perspective based on skills enhancement at its three levels. An alternative, but consistent, perspective can be gained by considering the delivery of systematic training in its modern context. The first perspective concerned the levels of operation; this second perspective concerns the sequence of activities.

Figure 10.3 shows this as a five-stage process. This is effectively an organizational adaptation of the systematic training model with its elements of identifying training needs, plan and design training; deliver training and evaluate outcomes. The identification of needs is now seen as a two-stage activity (the cascaded business needs and needs analysis), the design and delivery of training are expressed together as the determination and design of responses; the evaluation of training becomes much broader in scope. The subsidiary activities identified as bullet points underneath each of the main headings should not be taken to represent a complete list. This is not the intention. Instead, they focus on some prominent or difficult current issues.

I have already discussed most of the subsidiary bullet-points set out in Figure

The bullet points indicate significant current issues which should be considered at each stage.

1. Cascade of business issues into human resource development
- obtaining a clear indication of where the business is heading
- getting the training and development strategy considered at the appropriate stage.

2. Training needs analysis
- taking account of both organizational and individual needs (which arise from different sources)
- cannot be successful unless first cascade stage is right
- quality of appraisal information.

3. Determination and design of appropriate responses
- reinforcing on-the-job training/coaching
- delivery through distance/open learning.

4. Resourcing the responses/monitoring
- managing delivery and quality of outsourced training
- monitoring on-the-job training
- centralized or decentralized budgets/internal charging.

5. Communicating policies and responsibilities
- making known the availability of training opportunities
- distributing evaluation information/key training statistics
- disseminating reports on training activity.

Figure 10.3   **Stages of modern systematic training**

10.3 elsewhere in the book. Some aspects of the fourth and fifth stages, on information of statistics, budgeting and communications have not been discussed in detail. All are the subject of extensive literature, and the reader is referred to the *Gower Handbook of Training and Development* (see Ref. 1, Chapter 7) and the following discussion will be brief.

Adequate information on training is paramount. It allows the training professional to assess the extent to which the appropriate training culture is prevalent throughout the whole organization: the evenness of its permanence. It is a fact of organizational life that some senior managers are more committed to, and supportive of, training initiatives than others. Some senior managers may indeed become over-committed. This gives rise, particularly in large, decentralized organizations, both public and private, to training 'black holes' and 'random walks'. A 'black hole' is easily understood: it is a void in which nothing happens – the non-training or chronic under-training within the organization. A 'random walk' (a concept borrowed from operational research) is characterized by an individual heading off in a random direction for a randomly-chosen distance, stopping and then heading off on another walk in which direction and distance are again chosen randomly, and proceeding on the same basis again. A journey conducted as a series of random walks could end up anywhere, the destination with the highest probability being the starting point. Random walks in the training area are training events that have no relation to any evident broader business objectives and no synergy with other training events.

The (hopefully isolated) occurrence of both black holes and random walks is a likely consequence of a devolved responsibility to line managers. The training manager's information systems must be able to identify such aberrations at an early stage and begin corrective action.

The institution of training budgets is an automatic consequence of effective planning. Well-constructed training budgets held and managed at the right level are essential mechanisms in achieving three important objectives: cost control; the provision of information for decision-making by line managers; and the provision of information for decision-making by training managers.

The institution of a system of internal charging for courses delivered by in-house training staff (whether residential or not) is more controversial. None the less, internal charging has two considerable attractions. First, it allows a meaningful comparison to be made between the delivery of an in-house course and participation in a wholly external course. This may not always be a comfortable comparison for the training manager but the purpose of information systems is not to ensure that the training department enjoys a quiet life. The second argument for a system of internal charging is also hardly likely to offer the training manager a comfort factor. If the costs of an in-house course are made transparent to the line manager, they force a much harder focus on participation on the course. More questions are asked; more value is required from attendance.

In general, therefore, internal charging is to be welcomed. However, there is a case for maintaining a central budget for what might be described as broader development activity. For example, there is a movement among some progressive employers to send staff on external MBA courses – whether open courses or those customized for the employer. The costs involved here are likely to be carried on a central budget. Participation in such courses is often preceded by rigorous selection. Smaller departments could be required to spend a disproportionate part of their training budget if they carried the cost of a successful applicant; this could act as a disincentive to invest in development. The same argument can be extended to other activities that fall under the heading of broader development as distinct from training related to immediate job requirements.

The most appropriate way to communicate information on training must, more than any other aspect, depend on the circumstances. In some instances, where the attitude to training is well developed within the organization, there should, for example, be no need to 'sell' the plan. Line managers should see effective training and development of their staff as an essential part of their job. Senior directors, possibly through the use of the appraisal system, should ensure that this takes place.

Training departments in larger companies often produce guides or brochures. A typical contents list is set out in Figure 10.4. These guides are supplemented by information contained in office notices or whatever is the standard practice in the organization. Where technology networks are available, computer-based 'guidance booklets' and updates are used. Whatever the method the aim must be to make all staff aware that training takes place on a planned and systematic basis.

Introduction: including statement of endorsement by Chairman

Details of key contacts responsible for managing training

Guidance to managers, including pre- and post-course briefing

List of training events available by category:

- management and interpersonal
- technical
- information technology
- language training

Details of distance/open learning facilities

Statement of policy and approach on management development and careers

Statement of approach to qualifications

Figure 10.4 Typical contents of a training and development guide

The need to communicate and promote information on training is critical. Fortunately the literature is strong and readers are directed to Jessica Levant's *HRD Survival Skills*[3] (which is subtitled 'essential strategies to promote training and development within your organization').

THE SKILLS REQUIRED

Summary: *The ability to exert an influence in the organization beyond formal authority is the most important skill required by the trainer. Other skills needed are strategic awareness, diagnostic capacity and technical awareness – all of which have been looked at earlier in the book.*

The training manager, like every other manager, will need to be equipped with a new set of interpersonal skills to succeed in a rapidly changing environment.

Unless such skills are acquired the training manager's role will becom
and incidental. An outline list of requirements is presented in Figure 10.5.

The skills required of the training professional include:

- strategic awareness and understanding of the business imperatives
- dagnostic capacity and consultancy process skills
- technical expertise, which will increasingly involve the role of information technology

and the ability to exert an influence within the organization to manage the training culture.

Figure 10.5   The skills required of the training professional

The results of the survey of best practice organizations (see Appendix IV,
p. 269) expressed these requirements in terms of: consultancy skills and the ability
to make process interventions; a knowledge of business and commercial strategy;
knowledge and capability in information technology. The last of these three must
be recognized as the emerging technical skill requirement. The precise balance of
skills needed by the training professional will depend on the role that the individual is expected to play in the organization, in particular whether he or she is operating primarily as a strategic-facilitator or as a deliverer. However, strategic
awareness, diagnostic capacity and technical expertise will be required whatever
the role – though to different degrees. In all organizations the training function will
need to exert leverage beyond its formal status. Influencing skills are therefore
necessary to underpin the trainer's effectiveness, and the analysis will start with a
consideration of what is required here.

Rosabeth Moss Kanter, arguably the pre-eminent management writer of the last
decade, talks in terms of organizational power tools. Writing in *The Change
Masters*[4] she described them as three basic commodities:

- information (data, technical knowledge, political intelligence, expertise)
- resources (funds, materials, space, time)
- support (endorsement, backing, approval, legitimacy).

The training professional will have information, a facet of technical expertise that
will be discussed below; he or she is unlikely to have extensive resources at his
or her disposal, so support is essential. The training professional must achieve
influence and must recognize the value of choosing and using the appropriate
influencing tactics. A useful analysis of the alternative approaches has been
offered by Kipnis and others[5]. In the course of a research study of several hundred
managers they identified more than 1 400 different techniques by which managers
were able to exert influence. These were grouped into seven basic categories:

- reason, the use of facts and data to support the development of a logical argument
- friendliness, the use of flattery, goodwill and favourable impressions
- coalition, the mobilization of allies to support and therefore strengthen a request
- bargaining, the exchange of benefits and favours
- assertiveness, acting in a direct and forceful manner
- higher authority, the gaining of support from higher levels to back up requests
- sanctions, the use of rewards and punishments.

It is obvious, after the most cursory consideration of this list, that reason and friendliness are the first resort for the training professional. Reason can, however, only be used if the facts and data are there to support the argument – this underlines the importance of good information systems on training. The last resorts, higher authority and sanctions, are of less relevance to the trainer than to most other managers. Higher authorities are unlikely to welcome appeals. The only sanction that the training professional could have at his or her disposal is to bar someone from participating in training events – the equivalent of holding a gun to one's own head and threatening to shoot. Bargaining can be used to ensure participation in training events by trading cancellation charges when internal charging is applied; friendliness, and where necessary assertiveness, are the trainer's stock-in-trade; coalitions can be built, particularly with the more progressive and sympathetic line managers and other human resource professionals. The important point is that the training manager must recognize reality and use every means to achieve an influence beyond his or her status in the organization. As Robert Waterman put it:

> Every organization, no matter how well managed, has multiple goals, values and interests. It is never possible to align every person's objectives with every other's or with broader corporate goals. Political discussion, conflict, persuasion, bargaining and consensus building are the only way to resolve disagreement and get on with things.
>
> The convention you often hear in the well-managed companies is that the responsibility always exceeds the authority. If you see something that needs doing, do it, whether or not it fits your job description. In other words, if you have to operate outside channels, you have to work the informal organization in order to be an effective manager. That is not classic organization theory. It is political behaviour. The people who are good at it have a power that doesn't show up on the organization charts, but is power nonetheless. It is the way that much gets accomplished in this world (pp. 200–201).[6]

The training professional, then, must exhibit political behaviour and seek to promote the training culture through influence. He or she cannot achieve results by imposition.

INFLUENCING SKILLS: A US PERSPECTIVE

In Chapter 4, *Training in America: The Organization and Strategic Role of Training* was considered in the context of strategic human resources. This study for the American Society for Training and Development by Carnevale, Gainer and Villet analyses and stresses the importance of the training manager's capability to influence events.

The subtitle of the book is deliberate, and the text concentrates on a debate that is less well advanced in the UK. Evidence is presented and recommendations made on the way in which the training professional can achieve influence at the strategic level. Where the study is of particular value to the practising trainer, and repays examination, is that the tone is realistic. The question 'why should training and development advocates/professionals think strategically?' is dealt with and the answer offered in the following way:

> Training and development practitioners are, by and large, very good at what they do. They have defined their role as dealing with the humanistic part of the organization, the part charged with readying workers to assume new and increasing demands.
>
> This is an admirable viewpoint, but in today's modern business environment it is insufficient for success. Training and development professionals must transform themselves into savvy, knowledgeable business people who are not only competent in their functional roles but also understand the overall framework in which their business operates.
>
> Only with this understanding can training professionals gain the credibility to access the decision-making process inside a company. Only with a knowledge of strategic framework and company goals and strategies can the training professional help to develop the kind of organization wide environment that recognises the training professional as a major player on the organizational field (see Ref. 2, Chapter 3, p. 164).

The study characterizes the role of the training professional who is outside the strategic loop as that of the firefighter 'challenged to figure out how the unexpected implications of a strategic decision can be met after the fact'. Firefighters are expendable. In lean times they are the first to go; becoming part of the strategic loop means giving up the job of a full-time firefighter. The training professional must enter the strategic management process and be 'seen as an internal part of the organization's long-range picture'. This requires both an understanding of the strategic approach, and the ability to achieve influence – this is described as the ability to become an in-house lobbyist.

A successful internal lobbyist requires the same skills as the external lobbyist. He or she must gather intelligence and formulate a plan for influencing decision-makers. This requires information, persistence and patience. The recommended approach to influencing considered thereafter in the ASTD study repays reading in the original. It does not take support from the chief executive for granted, and it looks at the approach involved in building support in other ways. Success may require a pragmatic, almost cynical approach; it could come down to advancing the right alternative to the right person at the right time. The alternatives open to the training professional include:

- acting as a guerrilla, staging an underground effort to weave training throughout the fabric of the organization
- targeting the chief executive officer and launching an effort to influence his or her view of training
- engaging in institution building, building a training structure that connects with the strategic objectives of the organization
- co-opting outside influences to build a training infrastructure underpinned by government policies.

Most UK training professionals would recognize, and have practised to some degree, all four approaches. They have not, however, expressed them so eloquently.

STRATEGIC, DIAGNOSTIC AND TECHNICAL SKILLS

While influencing skills underpin the whole process, there remains the question of what other skills the training professional must deploy once that influence has been achieved. Here it is useful to return to Figure 10.5 and consider the three facets of the required skills.

The two main issues involved in developing strategic awareness have already been discussed. They are, first, the capability to translate the organization's business strategy into training terms through articulating a training strategy and developing a training plan; second, the need to position the training function in the organization in order to attain the right access to strategic information and to maintain the ability to implement strategic training plans.

The first issue was the subject of much analysis in Chapter 2. The bad news is that a much greater knowledge of business, economics and competitive strategy is required. This statement applies to both theory and practice. To summarize, the main conclusions that emerged from this discussion and from the first section of Chapter 4 are that:

- trainers should have a broad theoretical understanding of the strategic management process
- trainers should ascertain the methods used in their organization and stay close to the person responsible for strategic planning.

The positioning of the training function has been considered at several separate stages in the book. First, in Chapter 2 where the new human resources was outlined (p. 21). Second, in the first section of Chapter 4, where the link with strategic planning was reviewed (p. 73). Third, in the earlier section of this chapter, where I discussed the practical issues involved in repositioning the function (p. 234). This last section was concerned with developing a capability for the human resource department as a whole. The conclusion here was that the *process* of undertaking this exercise was as important as the *product*.

The capacity to diagnose what is needed to act in a way that meets organizational requirements underpins the effective delivery of human resource management in all its facets. Without that capacity the human resource professional will be production-oriented, unable to influence events within the broader organization. For the training professional this will mean performing an unsatisfactory reactive role in the ASTD terminology, acting as a firefighter rather than operating on a strategic level.

What is required to attain a diagnostic capacity is a particular set of consultancy skills. Although internal consultancy has been rejected as a model for training, all human resource professionals should nevertheless acquire a new set of skills similar to those used by external consultants.

These can be described as:

- entry skills, the need to gain acceptance within the organization in the defined role
- diagnostic or analytic skills, the ability to structure a problem through effective questioning
- intervention skills, establishing what needs to be done
- contractual skills, agreeing a firm commitment with the client
- transition skills, managing the continuous process of change.

The main emphasis, however, must be on the diagnostic or analytical skills. This involves a high degree of sophistication in the fact-finding interview – fortunately this is a skill that can easily be acquired through training.

The third facet, the skills required by the trainer, can be broadly described as technical expertise. The training professional must be able to bring something to the organization that is unique. He or she must have an expertise of value that no one else can offer.

Respect is gained within the organization only if the training professional is seen to know his or her business. The expertise that the trainer requires in the new context has been considered throughout this book. The requirements of modern training practice were presented in Figure 9.1 (p. 215), the role of the training professional in Figure 9.2 (p. 216) and the vital importance of training culture in Figure 9.8 (p. 228). Appropriate technical knowledge and skills are required.

Received wisdom on linking human resource management with strategy, on resource-based strategy, on knowledge management (to take just three examples), could be very different in five years' time. For this reason it is important that the training professional participates in the appropriate networks (for example, the Institute of Personnel and Development (IPD)). These provide opportunities ranging from formal continuing professional development to the informal exchange of views with others facing similar problems. Involvement is now high priority for the serious trainer.

Due to the emphasis on competition through people, perspectives on best practice training can be expected to emerge rapidly. Remaining abreast of the subject is demanding but it is also exciting. The agenda has changed and will continue to change – some speculation on the future issues will form the final part of this chapter. Discussion with other trainers – it is thankfully an open and supportive profession – will always help clarifying thoughts. Before this section on the skills of training is concluded, some final practical advice is offered. This comes, not from a currently fashionable management guru, but from General de Gaulle, who offered the following four aphorisms for managers:

- Exploit the inevitable
- Never relinquish the initiative
- Don't get between the dog and the lamp-post
- Stay in with the outs

The first three of these aphorisms could stand as a statement of the challenges facing the modern training professional. The fourth is a little more enigmatic, but may have some bearing on the following concluding discussion.[7]

A BROADER AGENDA

Summary: *Some key ethical issues facing the trainer are outlined. There is a danger of a growing division between organizations that demonstrate a high commitment to training and those that do not. Government policy may need to be reconsidered in the light of this problem.*

The topics of interest to the trainer are moving rapidly – hence the case for networking and participation in professional bodies given in the previous section. It is helpful to think in terms of multiple agenda. There is a technical agenda that is well covered in the professional journals and at conferences – topics like training and knowledge management, competencies and technology-based training would be included here. There is an organizational or business agenda that is centred on strategic and economic issues concerned with competitive success. This is a matter of general business education and updating. The training professional needs to know the literature and arguments that are well covered in journals and the heavy weekend magazines and newspapers. The third agenda is more elusive.

It can best be described as the ethical agenda. It is concerned with the effect that changing patterns of work have on individuals; it is concerned with equity in the workplace and with the use and abuse of power. The prediction is that these issues will become more important – the emergence of the psychological contract is an example (see Chapter 2, p. 32).

The past 15 years have been a period where there have been some more excessive management practices. Downsizing and delayering have been accompanied by a widening of reward and opportunity. In some cases management responses have been an inevitable reflection on the need to compete internationally; in others a necessary reaction to endemic inefficiency. However, there are many instances where management's right to management has not extended to a matching recognition of the obligations that brings. Over this period the human resource profession's interest in the ethical agenda can generously be described as dismal. With one or two exceptions, little question or challenge has been made to the more excessive management practices.

This will no longer be good enough. The new nature of competition, if it continues, will raise two compelling questions. First, for the competent and successful, work indeed has the potential to be fun, exciting and stimulating as well as rewarding. Nevertheless, there is a price to be paid for the high commitment required in terms of life balance and the dangers of stress and burn-out. Charles Handy has been well ahead of his time in recognizing and discussing these issues (see Refs 16 and 17, Chapter 1). Second, there are questions surrounding access to skills enhancement for those people who are not competent and successful. Such evidence as is available, which is considered more fully in Appendix I, gives no indication that, as a whole, the UK has embraced the new human resources. High-volume trainers, competing through people, are representative of best practice, not the norm. How, therefore, are the less able to avoid exclusion.

In his wide ranging attack on inequality of opportunity, *The State We're In*, Will Hutton states that: 'Society is dividing before our eyes, opening up new social fissures in the working population. The first 30 per cent are the disadvantaged ... the second 30 per cent are made up of the marginalised and insecure' (p. 106).[8]

The access to opportunities for skill enhancement reflects this division: 'In short training is in a mess, and highly inequitable in its distribution. Those without educational qualifications on low incomes and from unskilled families need training most. Yet it is precisely these workers who are unlikely to receive training' (p. 190).

More information would undoubtedly help, if only to focus on the extent of the problem. Over a decade ago one of the main recommendations of Charles Handy's important report *The Making of Managers*[9] was the establishment of an official statistical and information base, with statutory backing if need be, so that government and organizations can know what is happening to training in organizations. This was not implemented and subsequent official information is far less comprehensive.

The UK government's response is considered in Appendix II. This topic has been placed outside the main text, partly because the situation will change as the New Labour Government translates its intention into legislation, but also because this text is intended to appeal to an international readership. A brief summary focuses on one important issue.

As has been noted (and will be considered further in Appendix I, p. 255), there is as yet no evidence of a huge national commitment to employers' training. In the UK the previous Conservative Government and the New Labour Government, elected in 1997, understandably made exhortative voluntarism a key feature of the policies: this was described in Chapter 1 as the advocacy of best practice in the hope that it becomes universal. After much internal debate the New Labour Government rejected a compulsory training levy. It will introduce Individual Learning Accounts and the University for Industry. It has inherited, and will continue with, Investors in People and National Vocational Qualifications. The former has been commended throughout this book; the latter is briefly discussed in the context of this ethical agenda.

National Vocational Qualifications (NVQs) have received scant attention in this book. Yet they have been a significant feature of the UK training landscape since 1981, when the Manpower Services Commission, as the Government agency for training was then styled, produced its *New Training Initiative: An Agenda for Action*. This identified the need for a flexible, adaptable workforce achieved in part through a new set of training standards. Coincidentally the training community became interested in the idea of 'competencies' (see Chapter 5, p. 101) and the reform of qualifications became closely linked with this particular approach to measuring effectiveness. Since then successive Governments have encouraged the creation of industry Lead Bodies with the function of developing standards of occupational competence and approving a framework of NVQs.

The success of NVQs to date is considered in Appendix II, where National Training Targets will be discussed, and in Appendix III, where the critical Cambridge study is considered. However, an important question is raised in conclusion; how much can be contributed to the improvement of the nation's training problem though a restructuring of qualifications, on competency lines? Why do qualifications matter? In fact, the answer and emphasis differ from the perspective of the training manager, nation, employee or employer.

Clearly it is necessary that appropriate policies to support relevant qualifications (whether professional or vocational) are integrated into strategic plans for training. Part of the training manager's job will be to liaise with educational/ professional institutes. Often he or she will carry responsibility for determining who should be supported to seek qualifications and to what extent. This generates possibilities for improving the profile of training and supporting and modifying – interventions. Mishandled it can produce the opposite effect. To the nation, qualifications are important if they provide a stimulus to achieving a more flexible and competent workforce. This can arise in two ways. First, if recognized qualifications, which have a value or currency, are accessible the individual is more likely to want to attain them – and thus be more receptive to training. Second, if a national structure of qualifications encourages compatibility and flexibility across different sectors, the individual is more likely to retrain or to accept retraining. It is these arguments that have found favour with the government and trade unions.

For the employee, qualifications are also important for two reasons: they confer status and make the individual more attractive in the employment market. For the employer, at a cynical level, qualifications as such do not matter. What does matter is the recruitment and retention of a trained workforce that can meet current and future needs. However, the structure of available recognized national qualifications has a considerable impact on how that objective is met. For example, an employer who does not offer staff access to these qualifications is likely to be at a disadvantage compared with competitors who do permit such access. As an illustration, many company-based MBAs were introduced as much for recruitment and retention as for development. As a public-spirited citizen, the training professional may well be committed to the development of a more *qualified* workforce; as a company employee he or she is committed to providing the firm with a better *trained* workforce. The need to be sensitive to the developments in the national qualification structure, therefore, arises in part because of the considerable impact that they have on the appropriate training provision.

To many industries and sectors, the introduction of National Vocational Qualifications has undoubtedly provided a stimulus to the achievement of a more flexible and competent workforce – particularly at lower levels (retail and hairdressing are often cited as examples). In other situations, and at the highest levels, NVQs have not found favour and it is important to consider why.

Many leading-edge organizations regard competency frameworks as an important tool in the new human resources. They are a signal to employees of the skills they should acquire and demonstrate, and they must therefore reflect the business drivers. Many transnational organizations, for example, have deliberately set out to achieve international consistency in their competency frameworks because this is a way of reinforcing a key business objective. Many other organizations have, as part of their new approach to careers, supported staff in attaining qualifications with 'currency' – these have value in the labour market so that the individual's employability is increased. MBAs and relevant professional qualifications are examples. For these organizations, NVQs are unlikely to contribute much to the training effort. It is no surprise therefore that the high-level generic NVQs, and the Management Charter Initiative, have made such limited impact.

The NVQ framework has absorbed a considerable amount of energy over the last decade. There is much effort invested and a lot of credibility at stake. Some organizations in some sectors have found the frameworks of value. The suggestion is not that the structure is scrapped. What is required is a more realistic recognition of what NVQs can achieve. Best practice organizations will continue to train to compete on the international market. It is the worst practice organizations that are the problem. In the first edition of this book the introduction of fiscal measures designed to ensure that employers invest a minimum amount in the training of their workforce was advocated. This is no longer likely to find political acceptability, though an alternative proposal that I have formulated, based on setting minimum standards, may be of interest to the reader.[10] This approach is built on the experience of financial regulation: here there is a clear signal that training is needed to maintain the required business standards. Trained staff and appropriate practices are required to protect consumers; the management of the training process is seen as vital to that task. The approach is a mixture of the prescriptive and descriptive: certain things must be done; how they are done will depend on the circumstances of the organization. The above idea was intended as no more than a basis for discussion. The firm conviction, however, is that the degeneration of the UK into a high-tier progressive sector of training firms and remainder of minimal trainers would have disastrous social consequences.

NVQs, then, if they are to be effective instruments of national policy, should be judged differently. To what extent do they create opportunities for people who would not otherwise receive training for skills enhancement? Hard facts and hard information is required. There may be less emphasis on exhortative voluntarism and more on minimum standards. Worst practice, not best practice, is the proper area for government focus. A repositioning of National Vocational Qualifications may be an inevitable result.

This excursion is now complete. Training is important. Job-related skills give people pride in their work. They can acquire a new self-respect as they have the confidence to deal with demanding situations (the awkward subordinate or colleague) or perform better in everyday situations (in some sectors the improvement in customer service has been remarkable). The challenge for the nation is to ensure that these opportunities for self-respect are not the preserve of a minority of the workforce.

REFERENCES

1. Horton, C. (1990), *The Training and Development of Trainers*, Sheffield: Policy Studies Institute/Training Agency.

2. Riley, K. and Sloman, M. (1991), 'Milestones for the Personnel Department', *Personnel Management*, **23** (8), August.
3. Levant, J. (1998), *HRD Survival Skills*, Houston: Gulf Publishing.
4. Kanter, R.M. (1984), *The Change Masters: Corporate Entrepreneurs at Work*, London: Allen and Unwin.
5. Kipnis, D., Schmidt, S.M., Swaffin-Smith, C. and Wilkinson, I. (1984), 'Patterns of Managerial Influence: Shotgun Managers, Tacticians, and Bystanders', *Organizational Dynamics*, **12** (3), Winter.
6. Waterman, R. (1988), *The Renewal Factor*, London: Bantam Press.
7. I am grateful to Dr Al Vicere of the Smeal College of Business Administration, Penn State, for drawing my attention to General de Gaulle's aphorisms.
8. Hutton, W. (1995), *The State We're In*, London: Jonathan Cape.
9. Handy, C. (1987), *The Making of Managers*, London: NEDO.
10. Sloman, M. (1996), 'Putting Training on Track', *New Economy*, London: Dryden Press/*IPPR*, **3** (3), Autumn.

Appendix I: National trends in employers' training

The focus for the book has been on the need for the training manager to determine and manage the training agenda for his or her organization. It is not a book about national training policy. Nevertheless, the wider debate will have an influence on what happens in the organization. Accordingly the next three of the four Appendices have been included to provide sufficient background information. Appendix I outlines such evidence as is available on national trends in employers' or corporate training. In particular, it considers whether there has been a significant change in employers' training consistent with the implementation of what has been called the new human resources (see p. 7 and Chapter 2, p. 21). Appendix II reviews the main elements of Government policy at the time of writing. Appendix III summarizes the findings of a Cambridge University study on the employers' response to the national training priorities.

The starting point must be a recognition that there is a paucity of information. During a period of urgent debate on the UK's training infrastructure in the late 1980s, Charles Handy produced the report, *The Making of Managers*.[1] One of his recommendations was the establishment of an official statistical and information training database, with official backing if need be, so that government and organizations can know what is happening – as was the case in France. This has never been implemented and much of the debate takes place against the background of a favourable interpretation of very limited facts.

The survey of training in the UK (hereafter referred to as the National Training Survey) published in 1989 remains the most comprehensive. It will be considered in detail for two reasons: first, because it offers a template for data collection on training; second, because it offers a benchmark on training costs and volume. The National Training Survey was commissioned by the relevant arm of the government's Department of Employment – then styled the Training Commission; the work was undertaken by the management consultancy, Deloitte, Haskins and Sells (DH&S) in conjunction with IFF Research.[2] Some 1700 employers were sampled, and these were taken to be representative of some 208 000 employers covering about 17.8 million employees. (The main categories excluded were the armed forces and related activities, agriculture and very small employers.) Interviews took place in spring and summer 1987. It was an ambitious undertaking covering costs, volumes and aspects of the management of training in the organization. The results were published in conjunction with five other surveys as part of a large-scale investigation into the arrangements for financing vocational education and training in Great Britain, known collectively as the Training Commission's Funding Study.

The National Training Survey used a comprehensive definition of costs: for the first time, all the important elements of labour costs were included – trainees' and trainers' time for instruction on- and off-the-job, also senior management time and other support costs. Using this wide definition it was estimated that some £14.4 billion was spent on training in 1986/7 by the employers covered by the survey. The average cost of training to the employer (net of grants and other income) amounted to £809 per employee and £1685 per employee who received training. Wages and associated labour costs accounted for about 75 per cent of expenditure, rising to 85 per cent if senior management costs were included.

The second significant point is reflected in the average cost of training figures presented above. There was a very wide spread in the commitment to training. The training recorded as having taken place in 1986/7 was given to 48 per cent of employees: the remaining 52 per cent received no training at all over the twelve-month period. The pattern varied by sector and by type of employee. For example, about a third of employees in the private manufacturing sector received some training, compared with a half in the private services sector and nearly 60 per cent in the public sector. Managerial and professional workers were more likely to have received training than skilled and semi-skilled manual workers; new recruits received more training than established employees.

However, the results showing the incidence of non-training made depressing reading. In another component of the Funding Study, the Policy Studies Institute (PSI) reported on the training experience of individual adults: one-third of the sample of adults interviewed claimed *never* to have received any training.[2] The PSI also reported that employer-funded training was more likely to be received by those in non-manual occupations and by younger adults. There was a higher incidence of professional staff receiving employer-funded training throughout their working life. Together with the National Training Survey, the PSI suggestion that the level of initial education and training appears to be strongly related to subsequent training participation underlined the national concern. It became apparent that the UK faced the real prospect of creating an underclass of people who would expect no training and might resist it if it were offered. On the other hand, there was considerable emphasis on training those of the workforce who were obviously trainable.

The data on volumes provided by the National Training Survey produced some valuable insights into training patterns. The average amount of training received across all types of employees was seven days in the year. Since it was concentrated on the 48 per cent of employees who received training, the average given to employees who received training was 14.5 days. For these staff an average figure as high as 14.5 days in a year may seem impressive. However, two facts should be borne in mind: much training is concentrated on trainee populations; it is split between off-the-job and on-the-job training. Certain populations, for example graduate trainees, received up to 40 days' off-the-job training a year. Not all these populations are small: student nurses constitute the largest trainee population in the UK with 40 per cent of their time being spent in training.

The split between off- and on-the-job training was one of the most interesting features of the study. Data-capture here was far from easy – organizations do not record on-the-job training. By extensive sampling, however, it was found that the overall average of seven days' training per individual split 3.4 on-the-job and 3.6 days off-the-job. In other words roughly half the training delivered in the UK is received by trainees at their normal place of work. Few commentators would have predicted this result.

All this suggests that the number of days' off-the-job training received by employees is a valuable index of training activity. First, because it is a clear measure and one that is recognized by line managers and trainees alike. Moreover, it seems that the general extent of other training activity is related to the prevailing level of off-the-job training. Certainly, at the extreme, organizations that undertake no off-the-job training may not offer much else beyond a primitive approach to on-the-job training. Organizations that are high-level trainers are more likely to have embraced the sophisticated approach to training actively advocated by the profession. For these reasons, it is suggested that the average number of days off-the-job training received should be given prominence as a measure of the health of the training effort in the organization.

Using the National Training Survey as a benchmark, it is now appropriate to ask two questions: first, has there been a significant increase in employer's training activity over the subsequent decade? In particular, what evidence is there to suggest that the step-change consistent with the demands of the new human resources has taken place? The Government-sponsored report, *Winning*, outlined in Chapter 1, p. 7 (see Ref. 1, Ch. 1), suggested that as much as 10 per cent of employees' time (over 20 days a year) could ideally be spent in training. The second question concerns the distribution of training: is training still concentrated on the trainable?

The problems caused by the paucity of data have already been noted. There is simply no evidence to come to a firm conclusion on the second question. Government policies on training (see Appendix II) have been in part designed to promote wider access to training opportunities but, as will be shown, their effects are likely to be indirect. There is no compulsion for employers to train. If, however, there has been a striking increase in the training provided by employers it seems reasonable to suppose that the access of the least able would have improved. If there has been not a striking increase it seems reasonable to suppose that the pattern of access to training has remained relatively undisturbed.

What then, within the context of such information as is available, can we say of overall trends in training volumes? This requires an examination of the two continuing statistical series and the occasional partial surveys.

Detailed labour market statistics are produced quarterly in the Labour Force Survey. This includes a question on the proportion of employees who had received training in the previous four weeks. The quality and reliability of deduction based on this data was subjected to an incisive critical analysis by three academics specializing in labour economics, Felstead, Green and Mayhew. The conclusions of their report, *Getting the Measure of Training*,[3] do not offer much comfort. They reinforce a central theme of this Appendix: 'Despite the prominence of work-based training in national policy debate the published statistics are poor. They fail to give solid information on either the volume or the quality of training' (p. v).

The authors then turn their attention to the inferences that can be drawn from information on the proportion of employees receiving training over the previous four weeks. Trend analysis of this series is complicated by a number of technicalities – notably a change in the positioning of this question in 1994. However, superficially there is evidence of an increase: in 1985 this figure was 9.5 per cent; there was a steady increase recorded to 15.2 per cent in 1994 and a plateau thereafter (the spring 1998 figure, the latest available, stands at 14.6 per cent). However, Felstead, Green and Mayhew cast doubt on the crude assumption that employers' training had increased by 50 per cent over the decade. The use of other data from the Labour Force Survey, led them to the following conclusion:

> The Labour Force Survey is commonly used to give a picture of increasing training ... But closer analysis shows that the *volume* of training did not rise: spread over all employees the average time spent on off-the-job training was 39 minutes per employee in 1985 and 40 minutes in 1994. The best available statistics fail to support the contention that there has been a training revolution in Britain (p. v).

The second continuing statistical series is continued in the Government-funded Skills Needs in Britain Survey. This survey is conducted on behalf of the Department for Education and Employment by IFF Research, and is based on telephone interviews with (in 1997) over 4 000 organizations employing 25 people or more. In this survey employees were asked to estimate the number of days off-the-job training provided per employee. The report warns that such estimates can be subject to large errors, but the longer-term trend does suggest that the average amount is increasing slightly. The distribution continues to give cause for concern: in 1997, at one extreme, 65 per cent of managers and administrators received off-the-job training; at the other end 9 per cent of plant and machine operators received off-the-job training.[4]

IFF Research also undertook the one comprehensive survey since the National Training Survey. In September 1996 figures derived from the European Commission sponsored Continuing Vocational Training Survey (CVTS) were published.[5] These figures related to data collected in 1993. The design of the survey was driven by European statistical requirements and did not correspond to the categorizations used in the National Training Survey – coverage, definitions and methodology were different. However, despite these qualifications, IFF were able to indicate that, in 1993, 88 per cent of employers with ten or more people provided some form of planned training for their employees compared with 80 per cent in 1987. However, the volume evidence could not be described as encouraging.

In 1993, the survey indicated, employers provided 49m training course days which was less than 65m recorded in 1987 – though the latter embraced much wider activity including in-house discussions. On average in 1993 each employee spent 2.7 days on training courses and 1.0 day being supervised during on-the-job training. Rather more encouragingly the proportion of employees participating had increased since 1987 – both in terms of participation in training courses (45 per cent in 1993 compared with 35 per cent in 1987) and on-the-job training (47 per cent and 33 per cent).

Other surveys, which are narrower in focus and more limited in sample size, do show a more positive picture. An Open University Business School/Institute of Management Study published in 1997 concentrated on management training and development.[6] This suggested that the priority given by organizations to management development has increased significantly compared to the situation a decade earlier – and is expected to rise in the foreseeable future. The amount of training received by individual managers had increased in both larger and smaller companies. The regular surveys undertaken by the Industrial Society, which are somewhat wider in focus but relatively small in sample size, also report positive trends.

One other piece of evidence, though of a different form, must be introduced, and it weighs firmly on the negative side of the balance. The Swiss-based Institute for Management Development (IMD) produces a survey of global competitiveness published as a World Competitiveness Yearbook. A league table is produced based partly on statistical data and partly on a survey from 4 000 business executives worldwide. In the 1997 survey the UK moved from 19th to 11th, slipping back to 12th in 1998 – 46 countries were included in the survey. However, and this has been a consistent pattern, the UK's strongest scoring is in the 'business' factors of internationalization and finance. The UK's ranking in the people category is its lowest: the UK scores highly for literacy and employment but relatively badly for the use of skilled labour and for the educational system. In the most relevant component for the purposes of this book, in-company training, the country was 33rd out of 46.[7]

This excursion into the available information is complete. The conclusion must be that, although the evidence is patchy and inconsistent, employer training activity in the UK remains a cause for concern. There is no hard data to support that a step-change improvement has taken place over the last decade – the more comprehensive the information the less likely this appears. Best practice employers may be pressing ahead; managers may be receiving more training both absolutely and relative. However, the extent of activity and its distribution continue to be a national problem. The new human resources with its high commitment to training may offer a beacon; it cannot be said to represent comprehensive reality.

REFERENCES

1. Handy, C. (1987), *The Making of Managers*, London: NEDO.
2. The Training Agency (1989), *Training in Britain, a Study of Funding, Activity and Attitudes*, London: HMSO. See also: The Training Agency (1989), *Training in Britain, a Set of Research Reports*, London: HMSO.
3. Felstead, A., Green, F. and Mayhew, K. (1997), *Getting the Measure of Training*, Leeds: Centre for Industrial Policy and Performance, University of Leeds.
4. (1998), *Skills Needs in Britain*, 1997, London: IFF Research.
5. (1996), *Employer-provided Training in the UK*, 1993, London: IFF Research.
6. Thomson, A., Storey, J., Mabey, C., Gray, C., Farmer, E. and Thomson, R. (1997), *A Portrait of Management Development*, Institute of Management/Open University Business School.
7. (1998), *World Competitiveness Yearbook*, Lausanne: IMD.

Appendix II: Government policy on employers' training

The starting point for an analysis of government policy must be a recognition of a degree of consensus that extends across and beyond the political spectrum. This is best described as 'exhortative voluntarism'. The basic tenets of competition through people and the new human resources (see Figure 1.1, p. 6 and p. 7) are accepted, hence a high volume and good quality of employers' training is essential for economic growth. This is to be encouraged by statements indicating best practice. Compulsion is unacceptable; intervention, particularly concerning standards, benchmarks and targets, is acceptable. The reform of qualifications can help promote training and is to be welcomed.

In the late 1980s an important debate on employers' training took place – among other outcomes this prompted the production of the National Training Survey discussed in Appendix I. Since then there has been a general feeling that something must be done: Government, employers and all those involved in vocational and management training in the education sector agree on this.

At the time of writing (December 1998), the New Labour Government is operating within a framework inherited from a predecessor of a different political persuasion. To some extent this framework can be expected to continue. New initiatives on individual learning have been announced but are not in operation. Significant differences between the Conservative Government and the New Labour Government elected in 1997 are the latter's determination to change the climate through learning initiatives focused on the individual and their insistence that changes in national training activity must support social inclusion. I outline the elements of the inherited framework and consider the initiatives in turn. The discussion is restricted to those elements and initiatives that have a potential impact on employers' training. The wider issues of education and employment lie outside the scope of this book.

The current Government's commitment to exhortative voluntarism was not always so secure. In 1993 the Labour Party National Executive proposed that 'Employers sufficiently irresponsible to fail to provide training should force a training levy'. This would involve the collection of monies across the spectrum and their return only to those organizations that were considered to be training effectively. This would probably have been expressed in terms of a percentage of payroll costs spent on training – a return to the position that prevailed in the late 1960s. In 1990 such a levy system was introduced in Australia but it was suspended until 1996 pending a review, and since then support for the system in Australia has diminished.

Labour Party policy in the UK also moved away from the levy – although the existing levies in the construction and engineering industries will remain in place. In March 1996 the Labour Party produced *Labour's Plan for a Skills Revolution*, which replaced support for a levy by three distinct sets of proposals. These were the introduction of 'Learn as you Earn' accounts; a new stimulus for the Investors in People programme and a way of making it more accessible to smaller organizations; the establishment of a University for Industry. New policies for Investors in People are currently the subject of consultation. Development on the first and third proposals are considered below. First, however, the framework inherited from the previous Government is outlined.

The most accessible expression of this framework is found in the National Targets for Education and Training. National targets were first introduced in 1991 and were revised in 1995. The approach was endorsed in principle by the New Labour Government in 1997 when it first issued a consultation document on targets,[1] and then published revised targets in November 1998.[2]

Six targets were put out for consultation in 1997. All were expressed as a desired outcome by the year 2000. Three were foundation targets (relating to young people). The other three are lifetime targets:

- 60% of the workforce to be qualified to NVQ level 3, advanced level GNVQ or 2 GCE 'A' level standard
- 30% of the workforce to have a vocational professional, management or academic qualification at NVQ level 4 or above
- 70% of all organizations employing 200 or more employees, and 35% of those employing 50 or more, be recognized as Investors in People.

At the time of consultation there was little prospect of the NVQ targets being achieved, but some optimism about the impact of Investors in People. The best estimate on the NVQ targets was 45 per cent to 47 per cent compared with the desired 60 per cent for the first lifetime target and 26 per cent compared with 30 per cent for the second. Despite huge promotional pressures it seems that NVQs have failed to ignite the imagination. As a result the new National Learning Targets, which were now to express desired outcomes by the year 2000, represent a significant downgrading of ambition. They were expressed in terms of:

Targets for organizations:

- 45% of medium-sized or large organizations recognized as Investors in People
- 10 000 small organizations recognized as Investors in People.

Targets for adults:

- 50% of adults with a 'level 3' qualification
- 28% of adults with a 'level 4' qualification.

A third adult target – for Learning Participation – is due to be announced during 1999. Targets have also been set for 11-year-olds, 16-year-olds and young people (19- and 21-year-olds).

Most NVQ awards are at the levels 1 and 2 (below 'A' level standard) and are awarded in the service section. 'Providing Business Services' and 'Providing Goods and Services' together account for over 60 per cent of the 1996/7 awards. The late 1980s intention to revolutionize management training through the introduction of NVQ-related management qualifications must now be deemed to have failed.

The New Labour Government is currently in the process of establishing 70 national training organizations (NTOs) for particular sectors. Together with reformed Training and Enterprise Councils (TECs)[3] they will form the basic framework in which the desired improvement must be secured.

What does mark a development, if not a departure, is the Government's approach to change the climate through the promotion of lifelong learning. In a Green Paper published in February 1998[4] the Government committed itself to developing a culture of lifelong learning and creating a framework of opportunities for people to learn. Learning must be the shared responsibility of employers, individuals, the education system and the wider community. In most cases employees and individuals (or just the latter) will bear the cost. The Government will, however, provide incentives through Individual Learning Accounts (ILAs).

The Green Paper made it clear that ILAs will be open to everyone, allowing individuals to save and borrow to finance their learning. Tax incentives will be available and the individual's contribution will be supported by public funds. Initial estimates were of an intention to create one million ILAs, each supported by £150 from public funds provided the individual contributes £25.

The second new initiative is the creation of a 'virtual' or electronic University for Industry (UfI). A pathfinder prospectus issued in 1998 suggested that the University will act as a broker (providing referral services), as a change agent (publicizing the value of lifelong learning for adults) and as a directing force (investigating skills shortages and coordinating actions to deal with them). It will rely solely on open and distance learning; it will concentrate on priority areas where there are potential large-scale demands and will reflect national strategic needs. These are basic skills of literacy and numeracy; information and communication technologies in the workplace; small- and medium-sized business; and four specified sectors of the economy. The targets are bold: the intention is that, by 2002, UfI services will be used by 2.5 million individuals and employers.

The current Government has placed high hopes on lifelong learning. Further infrastructure changes will take place if they can been seen to facilitate and support the success of this approach. Lifelong learning, training targets, NTOs and TECs are, however, only the means to an end. The two key objectives must be: uprating the skills of the workforce for competitive purposes; ensuring that all sections of the workforce have an opportunity to develop their skills. Success against these objectives must be the basis on which the effectiveness of national policies are judged. It is evident that, if the voluntarism approach, reinforced by a cultural change towards individual learning, does not prove effective, new initiatives will be considered. While compulsion in the form of a levy is unlikely, greater incentives or subtler penalties are distinct possibilities.

Details of a survey of employers' responses to the initiatives that are in place at the time of writing are now presented in Appendix III.

REFERENCES

1.   (1997), *Targets for our Future*, Sheffield: DfEE Publications.
2.   (1998), *National Learning Targets for England*, Sheffield: DfEE Publications.
3.   (1998), *TECs: Meeting the Challenge of the Millenium*, Sheffield: DfEE Publications.
4.   (1998), *The Learning Age: A Renaissance for a New Britain*, Cmd 3790 (a Government Green Paper), London: Stationery Office.

Appendix III: Employers' response to national training priorities

In 1998 The Cambridge University's Department of Geography undertook a survey that concentrated on employers' responses to national training priorities. The relevant results have been reproduced by kind permission of Professor Robert Bennett and Sian Bowen. The survey summarizes the findings based on the views of 60 organizations on three topics: business response to key education and training initiatives; the development of links with training and education and initiatives; ways of influencing the development of training and education into national policy. Only the findings from the first area will be considered here, and will be further restricted to those concerned with corporate training.

The main conclusion in this area is a far-reaching one, and one that is consistent with the results of the study described in Appendix IV. The Cambridge survey underlined the central importance within the organization of competitive forces in determining the training strategy for a company.

> Our concluding comment, based on these findings, is that business requirements from the education and training system, interaction with education and training institutions, and the success or failure of policy initiatives does not exist in some sort of separate box distinct from commercial considerations which affect other areas. True, the links may not always be as strong, or indeed so explicit as other areas which impinge directly on the internal management of business organisations. But they exist nevertheless, and there are some important implications for the way business and government co-operate to frame policy in order to support the 'economic competitiveness' goal (p. 30).[1]

The commercial imperative and the diversity of organizations have an inevitable impact on the effectiveness of national training policies. As a result, the researchers recommend that:

> government needs to recognize the increasing diversity of business organisations, and to deliver policies which appropriately reflect that diversity. This has implications in terms of the boundaries of 'national' policy-making, but also suggests a far more targeted approach where the government has a valid role to play in levering change (Executive Summary, p. 3).

The response to Government policy in general suggests that current effectiveness is open to doubt:

> With regard to key policy initiatives the survey reveals a mixed response. Investors in People appears most successful both from qualitative and quantative information gathered here. NVQs appear to have established widespread use with the business community but are far from the main vocational qualification that the original concept implied. There are ongoing issues with NVQs, particularly the criticism of 'bureaucracy' which show no signs of disappearing despite efforts to address this. Apprenticeship schemes have had some success, and there is some potential for further take up according to results here. The key issue with these and other initiatives is, how much impact have these had on employer training investment? There can be no doubt that government messages about the responsibility of employers for training and developing their workforce have been consistent since the mid-1980s. Few could argue that there is an 'information' problem. Rather, we can see that the mixed responses to IiP and NVQ suggest that different reactions are more likely to be linked to the economics of certain organizational characteristics. The main conclusion, though not the only one we draw from this, is that national level targets, at least in terms of the *training market*, are not appropriate (p. 29).

More specific findings from the survey are set out in Figure AIII.1. The conclusions are significant. Exhortative voluntarism is unlikely to be effective, and there is a need for a review of national training policy given the primacy of commercial drivers. I recommend readers to read the report in its original.

- The main concern of business is getting the outputs from the *education* system rather than various training initiatives (related to employer training behaviour).
- Literacy and numeracy issues still need to be addressed, but other core competencies such as communication and language skills are more important for transnational organizations and those companies with high reliance on individual human capital.
- NVQs, while they are now widely accepted by employers, are far from the national framework of vocational qualifications which was intended at the outset. From this, and other surveys, NVQs show little sign of assuming this position, particularly in relation to organizations where there is a high reliance on individual human capital.
- Investors in People, though receiving substantial support from business in terms of the concept and implementation, looks unlikely to achieve the coverage of sectors of the business community which could benefit most. Even where it does, the main effect is to *focus* training investment rather than increase it.
- The increasing diversity of the business world makes national targets for training inappropriate. Targets should only be developed for something over which there is reasonable degree of control. The highly specific nature of company training needs militates against this.

(Reproduced with permission from *Training, Education and Business Diversity* (see Ref. 1).)

Figure AIII.1   Issues on effectiveness of training policy

REFERENCE

1. Bowen, S. and Bennett, R. (1999), *Key Employer Survey: Training, Education and Business Diversity*, Cambridge: University of Cambridge, Department of Geography.

Appendix IV: How are organizations responding?

The theme of this book is that the competition through people, leading to a new human resources, offers a window of opportunity for trainers. However, it has been argued throughout that each training manager will face different circumstances, demanding contingent solutions. Certain key issues have nevertheless emerged which could be said to apply throughout all organizations – for example, the challenge of the new opportunities afforded through technology.

To give some further insight on current thinking, I undertook a short survey of some more thoughtful training organizations. In no sense did I intend this survey to be a comprehensive analysis of current practice. The intention, as is developed below, was to test reactions to the important issues – opportunities, influences and dilemmas – of modern training practice.

At a straightforward level, best practice in UK training can be now said to be represented by Investors in People and by the holders of National Training Awards. Investors in People has been commended throughout the book and represents a business-neutral framework in which the harder aspects of training management should be delivered. Not all best practice organizations have, of course, opted to secure IiP. Although the underlying framework for National Training Awards (NTAs) has been rejected as a training model (see Chapter 3, p. 50), organizations which have been awarded NTAs have frequently demonstrated leading-edge thinking. Readers are recommended to study the annual review of National Training Awards, which contains details of the approaches adopted by the winners. In general, current practice is more difficult to capture except in the crudest of statistical terms. This topic was considered in Appendix I, where I noted the absence of an official statistical and information base.

The issues raised by the new role for training may be expressed as a single frame (a summary of the major arguments set out on a single page). This formed the basis of the questions posed to a group of training managers. They received the single frame (reproduced in Figure AIV.1) and a questionnaire (reproduced in Figure AIV.2).

The opportunity	Critical influences	The dilemmas	Areas for investigation
The key source of competitive advantage is now embedded in the skills and capabilities of knowledge workers	Accomplished and marketable individuals seek employability – appropriate opportunities to develop their own capability in both the long and the short term	The need to maintain an appropriate balance between the requirements of the organization and the demands of the individual	Link with strategic planning process? – international links ————? Organization of training department?
The new global economy reinforced by the information/telecommunications revolution and by regulation has changed the nature of competition		Responsibility for the formulation of training policy and the management of its implementation has become diffuse: • a coordinated approach is needed on developing advantage through people • line managers carry more responsibility for developing their staff	Role of line managers ————? Development initiatives ————? – career management ————? – development centres ————?
Resource-based strategy shifts the competitive emphasis from an external response to market conditions to an internal response based on the development of internal capabilities	Technology permits new approaches to the delivery of training – particularly dispersed access across networks.	Targeting and monitoring of resource is more critical and more difficult: • more people initiate training interventions • much may be uncoordinated/unrecorded	Management information ————? – budgets, reports, evaluation ————? Major challenges over last two years and the next two. Implications for the skills of the trainers.

© **Martyn Sloman 1998**

Figure AIV.1 Issues in modern training practice

SECTION 1   About your business
First, we would like some background on your establishment.

Respondent's name: ....   Date: ....

Position: ....

Company: ....

Address: ....   Telephone number: ....

....

....

Company turnover		Number of employees	
less than £1m		less than 250	
£1m–£5m		250–750	
£5m–£20m		750–1500	
£20m–£50m		1500–5000	
£50m–£100m		5000–10 000	
		over 10000	

Have you secured Investors in People?
commitment   Yes/No   recognition   Yes/No

If your answer to the above question is yes:

Please indicate whether the IiP recognition/commitment applies to
the whole business   part of the business

SECTION 2   Training strategy
Now we would like to know something about the training strategy of your establishment

Does your organization have a training plan?   Yes   No

If your answer to the question is yes:

Does the plan take a form of a written document?   Yes   No

How are the resources for training identified in the plan?

Who has primary responsibility for the formulation of the plan?

How is your training strategy linked to the business/corporate strategy?

Figure AIV.2   Survey questionnaire

How important has each of the following been as an influence on your training policies in the last 5 years:

	very important	important	not very important
a) market competition			
b) labour market changes			
c) organizational changes			
d) increased emphasis on human skills			
e) internationalization/globalization			
f) new technology			

Of the 6 possible factors mentioned in the above question, please write in the letters of the three which you see as the most important in shaping your training policy.

most important [   ]   second most important [   ]   third most important [   ]

How, if at all has the use of competencies affected your training programmes?

Next we would like to find out more about the approach to training in your organization.

SECTION 3   Organization of training

Approximately how many staff in the organization are designated trainers (i.e. they spend most of their time in the delivery of training)? [   ]

How, if at all, do you see your line manager's role changing to make the training activities more effective?

What facilities, if any, are available, to develop a training capability among line managers in the organization?

How, if at all, has your training been affected by new approaches to career development/career management?

Have any specific career-related development interventions been introduced, e.g. use of assessment or development centres/career workshops/special training in coaching and counselling?

SECTION 4   Technology and training delivery

What proportion of training volume is delivered by external suppliers including consultants? (please express answer as an appropriate percentage) [   ]

For which training activities, if any, is the contribution from external suppliers of particular importance?

Approximately what percentage of your training programmes are computer-based/use advanced technology? [   ]

How is access to computer-based training rationed within the organization (e.g. open access/restricted access)?

How, if at all, is your training linked with knowledge management?

Has your company specific links with a particular business school?

Figure AIV.2   Continued

Has your company considered setting up your own corporate university

Have you any policy/plans on individual learning contracts?

SECTION 5   **Monitoring, evaluating and reporting training activity**

What central records are maintained of training activity? Are the costs of training recorded?
Are the volumes of training recorded?

Who in the organization receives information on costs and volumes? Are training budgets maintained?

If yes, who is held accountable for actual spend against budget?

Is there any charging system for internal training courses (e.g. are the costs of attendance at internally-run courses charged back to business areas according to participation)?

What proportion of training events are evaluated in any form (please express answer as an approximate percentage)

What proportion of training events are evaluated beyond the use of an end-of-course questionnaire (please express answer as an appropriate percentage)?

Who in the organization receives reports on training activity and how regularly?

In what form, if any, does the Board receive reports on training activity?

SECTION 6   **Challenges**

And, finally we would like to ask you about the challenges facing the training function in the foreseeable future.

What, over the last two years, have been the major problems faced by the training function?

Looking ahead, over the next two years, what do you see as the major challenges facing the training function?

What, if any, do you consider will be the major differences in the organization of the training function in five years' time?

What skills does a training manager need today, which he/she did not need to have 5 years ago?

What additional/different skills will be required of the training manager of the future?

Thank you for your cooperation.

Figure AIV.2   **Concluded**

Organization	No. of employees (range)	Commitment to Investors People	Training plan (written)	No. of designated trainers	Proportion of training delivered		Access policy for computer-based training	Proportion of training events evaluated		Charging system for training?
					By external supplier	Computer-based using advanced technology		In any form	Beyond the use of the questionnaire	
Turnover of £100m +										
BAT	10000+	✓	✓ (w)	20	60%	2%	Open	90%	50%	Yes
David Smith Packaging	1500–5000	✓	✓ (w)	50	90%	75%	Restricted access	100%	100%	Yes
MoD, Police	1500–5000	✓	✓ (w)	20	10%	5%	Restricted – due to security reasons	90%	10%	No
Prudential Life & Pensions	1500–5000	✓	✓ (w)	36	10%	3%	Open	99%	1%	Yes
Royal Bank of Scotland	10000+	✓	✓ (w)	40	60%	50%	Open	100%	20%	Yes
TNT	10000+	✓	✓ (w)	9	5%	5%	Open	100%	40%	No
Zeneca	750–1500	✓	✓ (w)	20	10%	5%	Open	50%	10%	Yes
Turnover of £50m–£100m										
Blue Arrow Personnel	750–1500	✓	✓ (w)	6	0	5%	Restricted	100%	80%	No
Eastern Generation	250–750	✓	✓ (w)	0	65%	25%	Open access	90%	90%	No

Figure AIV.3   Key indicators from survey returns

Pharmco*	5000–10000	✓	✓ (w)	3	80%	20%	No agreed policy	100%	70%	No
Gas Transco	5000–10000	✓	✓ (w)	40	7%	7%	Open	70%	30%	No
Turnover of £20m–£50m										
Lifespan NHS Trust	750–1500	✓	✓ (w)	7	40%	2%	Ad hoc	90%	20%	No
Turnover of £5–£20m										
Timsons	250	✓	✓ (w)	2	35%	45%	Not restricted	80%	30%	No
University of Exeter, Domestic Services Division	250–750	✓	✓ (w)	1	50%	5%	Restricted	90%	30%	No
Turnover of less than £5m										
Clar Donald Visitors Centre	>250	✓	✓ (w)	0	20%	20%	Restricted to computer users	100%	75%	No
King George V School, South Shields	>250	✓	✓ (w)	0	10%	10%	Open	90%	90%	No
Lancaster & Thorpe	>250	✓	✓ (w)	3	5%	5%	Mixed – depends on programs	100%	100%	Yes
Queen Elizabeth's School, Barret	>250	✓	✓ (w)	3	60%	–	Open	90%	–	No

Figure AIV.3   Concluded

* pseudonym, the company did not wish to be identified

The single frame and questionnaire were sent to 82 organizations. Fifty-seven were chosen from among recent winners of the Employers' Section of the National Training Awards. Nineteen were significant organizations chosen across industrial sections (all of whom appeared in the FTSE 100 Index of the largest capitalized UK private companies). To add a balance to the large private sector firms six other organizations taken from the public sector were sent the frame and questionnaire and invited to respond.

Eighteen organizations (22 per cent) responded positively to the invitation to comment on the frame and completed the questionnaire – a virtually identical response to the survey as for the first edition. The list of respondent organizations is set out in Appendix AIV.3. The survey was therefore restricted to those training managers who felt sufficiently interested in the single frame to respond without prompting.

Figure AIV.3 (pages 274–75) sets out some key indicators from the returns. From the information, however, a confusing pattern is emerging. In some respects there is a high degree of consistency: in others there is a great deal of diversity. Some problems have demanded attention irrespective of the nature of the organization; in other respects the agenda has been determined by the specific circumstances facing the training manager. Nevertheless, there is a large measure of agree-ment on the challenges faced by trainers and the implications for their skill-set. This contradiction between consistency and diversity is illustrated in the discussion under the topic headings. This overall pattern is summarized in Figure AIV.4.

Best practice organizations:

- prepare a written training plan
- place considerable emphasis on improving the line management contribution to corporate training
- are concerned to demonstrate value for money from training.

Beyond this the pattern of training is determined by the business imperative facing the organization – and any related change management process.

This has led to considerable diversity in approach on such issues as:

- the extent to which the delivery of training is outsourced
- the use of technology-based training.

Figure AIV.4   Consistency and diversity of modern training practice

STRATEGIC PLANNING PROCESS

The clear indication is that a written training plan is in place to best practice organizations. This is not as conclusive a result as might at first appear. It is one of the conditions for securing Investors in People recognition and all the organizations, with one exception, had committed to IiP (the one exception had chosen to concentrate on securing accreditation for the European quality standard).

However, the written plan was almost universally a feature of best practice on the predecessor survey (for the first edition of the book), which was undertaken five years earlier. A written statement of intent can now be regarded as essential.

Moreover, a clear pattern has emerged in all except the smallest organizations. The preparation of the training plan is the responsibility of the human resource training manager; the exceptions are where this is undertaken in conjunction with designated line managers or an internal steering group. The plan is expressed in budgetary terms. It is explicitly linked to the commercial needs of the business and change management initiatives, but often on a reactive basis. The following quotations capture the flavour:

> Training and development programs are developed to support strategic and operational plans at Corporate and Department level (Lifespan NHS Trust).

> The training plan is a direct result of needs identified in the business plan (TNT UK).

> The business plan defines corporate objectives linked to corporate training objectives. These are cascaded to departments and individuals. These, along with the annual skills audit, determine our training plans (David S. Smith, Packaging).

INFLUENCES ON TRAINING

A series of questions was designed to identify the basic influences on training strategy. Two powerful influences were identified: market competition and organizational change. These dominated the replies and can be interpreted as a need for the training function to be in a position to respond to the requirements of the business.

> Training is embedded into 'plans for change' for key activities (Zeneca).

> Training is directly linked to the goals of the company (short, medium and long-term) and therefore integral to corporate strategy (Blue Arrow Personnel Services).

> The training plan echoes business needs (Lancaster and Thorpe).

The primary drivers are therefore internal to the organization rather than arising from developments in the broader external training arena. This finding is consistent with the Cambridge survey on responses to national policy considered in Appendix III. Few organizations mentioned NVQs as an influence.

One exception to the 'internal competitive focus' has been the impact of new technology on training policy, which was mentioned as an influence, to some extent, by almost half of the respondents. By contrast, internationalization/globalization cannot be said to have had any significant impact so far.

THE ORGANIZATION OF TRAINING

Figure AIV.3 shows that there is a wide diversity of approach to the organization of training and to its delivery. The number of staff who act as designated trainers (defined as spending most of their time in training delivery) varies enormously. At first glance, the implication would appear to be that some organizations have chosen the approach of total outsourcing of delivery, while others have maintained an extensive in-house capacity.

However, this first analysis does not appear to be consistent with the proportion of training delivered by external suppliers. These figures show a considerable difference across respondent organizations: from 90 per cent at the highest to zero at the lowest with a large spread in between. Certainly this indicates that attitudes on the benefits of using full-time in-company trainers differ considerably. The logical co-relationship between a low population of internal trainers and a high proportion of outsourcing is not evident from Figure AIV.3. One explanation, could, of course, be a misunderstanding of the relevant questions. There is, though, a more subtle explanation that follows from another evident trend. Many organizations have consciously sought to promote line management ownership of, and involvement in, training. This extends well beyond a corporate responsibility for developing subordinates into a role of training delivery and even evaluation.

Facilities to develop a training capability among line managers include:

to educate line managers to understand the entire training project: link with business strategy, training needs identification, implementation, and evaluation. To make them see training as an investment and understand the returns (Royal Bank of Scotland).

training material/internet/self-teaching/training centre (Zeneca).

training in feedback skills (British Gas Transco).

workshops in the manager's role as a developer (Lifespan NHS Trust).

all attend coaching skills and 'train the trainer' seminars and 'making performance appraisal work' seminars (Lancaster & Thorpe).

we train managers as D32 Assessors for NVQs and as craft trainers and group trainers to ensure the standard of training is as good as possible (University of Exeter, Domestic Services Division).

Training delivery, then, may be increasingly shared between a cohort of full-time in-house trainers, outsourced external suppliers, and the contribution of line managers at various levels in the organization.

USE OF TECHNOLOGY

As has been noted, some respondents have indicated that new technology has been an influence on training policy. However, Figure AIV.3 shows that very few organizations have wholeheartedly embraced technology as a means of delivery. All bar three respondent firms used technology for less than a quarter of their training.

A high proportion of usage of technology-based training was associated with the specific circumstances of the organization. CD ROM material for technical training (David S. Smith Packaging); CNC (computer numerically controlled) training connected with manufacturing advanced technology printing machinery (Timsons). About half the respondents allowed open access to computer-based training material that was held centrally.

The answers to the question on the link between training and knowledge management produced little evidence of significant current initiatives. Some respondents referred to the intention to advance individual capabilities through training (sometimes linked with qualifications; sometimes with personal development plans). Many ignored the question altogether and at least one respondent admitted to a lack of understanding of the term.

Generally, the use of technology emerged as an area of interest and concern, but few respondents appeared to display a current confidence that they have found the answers. The mood was captured by one of the two respondents from the educational sector who described the challenge as follows:

> this is the holy grail: to find the saturation points in each area of learning where open/distance learning can be more effective (Queen Elizabeth School, Barnet).

MONITORING/EVALUATION/REPORTING

One strong feature of best practice training organizations is their concern to demonstrate value. Only two organizations reported the proportion of training evaluated in any form at below three-quarters. The proportion evaluated beyond the use of end-of-course questionnaires varies considerably and improved practice is firmly on many organizations' agendas. About half the respondent organizations use internal charging as a method of focusing training spend.

The preparation of training reports is almost always the responsibility of the training manager. Practices in distribution vary, with some organizations circulating information widely and recording it for internal training department users.

THE CHANGING FUNCTION: SKILLS

There was some variance of views on the major challenges facing the function, but agreement on the additional/different skills required of the training manager of the future. When considering important challenges both greater centralization and decentralization appeared on the responses as did greater use of IT and consultants. However, again, many of the concerns expressed were related to the circumstances of the particular organization. Three areas dominated in the discussion of the skills required of the future training manager: all received equal weighting. The three were: first, consultancy skills and the ability to undertake process interventions; second, a firm knowledge of business and commercial strategy; third, knowledge and capability in information technology.

The conclusion must be that the training function is at a pivotal phase. Some aspects (like the place of planning and the importance of demonstrating value) are clearly recognized as important. Nevertheless, the function is wrestling with some important change issues: it needs to understand business strategy, grasp the opportunity of technology and develop the consultancy skill-set needed to establish credibility.

Index

Another 75 Ways to Liven Up Your Training

A Second Collection of Energizing Activities

Martin Orridge

In 1996 Gower published 'a collection of energizing activities' under the title *75 Ways to Liven Up Your Training*. It was an immediate success.

Now the same author has compiled a further collection. As with the first, most of the activities in this book require little in the way of either expertise or equipment. Yet they provide a powerful means of stimulating creativity, helping people to enjoy learning, or simply injecting fresh momentum into the training process.

Each activity is presented using the same standard set of headings as before. They include a brief description, a statement of purpose, likely duration, a note of any materials required and detailed instructions for running the event. In addition there are suggestions for debriefing and possible variations.

The activities are arranged by type or process which helps users to select the most appropriate. There are exercises for individuals, pairs and large groups and they range from icebreakers to closing events.

This second volume will surely prove a worthy successor to *75 Ways*.

Gower

90 Brain Teasers for Trainers

Graham Roberts-Phelps and Anne McDougall

The activities and exercises in this collection are designed to broaden perception, and improve learning, thinking and problem-solving skills. Using them is also a valuable way to boost energy levels at the beginning, middle or end of any training session.

The collection will help any group engage all five senses in their learning, and develop creative and lateral thinking, word usage, mental dexterity and cooperative team skills. Most of the activities require no more than a flip chart or OHP to run. And because they need only a few moments preparation, they can be planned into sessions in advance, or simply introduced to fill gaps, or to signal a change of direction, as appropriate.

Trainers, teachers and team leaders will find *Brain Teasers for Trainers* a rich source of simple, flexible, and easy-to-use exercises, as well as the inspiration for their own variants.

Gower

A Consultancy Approach for Trainers and Developers

Second Edition

Keri Phillips and Patricia Shaw

The first edition of this book, published over ten years ago, accurately predicted the significance of the transition from trainer to consultant and from training to learning. And, as the role of trainers has changed, so the responsibility for development has expanded to involve managers at all levels within the organization.

This Second Edition has been written to help you, whatever your particular responsibility as a trainer or developer, to plan your professional development. Using an original framework, the authors describe three approaches to consultancy designed to help you undertake increasingly complex assignments. With the support of case studies, they explain what each approach involves and illustrate the problems and opportunities the trainer is likely to face. A detailed self-development plan is contained in the appendices.

The fully updated text reflects the authors' experience in a changing profession over the last ten years, and includes two completely new chapters.

Gower

The Excellent Trainer

Putting NLP to Work

Di Kamp

Most trainers are familiar with the principles of Neuro-Linguistic Programming. What Di Kamp does in her book is to show how NLP techniques can be directly applied to the business of training.

Kamp looks first at the fast-changing organizational world in which trainers now operate, then at the role of the trainer and the skills and qualities required. She goes on to deal with the actual training process and provides systematic guidance on using NLP in preparation, delivery and follow-up. Finally she explores the need for continuous improvement, offering not only ideas and explanation but also instruments and activities designed to enhance both personal and professional development.

If you are involved in training, you'll find this book a powerful tool both for developing yourself and for enriching the learning opportunities you create for others.

Gower

The Gower Handbook of Management

Fourth Edition

Edited by Dennis Lock

'If you have only one management book on your shelf, this must be the one.'

Dennis Lock recalls launching the first edition in 1983 with this aim in mind. It has remained the guiding principle behind subsequent editions, and today *The Gower Handbook of Management* is widely regarded as a manager's bible: an authoritative, gimmick-free and practical guide to best practice in management. By covering the broadest possible range of subjects, this handbook replicates in book form a forum in which managers can meet experts from a range of professional disciplines.

The new edition features:

- 65 expert contributors - many of them practising managers and all of them recognized authorities in their field
- many new contributors: over one-third are new to this edition
- 72 chapters, of which half are completely new
- 20 chapters on subjects new to this edition
- a brand new design and larger format.

The Gower Handbook of Management has received many plaudits during its distinguished career, summed up in the following review from *Director*:

'... packed with information which can be used either as a reference work on a specific problem or as a guide to an entire operation. In a short review one can touch only lightly on the richness and excellence of this book, which well deserves a place on any executive bookshelf.'

Gower

Handbook of Management Games and Simulations

Sixth Edition

Edited by Chris Elgood

What kinds of management games are there? How do they compare with other methods of learning? Where can I find the most suitable games for the training objectives I have in mind?

Handbook of Management Games and Simulations provides detailed answers to these questions and many others.

Part 1 of the *Handbook* examines the characteristics and applications of the different types of game. It explains how they promote learning and the circumstances for which they are best suited.

Part 2 comprises a detailed directory of some 300 games and simulations. Each one is described in terms of its target group, subject area, nature and purpose, and the means by which the outcome is established and made known. The entries also contain administrative data including the number of players, the number of teams and the time required. Several indexes enable readers to locate precisely those games that would be relevant for their own needs.

This sixth edition has been revised to reflect recent developments. And of course the directory has been completely updated. Chris Elgood's *Handbook* will continue to be indispensable for anyone concerned with management development.

Gower

Handbook of Technology-Based Training

Edited by Brian Tucker
The Forum for Technology in Training

Technology-based training (TBT) has moved a long way since the early days of computer-based training in the 1960s and 1970s. Today it offers a flexible, cost-effective way of meeting the ever increasing need for people to re-skill.

Handbook of Technology-Based Training provides an accessible guide to the potential benefits and pitfalls of this form of training. It describes the evolution of technology-based training; the various technologies and their uses; the benefits of using such flexible learning; the important issues of how to use the technology; how to implement TBT in an organization and where the future might lie. Brian Tucker also deals with choosing and evaluating generic training and the issues of bespoke training, either produced in-house or outsourced.

The *Handbook* is not highly technical, and deals with the issues in a readily understandable way. It uses examples and detailed case studies to demonstrate how nine leading organizations have managed the various issues and how they have benefited from this approach to training. These include Sun Life, Vauxhall, Lloyds Bank, Argos, British Gas and British Steel.

Structured in two parts, the first provides a complete overview of the subject. The second consists of a directory of over 700 generic TBT courseware titles, indexed by subject, title, medium, and producer. Each entry includes the title of the courseware, its purpose and suitability, a brief description, delivery methods, hardware requirements, price and supplier details.

Gower

How to Deliver Training

Martin Orridge

'The aim of this book is to provide both managers wishing to run 'in team' exercises and those entering the training profession with a practical guide to delivering successful developmental events', says Martin Orridge in the Preface.

He writes as an experienced trainer and consultant, producing a very human guide to the realities of running a training event. In a brief introductory section he explains the need for training and the benefits it can bring. Part 1 of the main text shows how to design a successful training session and Part 2 deals in detail with preparation and delivery. At the end is a collection of model documents and forms that can be used at various stages of the training cycle. The text includes tips, tools, checklists, examples and exercises throughout, together with real-life anecdotal 'cameos' to help make the points memorable.

Martin Orridge's style is at all times practical and friendly. *How to Deliver Training* will be welcomed not only by professional trainers, but by all managers and team leaders concerned with staff development.

Gower

Planning and Designing Training Programmes

Leslie Rae

The quality of the planning will be instrumental to the ultimate success of any training or development programme, yet as the demands on today's trainers are constantly changing, the pressure to devise effective training, often at short notice, is increasing.

This latest book by one of the UK's leading training authors looks in detail at the entire planning process, set very much within today's challenging corporate context. Following the book will enable any trainer to devise a professional training and development programme, by:

• identifying and analysing training needs
• designing and planning a programme to meet them
• designing and planning the individual sessions within it
• evaluating success - at the start, during, and at the end of the programme.

Included are all the considerations a trainer needs to be aware of, ranging from skills assessment and learning styles, to relative benefits of on the job and off the job training, and the value of different types of training formats. Finding time for proper evaluation is crucial too, and Leslie Rae highlights a wide range of options. Also included is a unique index of available training resources.

This exceptionally practical structured approach will help any trainer to shorten the planning time involved whilst improving the quality of that preparation.

Gower

Team Development Games for Trainers

Roderick R Stuart

If you're involved in designing or delivering interpersonal skills training you will know that there are two perennial problems. The first is finding material that matches your objectives. The second is finding material that will be unfamiliar to the participants.

The 59 games in Roderick Stuart's collection have not appeared in print before. Based on the author's experience with a wide range of organizations and participants, they cover the entire gamut of skills associated with team development, including assertiveness, communication, creativity, decision making, influencing, listening, planning, problem solving and time management.

Each game is presented in a standard format, with an indication of objectives, timing and group size, detailed step-by-step guidance for the trainer or team leader, and ready-to-copy masters for all participants' material. An index of objectives makes it easy to select the most suitable items for your training needs and to compile complete workshops or more extensive programmes. In addition the author provides a four-stage model that relates learning to the requirements of the workplace, and a set of checklists for facilitating the learning process.

Gower

75 Ways to Liven Up Your Training

A Collection of Energizing Activities

Martin Orridge

Most of the activities in Martin Orridge's book require little in the way of either expertise or equipment. Yet they provide a powerful way of stimulating creativity, helping people to enjoy learning, or simply injecting new momentum into the training process.

Each activity is presented under a standard set of headings, including a brief description, a statement of purpose, likely duration, a note of any materials required and detailed instructions for running the event. In addition there are suggestions for debriefing and possible variations.

To help users to select the most appropriate activities they are arranged in the book by type or process. There are exercises for individuals, pairs and large groups and they range from icebreakers to closing events.

Trainers, managers, team leaders and anyone responsible for developing people will find this volume a rich store-house of ideas.

Gower

Web-Based Training

Colin Steed

Web-based training is becoming one of the most important tools for trainers and courseware developers. The ability to deliver training and learning online to an individual's desk offers enormous flexibility for the organization as well as the employee, cost and time savings and the opportunity to keep pace with constant changes required for today's organizations to remain competitive.

Colin Steed explains how trainers can use self-paced, online learning to develop and train employees and improve their performance. He outlines the benefits and drawbacks of web-based training, looks at the cost considerations, and examines the elements that make up a programme. There is plenty of coverage of what is currently available on the market as well as in-depth case material drawn from organizations that have already begun to use the technology. Using step-by-step procedures, and assuming no technical knowledge, this practical and timely book will help you design you own web-based training strategy.

If you want to know what web-based training is all about and whether its right for your organization, this book provides all the answers.

Gower